The
Deliciously
Conscious
Cookbook

The
Deliciously
Conscious
Cookbook

Over 100 vegetarian recipes with gluten-free,
vegan and dairy-free options

BELINDA CONNOLLY

HAY HOUSE

Carlsbad, California • New York City • London • Sydney
Johannesburg • Vancouver • Hong Kong • New Delhi

First published and distributed in the United Kingdom by:
Hay House UK Ltd, Astley House, 33 Notting Hill Gate, London W11 3JQ
Tel: +44 (0)20 3675 2450; Fax: +44 (0)20 3675 2451; www.hayhouse.co.uk

Published and distributed in the United States of America by:
Hay House Inc., PO Box 5100, Carlsbad, CA 92018-5100
Tel: (1) 760 431 7695 or (800) 654 5126; Fax: (1) 760 431 6948 or (800) 650 5115
www.hayhouse.com

Published and distributed in Australia by:
Hay House Australia Ltd, 18/36 Ralph St, Alexandria NSW 2015
Tel: (61) 2 9669 4299; Fax: (61) 2 9669 4144; www.hayhouse.com.au

Published and distributed in the Republic of South Africa by:
Hay House SA (Pty) Ltd, PO Box 990, Witkoppen 2068
Tel/Fax: (27) 11 467 8904; www.hayhouse.co.za

Published and distributed in India by:
Hay House Publishers India, Muskaan Complex, Plot No.3, B-2,
Vasant Kunj, New Delhi 110 070
Tel: (91) 11 4176 1620; Fax: (91) 11 4176 1630; www.hayhouse.co.in

Distributed in Canada by:
Raincoast Books, 2440 Viking Way, Richmond, B.C. V6V 1N2
Tel: (1) 604 448 7100; Fax: (1) 604 270 7161; www.raincoast.com

A catalogue record for this book is available from the British Library.

ISBN: 978-1-78180-276-2

Interior design: Leanne Siu Anastasi
Interior photography: 32tr, cl, bl; 146tr, b; 158bcr; 188tl, tr, cl; 208bl: thinkstockphotos.co.uk; All other photography © Carole Salmon, John Meredith and Rick Smaridge
Interior illustrations © John Platt

Printed and bound in Great Britain by TJ International Ltd, Padstow, Cornwall

CONTENTS

INTRODUCTION

The idea of making and selling high-quality food from a market stall first came about in response to the needs of my family. My partner and I had moved, together with our six-year-old twin daughters, to Totnes in Devon, and I needed a flexible, part-time income that would allow me to be at home with my children. As a trained chef with a lifelong interest in culinary creativity, a regular market stall seemed like a good way to begin.

Totnes is a thriving centre for natural health, so there was demand for quality, gluten- and dairy-free dishes, lower-sugar cakes and vegan alternatives. I wanted to embrace all dietary conditions, so the challenge was to satisfy all demands with wholesome food cooked with integrity. As time progressed, I had the idea of making all our cakes – and many of our savoury foods – gluten-free, provided there was no sacrifice in taste or texture. This step further influenced the format of *The Deliciously Conscious Cookbook*, as I have been able to include vegan and gluten-free options with many of the original master recipes, giving a wide range of flexibility for cooks.

Also important was the responsible use of consumer power in making food purchases, an ethical benefit we pass on to our customers. We choose as many ingredients as possible from the seasonal supply, and source organic fruits and vegetables, eggs, cheeses and whole foods from local suppliers. Finally, a message about how to use the recipes in this book:

'Let faithful imitation be followed by carefree improvisation.'

Have lots of fun!

Belinda

WHY FREE-FROM?

I wrote *The Deliciously Conscious Cookbook* in response to the growing need for delicious food that's free from gluten, dairy, animal products, cane sugar and nuts. My aim was to bring together a collection of recipes that everyone could eat, and at the same time offer the vegetarian cook extensive freedom of choice when catering for those with diverse dietary needs.

The subject of food allergies and intolerances can present considerable difficulties for the uninitiated cook, and also embarrassing moments for their prospective guests. It took me a while to understand the difference between dairy-free and vegan diets – that eggs can be eaten as part of a dairy-free diet, but vegans consume no part of any animal. I had wrongly assumed that eggs were classed as dairy, but have since learned that many people following a dairy-free diet don't want to be excluded from the egg-eating population. Why should they?

Many people choose a gluten-free diet for reasons other than necessity; sometimes they just feel more healthy, or they need to lose weight. Others do so because they have been diagnosed as being sensitive to gluten or, more seriously, having an auto-immune response to gluten, commonly known as coeliac disease, a condition some are born with and others acquire. Gluten is found mainly in wheat and barley, but also, in lesser concentrations, in rye. It is a complex combination of proteins, one of which – gliadin – is thought to be responsible for triggering an allergic response in the small intestine. The remedy for coeliac sufferers is to eliminate gluten from their diet.

Modern hybrid wheat contains a higher ratio of gluten than older strains, such as kamut and spelt, which are better tolerated by those who are sensitive, but not fully allergic, to gluten. Certified gluten-free oats are mostly well tolerated when harvested and milled in a manufacturing environment that is uncontaminated by gluten. However, 2 per cent of people are also allergic to avenin, a protein found in oats. Trial and error usually defines the safe parameters.

For many people, the choice of a vegan diet extends beyond reasons of personal health. For them, it is a powerful empathic act to live a life free from using animal products. Even the word 'empathy' is a relatively recent addition to the dictionary, and the practice of it empowers those who want to take on new responsibilities, often in the face of negative reactions from those who hold on to tradition. Whatever diet you choose to follow, the health benefits of eating a diet rich in whole foods and complex carbohydrates are now widely recognized. The issue of sustainability is also one of growing importance – we not only want to eat delicious, wholesome food, we also want to know where it's come from.

More people are now beginning to explore their unhelpful relationships with food, asking questions such as: 'Who's really in charge of what I eat?' 'Is quality or quantity more important?' 'Which part of me really needs feeding, and with what?' The weaning process from emotional and energetic dependence on a diet high in refined sugar can be a long journey, but one I hope it will be easier to make with the help of this book. A large number of my cake recipes have lower-sugar options made with lower glycaemic index sweeteners, such as xylitol, pomegranate molasses, or agave or rice syrup. Some of my lower-sugar cakes are an acquired taste for those used to sugary foods. I know of young children who adore my vegan lower-sugar cake; my own had to go on a low-sugar diet to appreciate it!

As you explore these recipes, I advocate mindful experimentation to discover new ways to meet your particular needs. The idea is that you are free to experiment based on how you feel and what your body tells you it needs. Here is not the place to go into a detailed nutritional analysis, but to consult your inner nutritionist!

AUTOBIOGRAPHY OF
A JOBBING CHEF

My lifelong fascination with the alchemical art of cooking was initially inspired by the myriad dishes prepared before my childish eyes in my mother's and grandmother's homes. Both were mistresses of large and productive vegetable gardens, which were maintained by family members and part-time gardeners. I have verdant memories of lazy days spent sneaking raw, sweet garden delights, followed by endless shelling and slicing while perched on rattan chairs in the sunny conservatory.

In 1967, my sister Sarah was diagnosed as suffering acutely from coeliac disease. Our mother had to expand her culinary repertoire accordingly, and I remember her swearing mightily over a succession of white sauces that refused to play ball. In the 1960s, public awareness of the needs of coeliac sufferers was practically nonexistent. Eating out was difficult and my poor sister suffered cruelly at birthday parties, where she was often faced with an entire table groaning with fabulous food, none of which she could eat.

Family Culture

My mother considered waistlines important, and so puddings only made an appearance on special occasions. That is, until I hijacked Marguerite Patten's post-war cookery bible for the British housewife, *Cookery in Colour*, and subjected my family to endless variations of blancmange and bavarois made with whipped jelly and evaporated milk. Next came sweets and puddings, followed by more grown-up imitations of dinner party extravaganzas.

When I was eight years old, we dined as guests of my grandparents at Sharrow Bay hotel in the Lake District, and I first experienced food preparation raised to an art form. It was to prove a life-changing event. Even now, I can remember digesting that first thrilling mouthful of the now-famous sticky toffee pudding. Inspiration and curiosity led me to the hallowed tome of my grandmother's kitchen bible, *The Constance Spry Cookery Book*, co-written by a principal of the Cordon Bleu School of Cookery in London. The recipe for grilled mackerel with gooseberry sauce went down very well at home! Encouraged, I soon began to make my own charcuterie, hanging it to cure from the laundry pulley, having graduated to cooking my way through Julia Child's *Mastering the Art of French Cookery*, courtesy of Auntie Sue, who was also a keen cook.

Peaks & Troughs

There were several scarring moments along the way, including the time when our cleaner inadvertently poured away my first attempt at a crystal-clear consommé, wasting hours of dedicated simmering, skimming and straining involving complicated manoeuvres using crushed eggshells and muslin!

As my teens progressed I delved into the world of Auguste Escoffier, the father of modern French cuisine, and imagined myself preparing fabulous *pièces montées* for crowds of glittering guests. Little did I guess that such aspirations would lead me, at the age of 16, to experiment with elaborate aspic work and cake decoration, which found appreciative outlets at family celebrations and earned remuneration from grateful neighbours.

It was at boarding school that I began to suffer from a compulsive eating disorder, caused by separation anxiety amongst other issues, which was to remain with me for the next 14 years. This need to be close to food undoubtedly affected my future choice of career. I realized that I was not, as I saw it, marriage material waiting to be transformed into the perfect hostess, so I chose not to enter cookery school and instead trained for three years as a nurse at the Royal Free Hospital in London.

However, the ghost of culinary creativity would not rest, and so from my north London flat and with more chutzpah than know-how – mainly to prove to myself and my parents that a career change was viable – I boiled luscious Christmas puddings and sold them to Covent Garden foodie shops, and trudged a snowy 'millionaires' avenue' in Hampstead, dropping posh leaflets advertising my extravagant wares. Soon I had acquired a small but exclusive following for whom I created Grand Marnier mousses encased in dark chocolate baskets, and Genoise cakes smothered in homemade custard and butter-cream icing.

My father, generously, and perhaps in a desperate bid to see his wayward daughter in gainful employment, offered to send me to a cookery school. I applied to Leith's School of Food and Wine with a list of everything I had ever cooked. To their lasting credit, my interviewers declared that if indeed I could prepare all that I had shown them, then they had nothing to teach me. With this ringing in my ears I set off, armed with the same list, to my interview at the Cordon Bleu Cookery School, only to be bluntly informed that I would have to start with the beginners' course. I had proved my long-suspected point that culinary school was not for me!

Outward Bound

My horizons expanded, I began working as the only female chef in the kitchen of the highly regarded Le Talbooth restaurant, in Colchester. I was thrown in at the deep end, and given sole charge of the starter section of a busy 80-cover restaurant. I was very inexperienced in kitchen brigade etiquette and was often derided for unwitting breaches. My most memorable gaffe was daring to bring my food processor into the kitchen, for which I was roundly criticized for 'not using proper knife skills'. However, on return from holiday, I discovered that much unauthorized use had been made of my despised machine, after which the subject was never mentioned again.

During the next six months, I learned how to work as part of a perfectly orchestrated kitchen brigade. I made (and occasionally ruined) terrines of everything, encountered fresh truffles, foie gras and live lobsters; worked hours of unpaid overtime rectifying mistakes and eventually discovered how to deliver accurate dishes at high speed. Having absorbed much of the restaurant's repertoire I began to look further afield and, much to my surprise, was offered a transfer as head chef to the noble Althorp kitchens of the Earl and Countess Spencer. This was my ticket to ride.

Onwards & Upwards

At Althorp I realized my dream, catering for innumerable private, royal and public parties, banquets and corporate events, all under the watchful and sometimes wrathful eye of Raine, Countess Spencer, who found me 'well bred but arrogant'.

I set myself the challenge of spinning sugar veils over lychee sorbets in tuile baskets nestling in chopped jelly atop silver salvers. For royal house parties I served the now-perfected, crystal-clear Consommé Madrilène in original East India Company china soup bowls to the Prince and Princess of Wales. However, my most treasured memory is of the French ambassador, who was flabbergasted to discover that I had never set foot inside a French kitchen! My duties included the provision of interesting meals for a large, mostly live-in staff, who were like my extended family. The trials and tribulations of 20th-century, upstairs-downstairs life cemented lifelong friendships, and the rich store of memories are still revisited at periodic reunions.

Since then I have globetrotted from Monte Carlo to the Cayman Islands, working in cramped and impossibly humid galleys to provide haute cuisine for the elite aboard billionaires' yachts. With the generous help of my long-suffering father, I also started my own catering company, A Private Function. Work included, among the usual business and private jobs, in-house events for local music celebrities, including Peter Gabriel, Tears for Fears, Morrissey and Van Morrison; and location work for film and television. I also catered events for the now Duchess of Cornwall and Jane Seymour, and worked for a short time at the Bristol Cancer Help Centre.

New Horizons

When business slowed during the early-1990s recession, my friend Belinda and I made the bold decision to open an art gallery and dining club in the French Alps.

There I met my partner, Brian, who was en route from Italy to England. After a few brief adventures we chose to start a family and decamped back to the UK, eventually taking root in Totnes, Devon, for our children's holistic education at the local Steiner school. I chose to stay at home, cooking for live-in students, and then started the market stall to share the art of producing wholesome relevant food in the thriving alternative community. I was home at last!

Having become practised in cooking for family, friends and students, my repertoire was further transformed by very different needs. I cooked for the Devon School of Shiatsu and also studied macrobiotic cooking at The Holistic Cooking School, learning about the energetics of food and their therapeutic combinations. At home, organic baby food and individual twin palates offered special challenges in both imagination and endurance. I shall never forget the relief when my daughter India – in those days never keen on anything green – began to eat lettuce after she had helped to prepare it. For her the key was to be included in the natural rhythmic cycle of earth to table.

I have since publicly demonstrated my recipes and devised cookery courses for single people, teenagers and those needing vegan, gluten- or dairy-free inspiration; but mostly what I find myself teaching is a way through the conceptual maze that lies behind cooking food without common ingredients. This new-found skill encourages the confidence to cook nourishing food, and this naturally leads to a more appreciative approach to life. I enjoy enabling people to trust themselves enough to have a go, even if they make mistakes. My culinary motto is: 'It's only a disaster when somebody else tells me it is.' Burned? Well, call it smoked!

Recently, I have become more active in spreading awareness of just how fragile, since the green and GM revolutions, our healthy food sources have become. I am also beginning to work therapeutically as a psychophonetics practitioner. This modality uses conversation, intention, alphabetical sounds and movement based on Rudolf Steiner's Psychosophy, and I hope to enable those suffering from eating disorders and nourishment-related issues to have an empowered future.

FROM PLATE TO PAGE

The motivation to write and publish my first book, *Belinda's Totnes Market Cookbook*, was inspired not only by repeated requests from customers at the market stall, but also by my friend Carole, a woman of vision, talent and no little enthusiasm. She photographed my food and encouraged me to imagine my book on the shelves of Waterstones and Barnes & Noble. In the summer of 2007 I began writing on one day a week, and it took almost two years to complete the manuscript, squeezed in as it was between school runs, visiting students, family meals and running the market stall.

In 2009 I was due to begin my psychotherapy training, and so made a monumental effort to complete the book beforehand. I asked for, and received, much skilled help from fellow parents within the Steiner school community, for which I paid mostly with cake! Two years later emerged a great-looking cookbook, which I sold from the market stall and encouraging local shops. Sales continued, and people often returned to buy a second copy for family and friends. After a year it became evident that a reprint would be needed, so I took a deep breath and ordered a larger quantity than the first print-run, praying that I hadn't made an expensive mistake. I hadn't – the cookbook went on to sell 1,000 copies.

By 2011, I began to feel that I had taken the book as far as I could and resolved to find a publisher. The initial response was less than encouraging. It seemed that nobody was interested in multi-functional, all-singing, all-dancing recipes, and agents weren't looking for new cookery authors. As time passed I felt increasingly despondent about the lack of progress, but my inner voice urged me to remain committed. I wrote another e-mail to a publisher, and then decided to stop worrying.

The dry, bright afternoon of 9 November 2012 found me selling an unexpected flurry of cookbooks alongside the debut of my Cider Mango Mincemeat Cheesecake. A familiar customer appeared with her friend, who seemed extremely interested in my cookbook. She handed me her card, and I realized in that here was the publisher I had been waiting for.

March 2014

MY PHILOSOPHY OF COOKING

For me, cooking and eating are flip sides of the same coin. When creating a dish, I allow my whole being to be guided intuitively by what pleases me. As I cook, I'm already seeing the result in my mind's eye. It is as if I am looking backwards from the future, watching others already enjoying the dish.

I love the immediate intimacy of the modern food culture which, since the advent of social media, now reaches into homes everywhere. I feel tingles of anticipation when, for example, a cranberry curd and walnut shortbread slice comes my way via the internet. It's new, fresh and invigorating, and it makes me want to meet the inventive cook who dreamed outside the box.

My most exciting explorations frequently bubble up from an inner picture inspired by, for instance, a meal out, a conversation or a food blog. One such impulse arose in response to my tired and fractious family on a recent chilly autumn evening. It evolved into a simple polenta sweetcorn slab topped with a quick roast vegetable sauce dreamed up in the moment. My mood became generous. I did it all – table setting, plate warming, lighting the candles – and was rewarded by an atmosphere of grateful ruminatory peace. The howling wind bayed in vain.

I never know how long the creative process will take to percolate. I remember waking up musing that I'd had a visitation from the pistachio-and-white-chocolate fairy, clad in a pale green gauze and creamy velvet party dress. I leaped out of bed – a rare occurrence – and into the kitchen where the blondie appeared an hour later.

Sometimes the process meanders along a winding path; my sweet vegetable cakes, for instance, have been evolving one after the other for 18 months. Lately I find my daughters are perfecting my recipes or busy creating their own, which feels wonderful, if not a touch alarming!

Like any parent, I have to balance my workload with the desire to provide wholesome, nourishing meals at every sitting. I have learned to enjoy cooking with the freshest of local seasonal produce, and now derive a deep satisfaction from tasting the simplicity of the land rather than being strung out between feeling the need to create something amazing for supper every night, or falling too frequently into pasta default mode.

My family all enjoy cooking, and my daughters' gorgeous, naturally iced Hobbity biscuits are currently occupying the transitional space between home and gap-year travels. I feel blessed to have been a part of bringing the simple art of self-nourishment home to roost. I will end with this J.R.R. Tolkien quote that echoes my sentiments exactly: *'If more of us valued food and cheer and song above hoarded gold, it would be a merrier world.'*

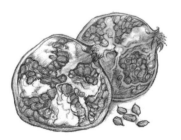

COOK'S NOTES

Flour

I use a variety of gluten-free flours, each with their own special qualities of taste and texture. I have found that they roughly divide into three categories, and that judicious mixes of the categories below make excellent substitutes for wheat flour:

Heavyweight flours: these are protein-rich flours that equate with whole-wheat flour and produce heavier bakes with less rise. They include buckwheat, millet, polenta, quinoa, teff, nut meal, hemp, and bean and legume flours.

Medium-weight flours: these broadly correlate with white (all-purpose) flour, and include sorghum or jowar flour; certified gluten-free oat flour; and coconut, chestnut and brown rice flour.

Lightweight flours: these are the featherweight, starchier flours, such as sweet rice flour, tapioca starch, cornstarch and arrowroot, and are used in some dishes for their binding properties.

My ideal cake mix consists of 50 per cent heavier flour mixed with 50 per cent comprising several of the medium flours listed above. You can also substitute a tablespoon or two of medium flour with maca, lucuma or baobab powders for added nutrition. You will find a big price difference between flours, so begin by experimenting with the cheaper bulk flours and then add smaller fractions of the exotics to taste. Or, if you prefer, you can use 100 per cent ordinary white (all-purpose), wholegrain, spelt or kamut flour and still enjoy my mouthwatering recipes.

The volumes of gluten-free baking powder I give in my recipes vary depending on whether they are bulked up with rice flour. I have used a middle-of-the-road measurement, so do increase or reduce as you see fit.

Fats & Oils

I use many different fats and oils at home. For everyday use, I keep a half-and-half, cold-pressed olive oil/sunflower oil mix made up in a large bottle corked with a wine pourer. For dressings, I use omega-rich oils such as flaxseed oil.

The wide-ranging health and ethical debates about hard fats continues apace. Tastes and needs are changing, and I find myself with a foot in both the culinary and sustainable wellbeing camps regarding the use of coconut oil and palm fat. Both lend themselves to pastry, sweet dishes and also to spicy and savoury food, yet I still prefer olive oil in traditional Mediterranean cuisine. I always recommend using GMO-free oils and margarine, sustainably sourced palm fat and raw organic coconut oil.

For sautéeing food over high heat, I used a mixture of butter and olive oil for years. However, in response to customer requests for a healthy, unprocessed saturated fat that produces fewer free radicals, I now often use unrefined raw coconut oil in place of butter or other oils. I also use it in baking, and you will find it in many of my recipes.

Please note that coconut oil is hard until melted; the measurements in the recipes do take this into account. It can be softened enough for perfect cake making by placing the jar in warm water for 20–30 minutes, or by popping the jar in the microwave for 30 seconds on a low power setting.

Lower Sugar… What Does that Mean?

In this book, 'lower sugar' means that cane sugar has been replaced with other sweeteners that are lower than cane sugar on the glycaemic index. These include rice, agave and date syrup, pomegranate molasses, apple concentrate and xylitol (I use one that's processed from birch sugar, not corn cobs).

Stevia drops or powder can also be used to sweeten fillings, cheesecakes, fruit purées and fruit juices; however, recipes that rely on higher concentrations of sugar, such as cakes and brownies, will suffer textural changes.

Pomegranate molasses can replace maple syrup any day of the week in my larder. Rich, sticky and darkly satisfying without even the slightest suggestion of cloying the palate, it's my most exciting new condiment! It adds both sweet and sour notes to savoury and sweet dishes alike. I use it in marinades, dressings, fruit salads, cake fillings, tomato sauces and anywhere a sweeter acidity balance is called for. If you can't find pomegranate molasses, then apple juice concentrate is the next best substitute.

If you are diabetic or following a restricted carbohydrate diet, you will need to decide which recipes in this book are suitable for you.

Thickening & Setting

I use ground psyllium husks to cleverly absorb runaway moisture from cold fillings and toppings. Psyllium is readily available in health food stores, but use it sparingly and wait couple of minutes before adding more or you could end up with a gummy finish!

Vegetarian gelling powders and crystals greatly vary in strength between brands, so please make sure you understand your packet instructions before attempting your recipe.

Chocolate

I buy organic Fairtrade chocolate whenever possible. I prefer 70 per cent organic dark chocolate because the flavour of the higher proportion of cocoa solids has an incomparably more penetrating flavour, and it is also freer from excess sugar.

It is increasingly possible to source no-added-sugar, dairy-free white and dark chocolate. Melting these can be a little tricky depending on your brand; however, I find adding a little sunflower oil works well. I recommend grating the white chocolate in most recipes, but feel free to experiment.

Nuts

Nut allergies are catered for in many of my recipes. I have listed seed options instead of nuts, so do experiment with anything else that appeals and remember that the fat content ratio is important to note when considering substitutes. Please note that seeds taste rancid after a few months, so it's better to buy them in smaller quantities.

Coconuts are considered nuts for the purposes of this book; consequently I have included a nut-free option for many recipes containing coconut products.

In the Kitchen...

For me, the essential power tools for your kitchen are a coffee/spice grinder, a food processor and a powerful hand blender.

Other items I wouldn't be without include a sharp, four-sided grater, a fat balloon whisk with a rubber handle, silicone rubber spatulas (these don't perish) and silicone baking parchment for lining tins.

The oven temperatures given in this book are for fan-assisted ovens. If you use a conventional oven, just set the temperature at approximately 20°C/70°F higher than indicated in your recipe. Adjust the cooking times to suit, and consult your cooker manual if you are in doubt.

My recipes include metric, imperial and cup measures. Please note that quantities for fruit and vegetables always reflect the *prepared weight*.

CHOOSING YOUR RECIPES

I compiled this chart to help you quickly and easily identify which recipes are dairy free, gluten free, lower sugar, nut free or vegan. Many recipes can be adapted to suit one or more of these requirements – see the Variations panels with each recipe and the 'options' listed below. Have fun selecting the right recipes for you!

SAVOURY RECIPES		Dairy free	Dairy-free option	Gluten free	Gluten-free option	Lower sugar	Lower-sugar option	Nut free	Nut-free option	Vegan	Vegan option
SOUPS											
Vegetable Bouillon	34	•		•				•		•	
Preserved Vegetable Bouillon	35	•		•				•		•	
Roasted Butternut Squash & Garlic Soup	36	•		•						•	
Leek & Potato Soup	37	•		•						•	
Thai Cauliflower, Coconut & Lime Soup	38		•	•				•			•
Country Potage	39	•		•				•		•	
Rich Carrot Soup	40		•	•				•			•
Kashmiri Root Vegetable Soup	41		•	•				•			•
Potato Goulash Soup	42		•	•							•
Soupe au Pistou	43		•	•				•			•
SNACKS & STARTERS											
Thai Butternut & Root Vegetable Pasties	46		•		•			•			•
Ratatouille & Lentil Pasties	48		•		•			•			•
Cranberry, Chestnut & Camembert Filo Pastries	50		•		•						•
Garlic-Mushroom Risotto & Cashew Filos	52	•			•				•	•	
Spinach & Ricotta Filo Pastries (Spanakopitas)	54		•		•				•		•

SNACKS & STARTERS (CONT.)		Dairy free	Dairy-free option	Gluten free	Gluten-free option	Lower sugar	Lower-sugar option	Nut free	Nut-free option	Vegan	Vegan option
Dal Fritters with Lime & Seed Yogurt	56		●	●				●			●
Sprouted Chickpea Falafel Pittas	58	●			●			●		●	
Pink Flush Falafels	59	●						●		●	
Butternut-kick Falafels	59	●						●		●	
Chilli Falafels	59	●						●		●	
Mini Millet Burgers with Tomato & Avocado Salsa	60	●		●						●	
Rainbow Superfood Muffins	62		●	●							●
Courgette or Spinach Superfood Muffins	63		●	●							●
Carrot & Tomato Superfood Muffins	65		●	●							●
Agrodolce Superfood Muffins	64		●	●							●
Beetroot Superfood Muffins	64		●	●							●
Black Olive Superfood Muffins	64		●	●							●
Japanese Superfood Muffins	64		●	●							●
Vegetable Pakoras	65	●		●						●	
COOKED SALADS											
Mushroom, Butter Bean & Seed Salad	68	●		●						●	
Beetroot, Kohlrabi & Potato Salad	69		●	●				●			●
Roasted Vegetable & Quinoa Salad	70		●	●				●			●
Seared Chicory & Orange Salad	72		●	●					●		●
Warm Ruddy Roasted Beetroot Salad	74		●		●				●		●
Mixed Bean Salad	76	●		●				●		●	
String Beans in Spicy Tomato Sauce	77	●		●				●		●	

SAVOURY RECIPES

SAVOURY SLICES		Dairy free	Dairy-free option	Gluten free	Gluten-free option	Lower sugar	Lower-sugar option	Nut free	Nut-free option	Vegan	Vegan option
Beetroot, Carrot & Potato Rösti	80	●		●					●	●	
Farinata with Spicy Tomato Sauce	82		●	●					●		●
Polenta, Fennel Caponata & Lentil Slice	84	●		●				●		●	
Giant Dolmada Cake	86		●	●					●		●
Giant Dolmada Roll	88		●	●					●		●
Butternut, Apple & Smoked Almond Roulade	89		●	●			●		●		
Char-grilled Pepper Polenta Cake & Tapenade	92	●		●				●		●	
Double Maize Bake with Spicy Tomato Sauce	94		●	●				●			●
Baked Ricotta Ring	96		●	●					●		●
Vegetable Quinoa Pizza	98		●	●				●			●
Sweet Quinoa Pizza	99		●	●						●	
CURRIES, STEWS & NOODLE DISHES											
Sweet-and-Sour Egg & Tofu Curry	102		●	●					●		●
Chickpea & Tofu Thai Green Curry	104	●		●					●	●	
Tempeh Goulash with Caraway Dumplings	106	●		●					●	●	
Tempeh Tagine	108	●		●					●	●	
Spätzle with Artichoke Salsa Verde & Greens	110	●		●					●		
Seaweed Noodle & Tofu Stir-fry with Satay Sauce	112	●		●					●	●	
Kashmiri Butter Bean & Vegetable Curry	114		●	●					●		●
PASTRY, TARTS, QUICHES & SAVOURY CHEESECAKES											
Spelt Pastry	122		●				●	●			●
Gluten-free Pastry	124		●	●			●	●			●

SAVOURY RECIPES

PASTRY, TARTS, QUICHES & SAVOURY CHEESECAKES (CONT.)

		Dairy free	Dairy-free option	Gluten free	Gluten-free option	Lower sugar	Lower-sugar option	Nut free	Nut-free option	Vegan	Vegan option
Gruyère, Almond & Thyme Pastry	126		●		●				●		●
Hazelnut Pastry	127		●		●		●		●		●
Beetroot & Butternut Tatin	128		●		●				●		●
Mushroom, Chard & Cheddar Quiche	130		●		●						●
Fennel & Adzuki Bean Pie	132		●		●			●			●
Herbed Potato Pie	134		●		●			●			●
Roasted Pepper & Goat's Cheese Quiche	136		●		●		●	●			●
Vegan Courgette & Cashew Quiche	138	●			●					●	
Chestnut, Cranberry & Onion Quiche	139	●			●					●	
Mushroom, Butter Bean & Seed Quiche	139	●			●					●	
Butternut, Berry & Goat's Cheesecake	140		●	●					●		●
Dolcelatte & Cucumber Cheesecake	142		●	●							●

SWEET RECIPES

SWEETHEART TARTS

		Dairy free	Dairy-free option	Gluten free	Gluten-free option	Lower sugar	Lower-sugar option	Nut free	Nut-free option	Vegan	Vegan option
Tarte au Citron Vert	148		●		●	●	●				●
Caramel Apple Tart	149		●	●				●			
Banoffee Pie	150		●		●			●			●
Mango & Cider Mincemeat Streusel Tart	152		●		●		●				
Pear & Chocolate Tart	154		●		●	●		●			●
Tarte Tatin with Hazelnut Pastry	156		●		●				●		●

SWEET RECIPES

ROULADES, DESSERT CAKES & CHEESECAKES

Recipe	Page	Dairy free	Dairy-free option	Gluten free	Gluten-free option	Lower sugar	Lower-sugar option	Nut free	Nut-free option	Vegan	Vegan option
Master Roulade Recipe	160		●	●				●	●		
Strawberry & Lemon Roulade	162			●					●		
Tiramisu Roulade	163		●	●				●	●		
Véronique's Chocolate Ganache Roulade	164		●	●					●		
Zesty Lemon Polenta Cake	166		●	●				●	●		
Zesty Tropical Polenta Cake	167		●	●							
Double Chocolate Truffle Torte	168		●	●				●			
Lucia's Chocolate Vegan Cake	171	●		●		●				●	
Vegan Nectarine Upside-down Cake	172	●		●		●				●	
Sticky Ginger & Prune Parkin	174	●		●				●		●	
Hazelnut Meringue Gâteau	176			●							
Quick Christmas Cake	178		●	●				●			●
Spiced Apple & Seville Marmalade Cheesecake	180		●	●				●			●
Lemon & Lime Cheesecake	181		●	●				●			●
Vegan Fruity Teasecake	182	●		●				●		●	
Mincemeat, Orange & Saffron Cheesecake	184		●	●				●	●		●
White Chocolate & Raspberry Cheesecake	186		●	●				●	●		●

SWEET VEGETABLE CAKES

Recipe	Page	Dairy free	Dairy-free option	Gluten free	Gluten-free option	Lower sugar	Lower-sugar option	Nut free	Nut-free option	Vegan	Vegan option
Beetroot & Chocolate Cake	190		●	●				●	●		●
Sweet Potato, Pecan & Cappuccino Cake	192		●	●				●			●
Tropical Parsnip & Polenta Cake	194		●	●				●	●		●

SWEET RECIPES

		Dairy free	Dairy-free option	Gluten free	Gluten-free option	Lower sugar	Lower-sugar option	Nut free	Nut-free option	Vegan	Vegan option
SWEET VEGETABLE CAKES (cont.)											
Courgette, White Chocolate & Mint Cake	196		●	●			●				●
Moroccan Aubergine & Rose Celebration Cake	198		●	●			●				●
Jamaican Sweet Potato & Orange Cake	200		●	●			●				●
Carrot Passion Cake	202		●	●				●			●
Macrobiotic Carrot Cake	203	●				●				●	
Vegan Beetroot & Chocolate Cake	204	●		●			●		●	●	
Vegan Sweet Potato, Pecan & Cappuccino Cake	206			●			●			●	
Vegan Tropical Parsnip & Polenta Cake	206			●			●			●	
Vegan Courgette, White Chocolate & Mint Cake	206			●			●			●	
Vegan Moroccan Aubergine & Rose Cake	207			●			●			●	
Vegan Jamaican Sweet Potato & Orange Cake	207			●			●			●	
Vegan Carrot Passion Cake	207			●			●			●	
BLONDIES, BROWNIES & FLAPJACKS											
Chocolate & Hazelnut Brownies	210		●	●					●		
White Chocolate & Pistachio Blondies	211			●							
Adzuki Bean Fudge Brownies	212	●		●			●			●	
Millionaires' Salted Caramel Brownies	213	●		●						●	
Pixie's Irresistible Vegan Chocolate Brownies	214	●			●		●			●	
Blackjack	215		●	●			●	●			●
Lovejack	216		●	●				●			●
Piña Colada Flapjack	217		●	●							●

Savoury Recipes

Soups

All the soups in this chapter have been tried and tested on the coldest and wettest of winter market days, and have never failed to draw cries of appreciation from chilled customers. Although a quick bowl of soup is always great on its own, you may want to combine it with a savoury slice or a cooked salad for a hearty meal.

Whilst puréed seasonal root soups form the rich heart of this repertoire, do try the evocative, summery Soupe au Pistou (page 43) where finely diced courgettes, French and fresh white beans bathe in a ground coriander, orange peel and saffron brew laced with a forceful garlicky tomato, basil and Parmesan pistou. Pure Provence!

A heavy-based, large saucepan with a lid makes the ideal cooking pot for soup. Quickly steam-fry the vegetables in a covered pan to release their aromas before adding the stock, and remember to scrunch up the fresh bay leaves, without breaking them, which helps liberate the fragrant volatile essential oils.

VEGETABLE BOUILLON

Makes about 1.5 litres/2½ pints/6⅔ cups | Prep 15 minutes, plus soaking the mushrooms and frying the vegetables (both optional) | Cook 40 minutes | Dairy free | Gluten free | Nut free | Vegan

Here is my infinitely variable template for vegetable stock, which I call bouillon, because it is richer than a simple stock. Get in the habit of popping clean vegetable peelings into a simmering pot of this bouillon and you'll have a ready supply for your everyday cooking.

6 dried or fresh mushrooms, wiped and quartered

125ml/4fl oz/½ cup boiling water

4 carrots, scrubbed and roughly chopped

4 celery sticks, scrubbed and roughly chopped

4 dried or fresh tomatoes, roughly chopped

2 unpeeled garlic cloves, smashed

2 unpeeled onions, roughly chopped

1 leek, roughly chopped and washed

225g/8oz/about 1⅔ cups chopped assorted root vegetables, such as beetroots (beets), celeriac (celery root), fennel, parsnips and swedes (rutabagas), or corn cobs (optional), scrubbed or peeled, as necessary

10 black peppercorns

4 thyme sprigs

2 bay leaves, scrunched

a handful of parsley sprigs, including the stalks

2 rosemary, oregano or marjoram sprigs, or ¼ tsp dried (optional)

1 tbsp olive or sunflower oil (optional)

2 litres/3½ pints/9 cups water

1. If using dried mushrooms, soak them in the boiling water for 20 minutes. Strain through a sieve lined with muslin (cheesecloth), then quarter them and set aside. Reserve the liquid.

2. If you have time, fry all the vegetables, including the soaked and drained mushrooms, with the peppercorns and herbs in the oil for a few minutes, stirring occasionally.

3. Add the water and any soaking liquid, cover and bring to the boil. Turn the heat down and simmer, with the lid ajar, for 40 minutes.

4. Strain and use according to your recipe, or leave to cool. This will keep in the fridge, in a covered container, for up to 3 days, or in the freezer for up to 6 months.

Cook's note:

You can omit step 2, but I include it because of the depth of flavour it adds.

PRESERVED VEGETABLE BOUILLON

Makes about 50 × 30g/1oz/2 tbsp portions | Prep 30 minutes | No cooking
Dairy free | Gluten free | Nut free | Vegan

Pondering the ticklish subject of reconciling time, great-tasting food and bouillon powder, I came across this salted, fresh vegetable bouillon mixture inspired by *The River Cottage Preserves Handbook* by Pam Corbin. Making and freezing a batch might just be enough to revolutionize your larder – and your taste buds.

55g/2oz/1 cup flat-leaf parsley sprigs, washed

1 garlic clove

85g/3oz/scant ½ cup sun-blush tomatoes or drained sun-dried tomatoes in oil

200g/7oz/1½ cups carrots, scrubbed and chopped

115g/4oz/1⅓ cups celeriac (celery root), peeled and chopped

55g/2oz/½ cup celery sticks, including the leaves, chopped

250g/9oz/1¾ cups sea salt

200g/7oz/2¼ cups fennel, including the small fronds, chopped

4 spring onions (scallions), chopped

140g/5oz/1½ cups leeks, sliced and washed

115g/4oz/⅔ cup shallots, chopped

1. Pulse the parsley in a food processor until finely chopped. Add the garlic and pulse again, then add the tomatoes and continue pulsing until they are finely chopped.

2. Add the carrots, celeriac (celery root) and celery and pulse until they are finely chopped. Add half the salt and pulse until roughly blended. Add the fennel, spring onions (scallions), leeks and shallots and pulse again, then add the remaining salt. The finished mixture should resemble a loose, moist paste.

3. Keep one-quarter of the mixture in a sealed jar in the fridge for up to 1 week and freeze the rest in a re-sealable bag, ready to add flavour to savoury dishes.

Cook's note:

This mixture has roughly half the strength of vegetable bouillon powder, so I use twice as much to compensate. It's very salty, so you will need to adjust the seasoning in your recipe accordingly.

ROASTED BUTTERNUT SQUASH & GARLIC SOUP

Serves 6–8 | Prep 10 minutes | Cook 30 minutes
Dairy free | Gluten free | Vegan

This is a velvety, flavoursome brew. The subtle tastes of roasted squash and garlic make a perfumed marriage, adding a warming glow to banish autumn chills. It's always a good seller. French bread, smothered in herb butter with a touch of turmeric and chillies, goes especially well.

1.3kg/3lb/10 cups butternut squash, peeled, de-seeded and cut into 5cm/2in dice

10 unpeeled garlic cloves

6 tbsp olive, sunflower or raw coconut oil

450g/1lb/2¾ cups onions, sliced

2 bay leaves, scrunched

about 1.8 litres/3 pints/8 cups vegetable stock, boiling

sea salt and freshly ground black pepper

2 tbsp finely chopped flat-leaf parsley, to garnish

6 tbsp rice or soya cream, to garnish

1. Preheat the oven to Fan 200°C/Fan 400°F/Gas 7.

2. Put the squash and garlic into a roasting tray (baking sheet) lined with a silicone mat. Toss in 2 tbsp of the oil and season with salt and pepper to taste. Roast for 15 minutes, or until the squash is just soft. Peel the garlic.

3. Meanwhile, heat the remaining oil in a saucepan over a medium-high heat. Add the onions and bay leaves and immediately turn the heat to medium-low. Cover and cook for 6 minutes, uncovering and stirring occasionally, until the onions are soft and translucent.

4. Add the squash and garlic to the pan with the onions. Stir in enough boiling stock to cover the vegetables by 10cm/4in. Bring the soup to the boil, then simmer, with the lid ajar, for 15 minutes to blend the flavours.

5. Remove the bay leaves, then purée the soup. Add extra boiling stock, as necessary, to make a velvety texture. Add salt and pepper to taste, and garnish with the chopped parsley and rice cream.

LEEK & POTATO SOUP

Serves 6–8 | Prep 20 minutes, plus making the bouillon (optional) | Cook 30 minutes
Dairy free | Gluten free | Vegan

I debated whether I should include my version of this classic. There were so many positive responses, however, that I decided another airing wouldn't harm. The taste is largely dependent on the quality of the ingredients, but the success lies in keeping the simmering to the minimum.

4 tbsp olive, sunflower or raw coconut oil

2 large bay leaves, scrunched

450g/1lb/5 cups leeks, thinly sliced and washed

450g/1lb/3 cups floury (Idaho or baking) potatoes, scrubbed and chopped

about 1.8 litres/3 pints/8 cups vegetable stock, boiling

125ml/4fl oz/½ cup rice or soya cream

sea salt and freshly ground black pepper

2 tbsp finely chopped flat-leaf parsley, to garnish

1. Heat the oil in a large, heavy-based saucepan over a medium-high heat until it shimmers. Throw in the bay leaves for a few seconds, then add the leeks and immediately turn the heat to medium-low, cover the pan and fry for 4 minutes, then stir the leeks again.

2. Add the potatoes, re-cover the pan and cook for 5 more minutes, then stir well.

3. Add enough boiling stock to cover the vegetables by 10cm/4in. Return to the boil and season with salt and not too much pepper. Turn the heat to low and simmer for 20 minutes, with the lid ajar, or until the potatoes are tender.

4. Remove the bay leaves, then purée the soup. Thin the soup with extra boiling stock if it is too thick. Add the cream, adjust the seasoning and keep hot, but do not re-boil. Scatter with the chopped parsley just before serving.

VARIATIONS
If you eat dairy products, replace the rice or soya cream with single (light) cream.

THAI CAULIFLOWER, COCONUT & LIME SOUP

Serves 6–8 | Prep 15 minutes, plus making the curry paste | Cook 35 minutes
Dairy-free option | Gluten free | Nut-free option | Vegan option

Cauliflower and coconut might sound like a surprising combination, but the flavours and texture are very successful, and the soup is so quick and easy to prepare. I serve this almost every Friday at the stall when the weather turns colder – and if I don't, I have unhappy customers.

4 tbsp raw coconut oil

450g/1lb/2¾ cups onions, thinly sliced

2 bay leaves, scrunched

1–1½ tbsp Thai Curry Paste (page 219), to taste

900g/2lb cauliflower, chopped into 12 chunks, including any green leaves

about 1.8 litres/3 pints/8 cups vegetable stock, boiling

250ml/9fl oz/1 cup plus 2 tbsp coconut cream

½ tsp sea salt

freshly grated zest and juice of 2 limes

125ml/4fl oz/½ cup crème fraîche

2 tbsp bottled sweet chilli sauce

freshly ground black pepper, to season

2 tbsp chopped coriander (cilantro) leaves, to garnish

VARIATIONS

Dairy-free and Vegan options
Replace the crème fraîche with rice or soya cream.

Nut-free option
Replace the coconut oil with sunflower oil, and the coconut cream with rice or soya milk.

1. Heat the oil in a large saucepan over a medium-high heat until it shimmers. Add the onions and bay leaves and immediately turn the heat to medium-low, cover and cook for 6 minutes, uncovering and stirring occasionally, until the onions are soft and translucent.

2. Stir in curry paste, re-cover and cook for about 3 minutes. Add the cauliflower, re-cover and cook for 5 minutes, uncovering and stirring occasionally, if necessary, so nothing burns. Add enough stock to cover the cauliflower by 10cm/4in.

3. Add the coconut cream, salt and lime zest, then simmer, with the lid ajar, for no more than 15 minutes, or until cauliflower is just tender. Do not boil or over-cook. Remove the bay leaves. Stir in the crème fraîche, lime juice and chilli sauce, then purée the soup.

4. Adjust the seasoning to taste and serve scattered with chopped coriander (cilantro). Do not re-boil the soup or it will curdle.

COUNTRY POTAGE

Serves 6–8 | Prep 20 minutes | Cook 40 minutes
Dairy free | Gluten free | Nut free | Vegan

Try this satisfying variation of a puréed mixed vegetable soup with the added nutritional boost of lentils. They add texture, while the garlic harmonizes with the rosemary, producing something a little different, which matures with keeping. Add a hunk of really good-quality sourdough bread and you'll have a wholesome, quick meal.

4 tbsp olive oil

4 onions, sliced

2 bay leaves, scrunched

4 garlic cloves, finely chopped

225g/8oz/1⅔ cups swede (rutabagas), peeled and cut into 4cm/1½in chunks

4 large carrots, scrubbed and cut into 4cm/1½in chunks

2 large potatoes, scrubbed and cut into 4cm/1½in chunks

2 large sweet potatoes, peeled and cut into 4cm/1½in chunks

50g/2oz/¼ cup dried red lentils

about 1.8 litres/3 pints/8 cups vegetable stock, boiling

a small bunch of rosemary sprigs, tied together

sea salt and freshly ground black pepper, to season

125ml/4fl oz/½ cup soya or rice cream (optional)

1. Heat the oil in a large saucepan over a medium-high heat until it shimmers. Add the onions and bay leaves and immediately turn the heat to medium-low, cover and cook for 6 minutes, uncovering and stirring occasionally, until the onions are soft and translucent. Stir in the garlic and cook for 1 more minute.

2. Add the root vegetables and lentils, re-cover and cook gently for 6 more minutes, stirring occasionally.

3. Pour in enough vegetable stock or water to come 10cm/4in above the vegetables. Add the rosemary, salt and 6 grinds of black pepper.

4. Bring to the boil, then simmer, with the lid ajar, for 30 minutes, or until the vegetables are tender. Remove the bay leaves and rosemary, then either mash or purée the soup. Stir in the cream, if you want, and adjust the seasoning.

> **VARIATIONS**
> If you eat dairy products, replace the rice or soya cream with crème fraîche.

RICH CARROT SOUP

Serves 6 | Prep 20 minutes | Cook 55 minutes
Dairy-free option | Gluten free | Nut free | Vegan option

The quality of the carrots affects the results of this simple soup, so I recommend home-grown or best-quality organic carrots, preferably with the soil still on them! Slowly cooking the carrots with the softened onions and garlic intensifies their flavour. Just watch closely so the onions do not burn.

1.3kg/3lb carrots, scrubbed

4 tbsp olive oil

4 large onions, sliced

2 bay leaves, scrunched

3 garlic cloves, chopped

about 1.5 litres/2½ pints/6⅔ cups vegetable stock, boiling

sea salt and freshly ground black pepper

2 tbsp chopped dill and chives, to serve

crème fraîche, to serve

1. Cut the carrots into 4cm/1½in chunks by slicing them on the diagonal and rotating a quarter turn – this guarantees even cooking the macrobiotic way – then set aside.

2. Heat the oil in a large saucepan over a medium-high heat until it shimmers. Add the onions and bay leaves and sweat (step 3 on page 36) for 6 minutes.

3. Add the garlic, re-cover the pan and continue to fry for 2 more minutes, stirring occasionally. Add the carrots and gently cook for 8 more minutes, stirring occasionally.

4. Pour in enough stock to come 10cm/4in above the vegetables, add salt and pepper to taste and bring to the boil. Simmer, with the lid ajar, for 40 minutes, or until the carrots are very tender.

5. Remove bay leaves, then purée the soup, adjusting the thickness with extra boiling stock, as necessary. Sprinkle with dill and chives and add a dollop of crème fraîche.

VARIATIONS

Dairy-free and Vegan options
Replace the replace the crème fraîche with rice or soya cream.

Stir in the freshly grated zest of 2 oranges in step 4 and add the juice just before serving.

KASHMIRI ROOT VEGETABLE SOUP WITH A HINT OF LEMON

Serves 6–8 | Prep 15 minutes, plus making the Kashmiri Spice Mix | Cook 55 minutes
Dairy-free option | Gluten free | Nut-free option | Vegan option

This is an unusual blend of warming spices and fresh lemon, which go very well together, transforming the humble swede into an exotic-tasting vegetable. I always sell out of this soup because of its interesting piquancy. If you can't find fresh galangal, use bottled galangal or replace it with grated fresh ginger.

4 tbsp raw coconut oil

2 large onions, sliced

2 bay leaves, scrunched

4 tsp Kashmiri Spice Mix (page 219)

4cm/1½in piece galangal or fresh ginger, peeled and finely grated

900g/2lb/6½ cups swede (rutabaga), peeled and chopped

225g/8oz/2 cups parsnips, scrubbed and sliced

about 1.8 litres/3 pints/8 cups vegetable stock, boiling

freshly grated zest and juice of 3 lemons

5 tbsp ground almonds

sea salt

115g/4oz/½ cup plain Greek yogurt

VARIATIONS
Dairy-free and Vegan options
Replace the dairy yogurt with soya or rice cream.

Nut-free option
Replace the coconut oil with olive or sunflower oil, and the ground almonds with finely ground sunflower seeds.

1. Heat the oil in a large, heavy-based saucepan over a medium-high heat until it shimmers. Add onions and bay leaves and immediately turn the heat to medium-low. Cover the pan and leave to cook for 6 minutes, uncovering and stirring occasionally, until the onions are soft and translucent. Stir in the spice mix and the galangal and cook for 3 minutes, stirring occasionally.

2. Add the swede (rutabaga) and parsnip, re-cover and cook for 5 minutes. Pour in the vegetable stock and add the lemon zest, ground almonds and salt to taste.

3. Bring to the boil, then simmer, with the lid ajar, for 40 minutes, or until all the vegetables are really soft.

4. Remove bay leaves and purée the soup, adding more boiling stock as necessary. Add the lemon juice and adjust the seasoning. Stir in the yogurt just before serving.

POTATO GOULASH SOUP

Serves 6 | Prep 15 minutes, plus making the bouillon (optional) | Cook 45 minutes
Dairy-free option | Gluten free | Vegan option

The rich scent and colour of smoked paprika and caraway, together with hearty chunks of potato, make this an ideal choice for a filling outdoor meal or a wholesome supper dish. I like to extend the Hungarian metaphor and serve with with toasted rye bread and gherkins.

2 tbsp olive, sunflower or raw coconut oil

2 large onions, finely chopped

2 bay leaves, scrunched

2 garlic cloves, smashed

4 carrots, scrubbed and finely diced

1 tbsp sweet paprika

1 tsp smoked paprika

1 tsp caraway seeds

2 red (bell) peppers, de-seeded and chopped

1–2 fresh red chillies, de-seeded and finely chopped

1 tsp marjoram or thyme leaves, or ½ tsp dried

900g/2lb/6 cups floury (Idaho or baking) potatoes, scrubbed and finely chopped

2 litres/3½ pints/9 cups vegetable stock, boiling

400ml/14fl oz/1¾ cups tomato passata (tomato puree)

1½ tbsp tomato purée (tomato paste)

1 tbsp red wine, white wine or apple cider vinegar

1 tsp blackstrap molasses

225g/8oz vegetarian frankfurters, chopped

sea salt and freshly ground black pepper

6 tbsp Greek yogurt or crème fraîche, to serve

1. Heat the oil in a heavy-based saucepan over a medium-high heat. Add the onions and bay leaves and sweat (step 3, page 36) until the onions are soft are translucent. Stir in the garlic and cook for 1 more minute.

2. Stir in the carrots, both paprikas and the caraway seeds. Re-cover and continue cooking for 5 minutes, stirring occasionally.

3. Stir in the peppers, chillies and herbs and cook for 2 minutes. Stir in the potatoes, then re-cover and cook for a couple more minutes.

4. Stir in the stock, tomato passata (tomato puree), tomato purée (tomato paste), vinegar and molasses, and add salt and pepper to taste. Re-cover and simmer for 30 minutes, or until the vegetables are soft. Add the frankfurters and warm through.

5. Ladle the soup into bowls and add a spoonful of yogurt to each one.

VARIATIONS
Dairy-free and Vegan options
Replace the Greek yogurt with soya yogurt.

SOUPE AU PISTOU

Serves 8–10 | Prep 20 minutes, including making the pistou | Cook 45 minutes
Dairy-free option | Gluten free | Nut free | Vegan option

I first had this aromatic soup, which is stuffed with seasonal goodies, in an unassuming restaurant in the mountain village of Vence in the south of France, when on a sunny day off from my live-in chef's job. It remains a perennial favourite, and I serve it with olive-oil brushed, toasted croûtes.

3 litres/5¼ pints/12½ cups water

225g/8oz/1¼ cups carrots, peeled and finely diced

225g/8oz/1⅓ cups onions, finely chopped, or 225g/8oz/2½ cups leeks, thinly sliced and washed

225g/8oz/1½ cups new potatoes, peeled and finely diced

a bouquet garni with 2 bay leaves, 1 thyme sprig and 1 orange peel strip, tied together

1 tbsp sea salt

1 tsp ground coriander

¼ tsp ground fennel

a small pinch of saffron threads

225g/8oz/2 cups courgettes (zucchini), finely diced

225g/8oz/2 cups thin green beans, ends trimmed, cut into 0.5cm/¼in pieces

225g/8oz/heaped 1 cup cooked or canned white haricot beans (navy or great northern beans), drained and rinsed, if canned

30g/1oz thin rice noodles, broken into bite-sized pieces

1 slice of gluten-free bread, crumbled into crumbs

8–10 grinds of fresh black pepper, to season

For the pistou:

4 garlic cloves

2 ripe tomatoes

2 tbsp tomato purée (tomato paste)

4 tbsp torn basil leaves

55g/2oz/½ cup freshly grated Parmesan cheese

150ml/5fl oz/⅔ cup fruity olive oil

1. Bring a large covered saucepan of water to the boil. Stir in the carrots, onions, potatoes, bouquet garni, salt, coriander, fennel and saffron. Simmer, with the lid ajar, for 20 minutes.

2. Stir in the courgettes, green and white beans, noodles and breadcrumbs and simmer for 10–15 minutes until all the vegetables are just tender.

3. Meanwhile, blend all the pistou ingredients together and season to taste.

4. Add the pistou to the soup and adjust the seasoning, if necessary.

VARIATIONS
Dairy-free and Vegan options
Replace the dairy Parmesan cheese with vegan-style Parmesan.

Snacks & Starters

Whether on the go or dining in, here is a tempting array of morsels to whet your appetite. The super scrumptious, versatile pasty fillings can also be used to stuff pancakes, a variety of whole vegetables, cabbage, lettuce or vine leaves. The adaptable Thai Butternut & Root Vegetable (page 46) and the Ratatouille & Lentil (page 48) pasty fillings make lovely lunches as well.

You will also find crispy fritters, baby burgers and a wonderful selection of tasty filo pastry parcels, which are perfect for snacking or serving as a starter. The succulent Falafels (page 58) come with a nutritious sprouting option and my own special sauce. The decorative Rainbow Superfood Muffins (page 62) decisively cross the line into savoury territory and come complete with a stunningly colourful array of unusual toppings.

These mini feasts can be enjoyed as soon as they come out of the oven or pan, but are good cold, too. Many can be made well in advance, freezing and reheating without losing either texture or flavour.

THAI BUTTERNUT & ROOT VEGETABLE PASTIES

Makes 6 | Prep 50 minutes, plus making and chilling the pastry and making the Thai Curry Paste | Bake 30–35 minutes
Dairy-free option | Gluten-free option | Nut-free option | Vegan option

Light, crisp, tasty pastry is one of the hallmarks that make my spelt pasties so popular; the other is the filling – this chunky, curried filling is by far the most popular choice. If you are serving these warm, transfer them to plates using a wide spatula as they are fragile.

1 quantity Spelt Pastry (page 122), chilled for at least 2 hours

white spelt flour, for rolling out

1 egg, beaten

black onion seeds, to garnish

For the filling:

2 tbsp sunflower or raw coconut oil

1 onion, chopped

1 bay leaf, scrunched

2 tbsp Thai Curry Paste (page 219), or to taste

150g/5½oz/heaped 1 cup carrots, scrubbed and chopped

150g/5½oz/1 cup potatoes, scrubbed and chopped

150g/5½oz/1 cup swede (rutabaga), peeled and cut into 1cm/½ in chunks

150g/5½oz/1 cup butternut squash, peeled, de-seeded and chopped

150g/5½oz/heaped 1 cup sweet potato, peeled and cut into 1cm/½ in chunks

1½ tsp sea salt

70g/2½oz/¾ cup grated block creamed coconut

freshly ground black pepper

1. Remove the pastry (dough) from the fridge 15–30 minutes before rolling out, if it has been chilled for 6 hours or longer.

2. To make the filling, heat the oil in a saucepan over a medium-high heat. Add the onion and bay leaf and immediately turn the heat down to medium-low, cover and cook for 6 minutes, uncovering and stirring occasionally, or until the onions are soft and translucent.

3. Stir in the curry paste and cook, covered, for 2 minutes. Stir in the carrots, potatoes and swede (rutabaga) and cook, covered, for 6 minutes, uncovering and stirring occasionally. Add the remaining ingredients, re-cover and continue cooking, stirring occasionally, for 10 minutes over a medium-high heat.

4. Turn the heat to very low and cook gently, covered, for 20 minutes, uncovering and stirring occasionally, or until all the vegetables are tender. If the mixture begins to scorch, moisten with a little water. Add salt and pepper to taste, and allow to cool before using.

Cook's notes:

To serve as a main meal, make double the quantity of filling, and add 400ml/14floz/1¾ cups water to the vegetables while they are cooking. Add 200ml/7fl oz/¾ cup plus 2 tbsp coconut cream along with the freshly squeezed juice of 2 limes just before serving, then scatter with chopped coriander (cilantro) and serve with rice or naan bread and pickles.

Another option for serving the filling as a main meal is to stir in 125ml/4fl oz/½ cup rice or soya (soy) cream or plain dairy yogurt, topping with chopped fresh coriander. Serve with rice, poppadoms and a selection of chutney.

All the pasties, including the Ratatouille & Lentil Pasties (page 48) can be glazed and frozen raw, then baked from frozen in a preheated Fan 200°C/Fan 400°F/Gas 7 oven for about 50 minutes.

VARIATIONS

Dairy-free option
Use 1 quantity Dairy-free Spelt Pastry (page 123).

Gluten-free option
Use 1 quantity Gluten-free Pastry (page 124) and use brown rice flour for rolling out.

Nut-free option
Use sunflower oil instead of coconut oil and omit the block creamed coconut.

Vegan option
Use 1 quantity Vegan Gluten-free Pastry (page 125) and omit the egg.

5. Meanwhile, preheat the oven to Fan 200°C/Fan 400°F/Gas 7 and line a baking (cookie) sheet with parchment paper.

6. On a lightly floured surface, roll out the pastry until it is 4mm/⅛in thick. Use an upturned 15cm/6in plate as a template and cut out 6 circles.

7. Hold a pastry circle in the palm of your hand and brush half the rim with beaten egg, then add one-sixth of the filling along the centre and firmly crimp the edge. Lay the pasty on a baking sheet. Continue until all the pasties are filled.

8. Generously brush with the egg to glaze, and scatter with black onion seeds.

9. Bake for 30–35 minutes until the pastry is golden brown. Leave to cool for at least 10 minutes before serving.

RATATOUILLE & LENTIL PASTIES

Makes 6 | Prep 40 minutes, plus making and chilling the pastry | Bake 30–40 minutes
Dairy-free option | Gluten-free option | Nut free | Vegan option

This filling has a rich flavour due to liberal use of olive oil and the browning technique. You may find browning the vegetables individually a bit puzzling, but it deepens the flavour. Just make sure the vegetables are browned as instructed in the method before you turn them over.

1 quantity Spelt Pastry (page 122), chilled for at least 2 hours

white spelt flour, for rolling out

1 egg, beaten

sesame seeds, to garnish

For the filling:
4 tbsp olive oil

115g/4oz/¾ cup onions, chopped

2 garlic cloves, smashed

115g/4oz/1½ cups aubergines (eggplant), chopped into 1cm/½in chunks

115g/4oz/scant 1 cup courgettes (zucchini), chopped into 1cm/½in chunks

115g/4oz 1 cup mixed (bell) peppers, de-seeded and chopped into 1cm/½in pieces

70g/2½oz/scant ⅓ cup floury (Idaho or baking) potatoes, peeled and coarsely grated

115g/4oz/slightly heaped ½ cup puy lentils

150ml/5fl oz/⅔ cup passata (tomato puree)

1 tbsp tomato purée (tomato paste)

200ml/7fl oz/¾ cup plus 2 tbsp water

4 tbsp dry red wine

2 tsp vegetable bouillon powder

1 bay leaf, scrunched

4 thyme sprigs, tied together

sea salt and freshly ground black pepper

1. To make the filling, heat 1 tbsp of the oil in a flameproof casserole (Dutch oven) over a medium-high heat until it shimmers. Add the onions and immediately turn the heat to medium-low, cover and leave to cook for 6 minutes, uncovering and stirring occasionally, or until the onions are soft and translucent.

2. Stir in the garlic and cook, uncovered, for 2 minutes, stirring occasionally. Transfer the onions to a bowl and set aside.

3. Heat 2 tbsp of olive oil until very hot. Throw in the aubergines (eggplant), stir, cover and cook for 5–8 minutes, uncovering and stirring occasionally, until they have taken on a golden brown colour and are soft; add to the onions. Preheat the oven to Fan 160°C/Fan 325°F/Gas 4.

4. Turn down the heat to medium and heat the remaining oil. Add the courgettes (zucchini) and (bell) peppers and cook for 8 minutes, stirring occasionally, or until they are soft and beginning to colour. Stir in the potatoes and lentils and cook for 1 minute.

Cook's note:

To transform the filling into a stew for an evening meal, double or triple the quantities and add extra water half way through the cooking.

VARIATIONS

Dairy-free option
Use 1 quantity Dairy-free Spelt Pastry (page 123).

Gluten-free option
Use 1 quantity Gluten-free Pastry (page 124) and use brown rice flour for rolling out.

Vegan option
Replace the spelt pastry with 1 quantity Vegan Gluten-free Pastry (page 125).

5. Return all the vegetables to the casserole. Add the passata (tomato puree), tomato purée (tomato paste), water, red wine, vegetable bouillon powder, bay leaf, thyme and add salt and pepper to taste. Stir well and cover.

6. Bring the mixture to the boil. Transfer the casserole to the oven and cook for 1 hour, stirring half way through, or until all the vegetables are tender, especially the aubergines. Add more water, if necessary, to stop the mixture catching on the bottom of the casserole. Leave the filling to cool completely before making the pasties.

7. Preheat the oven temperature to Fan 200°C/Fan 400°F/Gas 7 and line a baking (cookie) sheet with parchment paper.

8. Remove the pastry (dough) from the fridge 15–30 minutes before rolling out, if it has been chilled for 6 hours or longer.

9. Roll out the pastry (dough), then fill, shape and bake as described in steps 6–9 on page 47, sprinkling with the sesame seeds. Leave the baked pasties to cool for at least 10 minutes, before transferring to plates. If they are still warm, use a wide spatula as they are fragile.

CRANBERRY, CHESTNUT & CAMEMBERT FILO PASTRIES

Makes 12 | Prep 40 minutes | Bake 30–40 minutes
Dairy-free option | Gluten-free option | Vegan option

These might remind you of Christmas, but they taste good all year round, as the tartness of the cranberries cuts through the richness of the cheese. They also make an unusual harvest festival or Thanksgiving treat. Choose a ripe Camembert and include sourdough breadcrumbs, if you can.

125ml/4fl oz/½ cup olive oil

3 large onions, sliced

1 bay leaf, scrunched

2 tbsp finely chopped sage leaves, or 1 tbsp dried

175g/6oz/3 cups fresh wholegrain breadcrumbs

450g/1lb/4 cups cranberries, defrosted if frozen

225g/8oz Camembert, cut into 1cm/½ in cubes

225g/8oz/heaped 1 cup cooked and peeled chestnuts, chopped

225g/8oz filo pastry (phyllo pastry dough), defrosted if frozen, each sheet about 46x30cm/18½x12in

3 tbsp butter, melted

sea salt and freshly ground black pepper

black onion seeds, to garnish (optional)

1. Preheat the oven to Fan 200°C/Fan 400°F/Gas 7.

2. Heat 5 tbsp of the oil in a saucepan over a medium-high heat until it shimmers. Add the onions, bay leaf and sage and immediately turn the heat to low. Cover the pan and leave to cook for 6 minutes, uncovering and stirring occasionally, until the onions are soft and translucent. Remove the bay leaf.

3. Add the breadcrumbs, cranberries, Camembert and chestnuts to the pan. Stir together and moisten with water if dry. Season with the salt and pepper, then set aside.

4. Cut the pastry sheets into quarters – you should end up with 48 roughly equal, slightly rectangular pieces. Keep the filo pastry (phyllo pastry dough) you aren't working with covered with damp kitchen paper (paper towels). Lay 2 pieces of filo pastry on top of each other and brush with butter. Top with 2 more pieces, laid diagonally across the first 2 pieces. This ensures the layers fuse together and crisp while baking.

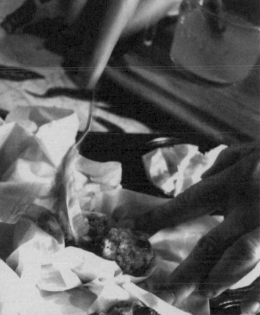

5. Press the filo pieces into one mould of a deep 12-cup deep muffin tray (muffin pan). Leave any over-hanging pastry. Use the remaining pastry and butter to fill the remaining moulds.

6. Divide the filling among the moulds, then fold the overhanging pastry over the top. Brush with the remaining oil and sprinkle with black onion seeds, if using.

7. Bake for 30–40 minutes until all the pastries are golden brown. Transfer the muffin tray to a wire rack and leave to cool for 5 minutes. Gently ease the pastries out of a pan, using a fork, and serve hot or warm.

VARIATIONS

Dairy-free and Vegan options
Replace the Camembert with 225g/8oz/1 cup vegan cream cheese.

Gluten-free option
Use gluten-free breadcrumbs in the filling, and replace the filo pastry with 12 round rice wrappers, about 16cm/6¼in in diameter and defrosted if frozen. Soak them in hot water for 20 seconds, then dry on kitchen paper. Add 1 tbsp filling to each, then roll into spring-roll shapes, sealing the edges with water, if necessary. Deep- or shallow-fry the stuffed rolls for 4 minutes, or until they are golden brown and crisp. Alternatively, they can be steamed for about 10 minutes until the filling is hot.

GARLIC-MUSHROOM RISOTTO & CASHEW FILO PASTRIES

Makes 12 | Prep 40 minutes | Bake 30–40 minutes
Dairy free | Gluten-free option | Nut-free option | Vegan

The mushroom risotto filling here is quite intense; the toasted nuts deepen the richness. Field mushrooms, such as chestnut (cremini) or portobellos, have a full flavour, but I like to add a few very finely chopped fresh shiitake mushrooms for the extra flavour they add.

225g/8oz filo pastry (phyllo pastry dough), defrosted if frozen, each sheet about 46×30cm/18½×12in

4 tbsp olive or sunflower oil, blended with 1 garlic clove and ½ tsp salt for brushing (use an electric hand-held mixer)

1 tbsp blue poppy seeds, for sprinkling

For the Mushroom-Garlic Risotto:

150ml/5fl oz/⅔ cup olive or sunflower, or 140g/5oz/½ cup raw coconut oil

8 garlic cloves, chopped

3 large onions, sliced

2 bay leaves, scrunched

175g/6oz/heaped ¾ cup arborio rice

450g/1lb/6½ cups mushrooms, wiped and chopped

1 tsp sea salt, plus extra for seasoning

300ml/10fl oz/1¼ cups (hard) cider or unsweetened apple juice, boiling

about 300ml/10fl oz/1¼ cups vegetable stock, boiling

115g/4oz/¾ cup cashew nuts, toasted and chopped

85g/3oz/1½ cups flat-leaf parsley, including stalks, finely chopped

freshly ground black pepper

1. To make the risotto, heat the oil in a heavy-based saucepan over a medium-high heat. Fry half the garlic for 1 minute, stirring, or until it begins to turn gold.

2. Immediately add the onions and bay leaf, stir well and turn the heat down to medium-low. Cover and allow to cook gently, uncovering and stirring occasionally, for 10 minutes, or until the onions are soft and translucent.

3. Add the remaining garlic and continue frying, uncovered, for 2 more minutes, or until it begins to soften.

4. Add the rice, stirring until it becomes translucent. Raise the heat, add the mushrooms and the salt and fry, stirring, until the juices run. Lower the heat again and stir in half the hot cider. Season with salt and plenty of pepper.

5. Cover the pan and leave the risotto to cook over a very low heat for 40 minutes, uncovering and stirring occasionally and adding the cider and the stock at periodic intervals, or until the rice is

tender but still with a little bite. Add more stock nearer the end of the cooking time, but only if the mixture begins to stick; you want a drier-than-usual risotto to fill the pastries.

6. Leave the risotto to cool completely. Stir in the cashew nuts and parsley and adjust the seasoning. You should be able to taste the pepper, so if not add more at this stage.

7. Meanwhile, preheat the oven to Fan 200°C/Fan 400°F/Gas 7.

8. Stuff, shape and bake the pastries as instructed in steps 4–7, pages 50–51, filling them with the risotto, brushing with the garlic oil and sprinkling with poppy seeds.

SPINACH & RICOTTA FILO PASTRIES (SPANAKOPITAS)

Makes 12 | Prep 40 minutes | Cook 30–40 minutes
Dairy-free option | Gluten-free option | Nut-free option | Vegan option

This recipe is slightly modified from the Greek classic. It uses ricotta instead of feta cheese, which produces a creamier result. You can, however, use well-drained feta or vegan cream cheese, if you prefer. Including the seeds creates a unique chewy texture – a welcome surprise.

2 tbsp cumin seeds

2 tbsp coriander seeds

2 tbsp fennel seeds

5 tbsp olive oil, plus extra for brushing

3 onions, thinly sliced

3 garlic cloves, finely chopped

900g/2lbs frozen leaf spinach, defrosted and very well drained

450g/1lb/2¼ cups ricotta or feta cheese, drained, if necessary

4 tbsp pumpkin seeds

4 tbsp sunflower seeds

1 tbsp vegetable bouillon powder

½ tsp freshly grated nutmeg

freshly grated zest and juice of 2½ lemons

225g/8oz filo pastry (phyllo pastry dough), defrosted if frozen, each sheet about 46x30cm/18½x12in

sea salt and 10 grinds of black pepper

55g/2oz/4 tbsp butter, melted, or raw coconut oil

1. Preheat the oven to Fan 200°C/Fan 400°F/Gas 7.

2. Dry-roast the spices in a frying pan over a medium heat for 3–4 minutes, stirring. Remove from the heat and grind the spices to a fine powder.

3. Heat the oil in a saucepan over a medium-high heat until it shimmers. Add the onions and immediately turn the heat down to medium-low, cover and cook for 4 minutes, uncovering and stirring occasionally. Add the garlic, re-cover the pan and cook for 2 more minutes, or until the onions are soft and translucent.

4. Stir in the spinach, ricotta cheese, pumpkin and sunflower seeds, bouillon powder, ground spices, nutmeg and lemon zest and juice, and season with salt and pepper. Stir until well mixed together, then set aside until cool.

5. Cut the pastry sheets into quarters – you should end up with 48 roughly equal, slightly rectangular pieces. Keep the filo pastry (phyllo pastry dough) you aren't working with covered with damp kitchen paper (paper towels). Lay 2 pieces of

VARIATIONS

Dairy-free and Vegan options
Replace the ricotta or feta cheese with an equal quantity of silken tofu or vegan cream cheese, drained if necessary, and the butter for brushing with 4 tbsp sunflower oil.

Gluten-free option
Use 12 round rice wrappers, each about 16cm/6½in in diameter, defrosted if frozen, and follow the instructions for soaking on page 51. Fill each one with about 1½ tbsp of the spinach and cheese mixture, then cook as instructed.

Nut-free option
Use sunflower or olive oil instead of coconut oil in the filling, and brush the pastries with melted butter or olive oil.

filo pastry on top of each other and brush with butter. Top with 2 more pieces, laid diagonally across the first 2 pieces. This ensures the layers fuse together and crisp while baking.

6. Press the filo pieces into one mould of a deep 12-cup deep muffin tray (muffin pan). Leave any over-hanging pastry. Use the remaining pastry and butter to fill the remaining moulds.

7. Divide the spinach and ricotta filling among the moulds, then fold the overhanging pastry over the top and brush with the remaining oil.

8. Bake for 30–40 minutes until the pastries are golden brown. Transfer the muffin tray to a wire rack and leave the filo pastries to cool for 5 minutes. Gently ease them out of a pan, using a fork and serve hot or warm.

DAL FRITTERS WITH LIME & SEED YOGURT

Serves 6–8 | Prep 10 minutes, plus at least 2 hours soaking | Cook 20–30 minutes
Dairy-free option | Gluten free | Nut free | Vegan option

I first made a version of these delicious lentil fritters when I worked at Willow vegetarian restaurant, here in Totnes. They are so simple to make and extremely moreish. Make these as a scrummy, gluten-free snack, a dinner party first course or as part of a hot grazing buffet.

225g/8oz/heaped 1 cup white urud dal, soaked for at least 2 hours in cold water to cover, then well drained

2 fresh green chillies, seeded or de-seeded as you like, and finely chopped

1 red onion, finely chopped

½ tsp sea salt

freshly grated zest of 1 lime

a pinch of dried fenugreek

sunflower oil, for frying

a handful of chopped coriander (cilantro) and mint leaves, to garnish

For the Lime & Seed Yogurt:

1½ tsp cumin seeds

½ tsp yellow mustard seeds

½ tsp black onion seeds

1 tsp sunflower oil

1½ tsp white urud dal

500g/1lb 2oz/2 cups plain sheep or goat's yogurt

freshly squeezed juice of 1 lime

Cook's notes:

You should be able to find the small white urud dal lentils at health food shops or in Indian grocery stores. Some traditional recipes instruct you to soak the fritters in the yogurt sauce for 20 minutes, then squeeze and serve. I prefer them hot, but you can serve them either way.

Deep-frying yields the best results, but the fritters can also be shallow-fried. Heat about 2.5cm/1in sunflower oil in a heavy-based frying pan over a medium heat. Fry the fritters, in batches, for 2 minutes on one side, then gently turn them over and fry for 2 more minutes, or until they are golden brown and cooked through. Keep them warm and serve as step 6 (right).

1. Grind the urud dal in a blender or food processor until you have a thick, white, smooth batter. Blend in the chillies, onion, salt, lime zest and fenugreek, then set aside.

2. To make the yogurt, fry the cumin, mustard and black onion seeds in the oil over a medium-high heat for 1–2 minutes until they splutter.

3. Add the urud dal and continue frying until they turn golden brown. Add the fried spices and dal to the yogurt, then stir in the lime juice and season with salt. Pour into a shallow serving dish, cover and chill until required.

4. Just before serving, heat enough oil for deep-frying in a heavy-based saucepan until it reaches 190°C/375°F, or a cube of bread sizzles and browns in 30 seconds.

5. When the oil is hot, carefully lower tablespoons of the batter into the oil and fry for 3 minutes, or until the fritters are golden brown all over and they float to the surface. If you find the batter sticks to the spoon, grease it with a little oil first.

6. Drain the fritters on kitchen paper (paper towels), then pop into a hot serving dish and keep hot in a Fan 160°C/Fan 325°F/Gas 4 oven, with the door ajar, while you fry the rest. Serve immediately, arranged on top of the yogurt sauce and sprinkled with coriander (cilantro) and mint.

VARIATIONS
Dairy-free and Vegan options
Replace the dairy yogurt with soya (soy) yogurt.

SPROUTED CHICKPEA FALAFEL PITTAS WITH TAHINI-LEMON DRESSING

Makes 15–20 | Prep 30 minutes, plus at least 4 hours soaking but, ideally, 24 hours, plus optional 2–3 days sprouting
Cook 20 minutes | Dairy free | Gluten-free option | Nut free | Vegan

This is the item I sell that has the most requests for the recipe. I discovered the special quality by deep-frying raw hummus made with sprouted chickpeas. Please resist the temptation to use either cooked or canned chickpeas in this recipe—they will not work out for you. You have been warned!

250g/9oz/heaped cup dried chickpeas, soaked in cold water to cover by 5cm/2in for at least 4 hours, but preferably 24 hours

85g/3oz/1½ cups flat-leaf parsley sprigs, stalks and leaves, washed and patted dry

1 onion, cut into 8 wedges

200g/7oz/1½ cups sesame seeds, freshly ground

4 tbsp freshly squeezed lemon juice

1 tbsp cumin seeds, freshly ground

1 tbsp sea salt

1–3 tbsp chickpea flour

sunflower oil, for frying

For the Tahini-Lemon Dressing:
400g/14oz canned chickpeas (don't drain – you need the liquid for mixing)

6 tbsp freshly squeezed lemon juice

2–3 tbsp tamari, to taste

2 tbsp balsamic vinegar

3 tbsp light tahini

1 garlic clove, smashed

To serve:
pitta breads, warm

bottled hot or sweet chilli sauce

salad leaves, chopped spring onions, sliced tomatoes and chopped cucumbers

1. If not sprouting the chickpeas, omit this step. Drain and rinse the soaked chickpeas, then leave them in a bowl in a cool place, covered with a clean cloth, for 2–3 days, rinsing them at least twice a day in a colander.

2. Meanwhile, to make the dressing, put the chickpeas and the liquid from the can in a blender or food processor with all the other ingredients and blend until the mix is the consistency of thick double (heavy) cream. If it is too thick, thin with a little water. Cover and chill until required. The dressing improves over a 24-hour period and keeps for up to 3 days in the fridge.

3. Once the soaked chickpeas have sprouted, drain and rinse them again. Put the parsley in a food processor, then add the onion and finally the chickpeas and pulse until you get a firm, chunky paste.

4. Add the sesame seeds, lemon juice, cumin seeds, salt and 1 tbsp chickpea flour, and blend again. If the mixture appears too wet, add more sifted chickpea flour. A perfect mixture should be moist

Cook's notes:

If you want to get ahead, shape the falafals and leave them covered with cling film (plastic wrap) in the fridge for up to 4 hours.

If you are new to sprouting chickpeas, you need to begin the sprouting process up to 3 days in advance for the extra nutritive sprouts to emerge. If you are in a hurry, however, a minimum 4-hour soak will suffice, but a 24-hour soak is preferable. The chickpeas begin sprouting at the end of 24 hours soaking and will continue to grow almost indefinitely. The 3-day sprouting process adds extra vitamins to the food, especially if you choose to eat them raw. It is important, however, the sprouting chickpeas are rinsed before eating.

VARIATIONS

Gluten-free variation
Use gluten-free pitta breads and gluten-free chilli sauce.

Pink Flush Falafals
Add 175g/6oz/1¼ cups finely chopped raw beetroot (beets) and 1 tsp wasabi powder or 1 tbsp bottled creamed horseradish to the chickpea mix when blending.

Butternut-kick Falafals
Add 175g/6oz/1 cup grated butternut squash and 1 tsp Piri-piri Spice Mix (page 220).

Chilli Falafals
Add 1 very finely chopped, de-seeded fresh red chilli, 2 very finely chopped garlic cloves and 1 tsp smoked garlic powder to the chickpea mix when blending.

but not runny; experience will allow you to find the best texture.

5. Form the mixture into the shapes you prefer, large or small balls or croquettes.

6. Heat enough oil for deep-frying in a deep-fat fryer or a heavy-based saucepan until it reaches 190°C/375°F, or until a cube of bread browns in 30 seconds. Line a colander with kitchen paper (paper towels) to drain the falafels in.

7. Gently slide in as many falafels as will comfortably fit in the fryer, then immediately lower the heat to 160°C/325°F. Fry for 5–6 minutes, using tongs to turn them over half way through. Cooking times will vary depending on the size of your falafel; you are aiming for darkish golden brown. Use a slotted spoon to transfer them to the colander. Keep the falafels warm in a Fan 160°C/Fan 325°F/Gas 4 oven, with the door ajar, until all are fried. Reheat the oil between batches, if necessary.

8. Serve the falafels in hot, split pitta breads with the salad ingredients. Add the Tahini-Lemon Dressing and drizzle with the chilli sauce.

MINI MILLET BURGERS WITH TOMATO & AVOCADO SALSA

Makes 24 | Prep 40 minutes, plus at least 2 hours chilling and making the salsa | Cook 16–20 minutes
Dairy free | Gluten free | Vegan

When my children were at the local school, I ran the burger stall at the summer fair, and this recipe was kindly donated by a fellow parent. The burgers were so popular that the recipe lives on in the local community and here it is for everyone to enjoy.

750ml/1¼ pints/3 cups vegetable stock

225g/8oz/heaped 1 cup millet

1 bay leaf, scrunched

115g/4oz flat field mushrooms, wiped and trimmed

5–6 garlic cloves, smashed

3 celery sticks, chopped

2 large onions, chopped

1 small green (bell) pepper, de-seeded and chopped

1 small red (bell) pepper, de-seeded and chopped

1 fresh red chilli, de-seeded (optional)

4–6 tbsp olive or raw coconut oil

55g/2oz/1 cup coriander (cilantro) leaves, finely chopped

freshly grated zest of 1 lime

sea salt and freshly ground black pepper, to season

sunflower oil, for frying

selection of salads, to serve

1. Put the stock, millet, bay leaf and a few grinds of pepper in a saucepan and bring to the boil. Cover and simmer for 25 minutes, or until the millet is tender and all the liquid has been absorbed. Set aside, covered with a clean kitchen towel. When cool, remove the bay leaf.

2. Meanwhile, place the all the vegetables and the chilli in a food processor and pulse-blitz to finely chop, or finely chop by hand. Do not purée or the burgers will be soggy.

3. Heat a 0.5cm/¼in layer of oil in a frying pan. Add the vegetables and fry, stirring, until they are very soft and turning golden. Lower the heat as necessary. When the millet is cool enough to handle, combine it with the vegetables, coriander (cilantro) and zest. Season and mix together.

4. Use wet hands to shape the mixture into 24 mini burgers, pressing together firmly. Place the burgers on a tray lined with parchment paper. Cover and chill for at least 2 hours, but no longer than 36 hours.

For the Tomato & Avocado Salsa:

1 garlic clove, smashed and finely chopped

1 small red onion, finely chopped

1 fresh red chilli, de-seeded and finely chopped (optional)

1 tbsp chopped coriander (cilantro) leaves

½ tsp smoked paprika

freshly squeezed juice of 1 lime

225g/8oz ripe tomatoes

2 ripe avocados

5. Meanwhile, to make the salsa, combine the garlic, onion and chilli, if using, in a non-metallic bowl with the coriander (cilantro), smoked paprika, lime juice, salt to taste and a few grinds of pepper.

6. Next, use a small curved knife to remove the tough core at the top of the tomatoes in a cone shape. Finely dice the flesh and add to the other salsa ingredients.

7. Split an avocado in half lengthways, then smack a large knife into the stone and twist – the stone should come out with ease. Repeat with the other avocado, then peel and dice them. Add to the salsa and gently mix together. Cover and chill until required.

8. Shallow-fry the burgers in batches over a medium heat for 4–5 minutes on each side until they are golden brown and crisp on both sides. Let a good crust form before attempting to turn them. Transfer to a warm oven and continue frying until all the burgers are cooked.

9. Drain the burgers well on kitchen paper (paper towels), then serve with the salsa and salads of your choice.

RAINBOW SUPERFOOD MUFFINS

Makes 12 | Prep 20–30 minutes | Bake 20–30 minutes
Dairy-free option | Gluten free | Vegan option

Let your creative impulses loose with these pretty, über-healthy savoury muffins. Here's the basic recipe and technique with a number of variations – experiment and make them your own. Why not throw a rainbow muffin and smoothie party for an original children's party? It doesn't have to be a kids-only affair, either!

115g/4oz/1⅓ cups soya (soy) flour

115g/4oz/¾ cup brown rice flour

5 tsp gluten-free baking powder

1 tsp sea salt

chopped herbs, ground spices, seeds and/or nuts of your choice (see variations, pages 63–64)

225g/8oz vegetables of your choice (see variations, pages 63–64)

175ml/6fl oz/¾ cup milk

125ml/4fl oz/½ cup sunflower, olive or groundnut (peanut) oil

2 eggs, beaten

fresh herb sprigs, chopped herbs, micro herbs and/or sprouts or cherry tomato roses, to decorate – use your imagination!

For the basic topping:

250g/9oz/1 cup plus 2 tbsp cream cheese, plain Greek yogurt or soft goat's cheese

ground spices, such as Kashmiri Spice Mix (page 219), za'atar or gomasio, to flavour and dust

sea salt and freshly ground black pepper, to season

1. Preheat the oven to Fan 180°C/Fan 350°F/Gas 6. Line the moulds of a deep 12-hole muffin tray (muffin pan) with paper cases (cups).

2. Mix the flours, baking powder, salt and your chosen flavourings together in a large bowl. Stir the vegetables into the dry ingredients.

3. Beat together all the wet ingredients in another bowl. Add the wet ingredients to the dry ingredients and stir just enough to mix together. Take care not to over-beat – it doesn't matter if all the flour isn't incorporated.

4. Spoon the batter into the paper cases, filling each almost to the top, then smooth the tops. Bake for 20–30 minutes until the muffins are firm to the touch. Leave the muffins to cool in the tray on a wire rack for 5 minutes, then turn out and leave to cool completely on the rack.

5. Meanwhile, to make the topping, beat your chosen topping mixture until smooth and creamy. Add the superfood powder, herbs and flavourings you have chosen and season to taste.

6. Spread or pipe the filling over the top of the muffins. Decorate with sprouts and dust with ground spices or whatever you like.

Cook's note:

Store the un-filled and un-iced muffins in an airtight container for up to 48 hours, and filled ones for up to 24 hours.

COURGETTE OR SPINACH SUPERFOOD MUFFINS

225g/8oz/1¾ cups courgettes (zucchini), grated, or 225g/8oz/4 cups chopped spinach, wilted in butter, drained and squeezed dry

30g/1oz/½ cup chopped flat-leaf parsley leaves

1 tbsp toasted tamari pumpkin seeds for sprinkling on the batter before baking

For the topping:

2 tsp green superfood, such as chlorella or spirulina

1 tbsp torn basil leaves

1 garlic clove, smashed with a pinch of sea salt

CARROT & TOMATO SUPERFOOD MUFFINS

225g/8oz/heaped 1¾ cups carrots, scrubbed and finely grated

1 tbsp chopped, drained sun-dried tomato in olive oil

1 tsp smoked paprika, plus extra for dusting

1 tbsp drained and chopped char-grilled (roasted red) pepper

For the topping:

1½ tsp tomato purée (tomato paste)

½ tsp vegetable bouillon powder

1 tsp pomegranate molasses or unsweetened apple juice concentrate

cherry tomato roses, for decoration

AGRODOLCE SUPERFOOD MUFFINS

115g/4oz/scant ¾ cup fine polenta, to replace the soya (soy) flour

225g/8oz/1½ cups onion, chopped and boiled for 10 minutes with 1 tbsp raisins, 2 tsp pomegranate molasses, 1 tsp tarragon vinegar, a small pinch of saffron and sea salt and freshly ground black pepper to taste

1 tbsp freshly grated Parmesan cheese and 2 tsp toasted pine nuts, for sprinkling over batter before baking

For the topping:

225g/8oz/1 cup ricotta cheese, drained

1 tsp finely chopped sage leaves

1 tbsp finely grated Parmesan cheese

2 tsp maca powder

BLACK OLIVE SUPERFOOD MUFFINS

1 tbsp chopped pickled garlic

½ tsp chopped rosemary leaves

2 tbsp black tapenade (add to the wet ingredients)

1 tbsp red pesto (add to the wet ingredients)

1 tbsp pine nuts, for sprinkling over the batter before baking

For the topping:

1 garlic clove, smashed

1 tbsp chopped basil

2 tsp lucuma powder

BEETROOT SUPERFOOD MUFFINS

225g/8oz/1¼ cups beetroot (beets) peeled, finely grated and cooked in boiling water for 4 minutes, then drained and squeezed dry

½ tsp wasabi powder, or 2 tsp creamed horseradish

½ tsp thyme leaves

For the topping:

2 tbsp grated red onion, fried in a little oil and patted dry

1–2 tbsp beetroot (beet) juice, just enough to make a spreading consistency

1 tbsp cashew nuts, toasted and chopped

beetroot powder or ground pink peppercorns, for dusting

JAPANESE SUPERFOOD MUFFINS

140g/5oz/heaped 1 cup daikon, peeled and finely grated

115g/4oz/⅔ cup cooked glutinous (sweet) rice, sprinkled with 1 tbsp rice vinegar, to replace the rice flour in the master recipe

1 tsp wakame flakes

½ tsp Chinese 5-Spice powder

For the topping:

½ tsp wasabi powder

1 tsp umeboshi plum paste

1 tbsp tamari

1 tsp black sesame seeds

2 tsp chlorella or spinach powder

ground Szechuan pepper, for dusting

VEGETABLE PAKORAS

Serves 6–8 I Prep 15 minutes, plus 15 minutes resting, making the spice powder and the yogurt sauce (optional)
Cook 15–18 minutes I Dairy free I Gluten free I Vegan

Made with a gluten-free batter, these make spicy, tasty snacks or a delicious first course for an Indian meal. You can use almost any firm, sliced raw vegetable, or even cooked artichoke hearts. I particularly like these made with aubergine, cauliflower and red onions.

280g/10oz/3⅓ cups chickpea flour

2 tsp sea salt

1 tsp turmeric

2 tsp Kashmiri Spice Mix (page 219)

500ml/18fl oz/2¼ cups water

1 tbsp sunflower or melted raw coconut oil

1 tbsp freshly squeezed lime juice

55g/2oz/1 cup shredded spinach leaves

2 garlic cloves, smashed

4 tbsp finely chopped spring onions (scallions)

sunflower oil, for deep-frying

600g/1lb 5oz assorted firm vegetables, such as sliced cooked artichoke hearts, aubergine (eggplant) slices, (bell) pepper slices, cauliflower florets, sliced red or white onions or cubed small waxy potatoes

Lime & Seed Yogurt (page 56), to serve (optional)

1. Sift the flour, salt and turmeric together in a large bowl, then stir in the spice powder. Slowly whisk in most of the water and the coconut oil to make a batter.

2. Add the lime juice, shredded spinach, garlic, spring onions (scallions) and beat, adding the remaining water as necessary until the batter is like thick cream. Leave the batter to rest at room temperature, covered, for 15 minutes.

3. When ready to cook, heat enough oil for deep-frying in a deep-fat fryer or heavy-based frying pan over a high heat until it reaches 190°C/375°F.

4. Stir your chosen vegetables into the batter. Lower tablespoonfuls of the mixture, in batches, into the oil and fry for 5–6 minutes until the pakoras are golden brown and the vegetables cooked through.

5. Drain the pakoras on kitchen paper (paper towels) and keep warm in a low oven, with the door slightly ajar, until they are all fried, if you want. Serve hot or at room temperature with the yogurt, if you like.

Cooked Salads

This chapter somehow wrote itself under the cooked vegetable umbrella, which has I think, on reflection, something to do with unexpected contrasts. Roast hot lettuce, chilled charred beetroot and al dente sauced green beans all pique the gastronomic curiosity.

Several composed salads multitask as a light or main meal in themselves, others form part of the salad table and several more offer interesting side accompaniments to a hot main menu.

I also really enjoy the cooking challenge of preserving the taste and texture of green vegetables by presenting them on the cusp between al dente triumph and mushy disaster!

MUSHROOM, BUTTER BEAN & SEED SALAD

Serves 4–6 | Prep 15 minutes | Cook 20 minutes
Dairy free | Gluten free | Vegan

This cooked salad is almost a meal in itself, tasty and filling with scope for mushroom experimentation. If you have been foraging in the autumn woods, use your mushroom stash in this recipe. If you prefer a raw salad, marinate the mushrooms with all the liquid ingredients for an hour.

4 tbsp olive, sunflower or raw coconut oil

450g/1lb/6½ cups chestnut (cremini) mushrooms, wiped and sliced

60g/2½oz/scant 1 cup shiitake mushrooms, wiped and finely chopped

225g/8oz/1¾ cups courgettes (zucchini), cut into matchsticks

1 tsp finely chopped tarragon leaves, or ½ tsp dried

2 garlic cloves, finely chopped

1 tbsp ground coriander

freshly grated zest and juice of 1 lemon

4 tbsp pumpkin or sunflower seeds

4 tbsp tamari

1 tbsp tarragon vinegar

300g/10oz/2 cups canned butter beans, drained and rinsed

2 tbsp chopped chives

3–4 tbsp hazelnut and flaxseed oils mixed together, to taste

sea salt and freshly ground black pepper, to season

1. Heat 2 tbsp of the oil in a wok over a medium-high heat until it shimmers. Toss in all the mushrooms and stir-fry for about 8 minutes until they are browned. Transfer to a bowl.

2. Heat the remaining oil. Add the courgettes (zucchini) and tarragon and stir-fry for 6 minutes, or until barely tender. Add the garlic and stir-fry for 1 minute. Stir in the ground coriander and lemon zest and continue stir-frying for 1 minute. Add to the mushrooms, then wipe the wok.

3. Re-heat the wok. Sprinkle in the seeds and dry-fry over a medium heat, stirring constantly, for about 4 minutes, or until they begin to colour.

4. Immediately splash in the tamari, vinegar and lemon juice and continue to stir until the liquid evaporates, then tip the seed mix over the courgettes.

5. Mix the beans into the bowl with the chives, and season to taste. Toss the salad with the hazelnut and flaxseed oils and adjust the seasoning, if necessary. Cover and chill until ready to serve.

BEETROOT, KOHLRABI & POTATO SALAD

Serves 10–12 | Prep 25 minutes, plus up to 24 hours chilling | Cook 20 minutes
Dairy-free option | Gluten free | Nut free | Vegan option

This is a fine-tasting, pink and chunky salad for a crowd, with kohlrabi giving an unexpected juicy bite. The colours of the salad intensify as the salad chills, which is what makes it an ideal party salad. Summer to early autumn is the time to catch these vegetables in their prime.

750g/1lb 10oz/5½ cups raw beetroot (beets), peeled and cut into bite-sized chunks

750g/1lb 10oz/5½ cups kohlrabi or broccoli stalks, peeled and cut into bite-sized chunks

750g/1lb 10oz/5 cups new potatoes, scrubbed and cut into bite-sized chunks

3 tbsp fruity olive oil

1 red onion, chopped

1 garlic clove, finely chopped

2 tbsp chopped chives or spring onions (scallions)

2 tbsp chopped flat-leaf parsley leaves

6–8 tbsp mayonnaise

sea salt and freshly ground black pepper, to season

1. Bring 2 large saucepans of salted water to the boil. Cook the beetroot (beets) and kohlrabi in one for 20–30 minutes until they are both tender.

2. Meanwhile, boil the potatoes in the other pan for 15–20 minutes until they are tender. Test all the vegetables near the end of their cooking time with the tip of a knife so they do not over-cook.

3. Drain the vegetables and place in a large bowl. While they are still warm, toss them with the olive oil, a sprinkle of salt and 5 grinds of black pepper, stirring to coat. Leave them to cool, covered with a towel.

4. Meanwhile, blitz the onion, garlic, chives and parsley in a food processor. Stir this mixture into the mayonnaise and season to taste, then toss with the vegetables. The salad is ready to serve, but best if chilled for at least 1 hour or up to 24 hours.

Cook's note:

If you keep the kohlrabi in the fridge for any length of time, remove the leaves as they suck moisture from the root. The leaves can be used in the same way as spinach in other dishes.

> **VARIATIONS**
> **Dairy-free and Vegan options**
> Replace the egg mayonnaise with vegan mayonnaise.

ROASTED VEGETABLE & QUINOA SALAD

Serves 4–8 | Prep 25 minutes, plus making the spice mix (optional) | Cook 45 minutes
Dairy-free option | Gluten free | Nut free | Vegan option

This is a modern classic for a very good reason – quinoa is wonderfully nutritious, especially when combined with such tasty companions. I like this for packed lunches, and it is always a welcome offering at parties. This serves four as a main meal or eight as a first course.

2 large red onions, peeled and chopped

2 red (bell) peppers, de-seeded and cut into 4cm/1½in pieces

280g/10oz/2¼ cups courgettes (zucchini), cut into 4cm/1½in dice

280g/10oz/2 cups sweet potatoes, peeled and cut into 4cm/1½in dice

280g/10oz/2½ cups butternut squash, skin on, de-seeded and cut into 4cm/1½in dice

8 unpeeled garlic cloves

2 tbsp olive, sunflower or flaxseed oil

2 tbsp tamari or liquid aminos

2 tbsp balsamic vinegar

1 tsp sea salt

1 tsp sugar or agave syrup

a small pinch of Piri-piri Spice Mix (page 220) or chilli flakes

1 tbsp olive or flaxseed oil

280g/10oz/1½ cups quinoa, rinsed and drained well, then rubbed to remove the coating

500ml/18fl oz/2¼ cups vegetable stock

1 tsp chopped rosemary leaves, or ½ tsp dried

sea salt and freshly ground black pepper, to season

1. Preheat the oven to Fan 200°C/Fan 400°F/Gas 7.

2. Put all the vegetables and the garlic into a roasting tin (roasting pan) lined with a silicone mat.

3. Add 2 tbsp of the oil, the tamari and vinegar and sprinkle with the salt, sugar and Piri-piri, then toss well to coat.

4. Roast the vegetables for 12 minutes, then remove the garlic, which should be soft. Turn the vegetables over and roast for a further 10–15 minutes until they are all tender.

5. When the garlic is cool enough to handle, pop the cloves out of their skins.

6. Meanwhile, blitz the garlic in a blender or food processor with all the dressing ingredients and seasoning to taste, but remember the capers are salty. Coat the vegetables with a couple tbsp dressing while they are still hot, then leave them to cool.

For the dressing:

6 tbsp olive oil

2 tbsp flaxseed oil

2 tbsp pomegranate molasses

2 tbsp chopped flat-leaf parsley

2 tbsp roughly chopped shallots

2 tbsp white or dark balsamic vinegar

2 tbsp white wine vinegar

1 tbsp capers, rinsed

To serve:

mixed salad leaves and flowers, such as comfrey, marigold, nasturtium and rose

450g/1lb/3 cups aged feta, drained and crumbled

10 purple or green basil leaves, torn

20 cherry tomatoes, halved

1 tbsp sesame seeds, toasted and ground (use a coffee grinder)

chopped chives

VARIATIONS
Dairy-free and Vegan options
Replace the feta with feta-style vegan cheese.

---

7. Heat the remaining oil in a saucepan over a medium-high heat. Add the quinoa and toast, stirring, until it is golden. Pour in the stock, rosemary and pepper to taste and bring to a rolling boil.

8. Turn the heat to the lowest setting and cook, with the lid ajar, for 15 minutes, or until the quinoa is tender and all the liquid has been absorbed. Cover tightly and leave for 5 minutes. Fluff up with a fork and allow to cool.

9. To assemble, arrange the leaves around the border of a serving platter or on individual plates. Gently fork the feta, if using, into the cooled quinoa. Add the cherry tomatoes and most of the torn basil, and season with pepper.

10. Spoon the quinoa into the middle of the dish and arrange the roasted vegetables on top. Scatter with the remaining basil, sesame seeds and some chopped chives. Drizzle with more dressing and serve the remainder on the side in a small jug.

SEARED CHICORY & ORANGE SALAD

Serves 6 | Prep 30 minutes | Cook 15 minutes
Dairy-free option | Gluten free | Nut-free option | Vegan option

I love cooked salads, especially in the winter. This one will enliven your palate, the charred bitter juiciness wooed by a nutty honeyed dressing, slaked with fresh goat's cheese. Even if you can't bear bitter flavours, I really do encourage you to try it at least once – or use bok choy and romaine lettuce instead.

4 navel or blood oranges

2 red onions, cut into 1cm/½in slices

3 chicory (Belgian endive), halved lengthways

3 Treviso radicchio, halved lengthways

seeds from 1 pomegranate

4 tbsp pecans halves, toasted

225g/8oz soft goat's cheese or dolcelatte

2 tbsp finely chopped chives

For the dressing:

6 tbsp hazelnut or walnut oil

2 tbsp sherry or raspberry vinegar

1 tbsp manuka honey

1 tbsp pomegranate molasses or maple syrup

1 tsp wholegrain mustard

1 tsp sea salt

6 grinds of black pepper

a pinch of smoked paprika

a dash of Angostura bitters (optional)

1. Bring a small saucepan of water to the boil.

2. While the water is coming up to the boil, zest the orange peel into very fine shreds. Plunge the shreds into the boiling water, then almost immediately drain and refresh them under cold water. Pat them dry and set aside.

3. Using a small serrated knife, slice the ends off the zested oranges. Carefully cut away all the pith, so you end up with skinless, pithless oranges. If you don't remove all the pith the oranges will taste bitter. Next, carefully remove the segments and set them aside.

4. Squeeze the juice from the membranes into a non-metallic bowl. Whisk all the dressing ingredients, including the bitters, if using, into the juice and season to taste, then set aside.

5. Heat a ridged, cast-iron griddle pan until it is very hot. Sear the onion slices for 2 minutes on each side, or until lightly charred and softened, then set aside.

6. Brush the endive and radicchio halves with the dressing and char-grill, cut-side down first, for 3–4 minutes each side until lightly charred and softened.

7. While the endive and radicchio are still hot, arrange the leaves on a platter or individual plates and add the orange segments and pomegranate seeds. Sprinkle with the nuts, dollops of cheese, chives and orange zests, then drizzle with the remaining dressing.

WARM RUDDY ROASTED BEETROOT SALAD

Serves 6–8 | Prep 40 minutes, including cooking the spinach | Cook 1 hour
Dairy-free option | Gluten-free option | Nut-free option | Vegan option

This is a special, elegant side dish or first course, and you can enjoy it cold in hotter weather. It's crunchy, soft, fruity, sweet and sour, all offset by dabs of garlic-scented cheese... yummy. I do enjoy roasting the beetroots over an open fire at least once every winter, especially with friends.

1kg/2lb 4oz beetroot (beets), preferably large and the same size, trimmed with leaves reserved

1 tbsp walnut oil, lightly seasoned

115g/4oz/2 cups beet greens or fresh spinach

500g/1lb 2oz shallots or small onions, peeled

4 unpeeled garlic cloves, plus 1 or 2 extra, peeled

4 tbsp olive, sunflower or flaxseed oil

2 tbsp raspberry or red wine vinegar

2 tbsp tamari

1 tsp pomegranate molasses, or 1 tsp sugar

1 bay leaf, scrunched

½ tsp fresh thyme leaves

½ tsp juniper berries

olive oil, for brushing

140g/5oz/heaped ½ cup soft sheep or goat's cheese

3–4 slices sourdough bread

100g/3½oz/½ cup cooked, peeled chestnuts (optional)

sea salt and freshly ground black pepper, to season

1. Preheat the oven to Fan 200°C/Fan 400°F/Gas 7.

2. Scrub the beetroot, trying not to break the skins, and leave them wet. Loosely wrap them individually in foil, place in a roasting tin (not too close together) and roast for 1 hour, or until tender – a skewer should pass through the centres without any resistance.

3. When they are cool enough to handle with a cloth, use the foil to rub off the skins. Cut each beetroot into thick wedges, brush with the seasoned walnut oil and keep warm by re-wrapping them in the foil.

4. Meanwhile, put the shallots and unpeeled garlic cloves in a roasting tin lined with a silicone mat. Sprinkle over the oil, vinegar, tamari and pomegranate molasses, then add the bay leaf, thyme and juniper berries, and mix well.

5. Put the pan in the oven while the beetroot are cooking and roast for 20–30 minutes, turning them once after 15 minutes. Remove the garlic at the turning stage and add the chestnuts to the onions,

To serve:

mixed bitter salad leaves

2 tbsp walnut oil

½ tbsp balsamic vinegar

seeds from 1 small pomegranate

chopped chives or spring onion (scallion) tops

½ tbsp sloe gin (optional)

coating them with the juices. Return the pan to the oven until the onions are golden brown.

6. Rub the bread with the raw garlic cloves on one side, grind pepper over and brush both sides with olive oil. Place them in the oven and toast for 10–15 minutes until crisp.

7. Meanwhile, pop the roasted garlic cloves from their skins and blend with the cheese. Season with a little salt and pepper, then set aside until ready to serve. Remove the onions from the pan and discard the juniper berries and bay leaves.

8. If you have any reserved beetroot leaves, wash them in cold water, then dry well and shred, otherwise shred the spinach, and steam for 5 minutes.

9. To assemble, toss the salad leaves in a bowl with the oil, vinegar and seasoning until well coated. Arrange the leaves around the edges of a serving dish or on individual plates. Add the beetroot in overlapping slices and spoon the hot onions, chestnuts and spinach over the top.

10. Dice the toast and scatter over, then dot with dabs of the garlic cheese. Grind a little pepper over the cheese and finish with the pomegranate seeds and chives and a sprinkle of sloe gin, if using.

VARIATIONS

Dairy-free and Vegan options
Replace the cheese with herbed vegan cream cheese, and be sure to use bread made without milk or butter, and without eggs for the vegan option.

Gluten-free option
Use gluten-free bread.

Nut-free option
Replace the walnut oil with olive oil.

MIXED BEAN SALAD

Serves 6–8 | Prep 15 minutes, plus, ideally, at least 1 hour marinating | Cook 6 minutes
Dairy free | Gluten free | Nut free | Vegan

This quick-cooked salad is filling as it is, but you can add boiled baby new potatoes or hard-boiled eggs, if you eat them, for a more substantial dish. It's a welcome favourite at the stall, being generally less commercially available, and is ideal for a nutritious packed lunch.

225g/8oz/scant 1½ cups shelled broad (fava) or edamame beans, defrosted if frozen

225g/8oz/2 cups long green beans, defrosted if frozen, topped and tailed and cut into bite-sized pieces

225g/8oz/heaped 1 cup mixed canned pulses (legumes), such as chickpeas or kidney, pinto or soya beans, drained and rinsed

3 spring onions (scallions)

30g/1oz/½ cup torn basil leaves, or 1 tbsp vegan pesto sauce

30g/1oz/½ cup flat-leaf parsley leaves

225g/8oz bottled char-grilled red (bell) peppers, drained and diced

1 tbsp balsamic vinegar

2½ tbsp fruity, cold-pressed olive oil

½ tbsp tamari

sea salt and freshly ground black pepper, to season

Cook's note:

The flavours improve if this salad is left to marinate for at least an hour, or overnight in the fridge, in a covered container.

1. Bring a saucepan of salted water to the boil. Add the broad (fava) and green beans and boil for 5 minutes, uncovered, or until they are just tender. Begin the cooking time from the time the water returns to the boil.

2. Immediately drain the beans and plunge them into a bowl of iced water to stop the cooking and set the colours. Drain again, shaking off the excess water, then transfer to a large serving bowl.

3. Meanwhile, blitz the spring onions, basil and parsley in a blender or food processor until finely chopped.

4. Add the vinegar, oil and tamari and blitz again to complete the dressing.

5. Add the peppers and dressing to the ingredients in the bowl and thoroughly mix together. Season to taste. Cover and chill until ready to serve.

STRING BEANS IN SPICY TOMATO SAUCE

Serves 6–8 | Prep 10 minutes, plus making the tomato sauce and at least 1 hour infusing | Cook 40 minutes
Dairy free | Gluten free | Nut free | Vegan

This recipe is indispensible at the height of summer when it seems impossible to keep up with those summer gluts of tomatoes and beans. I keep a large bowl of this in the fridge for instant meals on the days when it's so hot I would rather sit in the garden than be in the kitchen.

900g/2lb/heaped 8 cups string beans, topped and tailed with strings removed and thinly sliced

1 quantity Spicy Tomato Sauce (page 83), cold

1 tbsp chopped basil or parsley leaves, to garnish

1. Bring a large saucepan of salted water to the boil. Add the beans and boil, uncovered, for 6–10 minutes until tender but still slightly crunchy.

2. Meanwhile, fill a large bowl with cold water. Drain the beans, then immediately put them into the water to stop the cooking and set the colour.

3. Drain them again, shaking off all the water, then put them in a bowl and mix with enough tomato sauce to coat.

4. Leave the salad to infuse for at least an hour. Garnish with the basil or parsley leaves just before serving.

Savoury Slices

Here is plentiful provender for posh picnics, packed lunches, fork buffets, light lunches or tasty supper dishes. You will discover I have plundered Middle Eastern street food, Mediterranean cuisine and the Swiss Alps, adding a few home-grown touches along the way!

These unusual savoury creations are a far cry from traditional, wheat-laden buffet fare. They also look heavenly, can be eaten hot or cold and pack a gastronomic punch wherever they go. Cook your way through a variety of succulent vegetable slices and stuffed polenta cakes, and discover the crispy, life-enhancing quinoa pizza and its creamy, sweet, avocado twin. Bring them to gatherings and watch your friends' eyes light up!

I often serve these slices accompanied with a selection of salads, a spoonful of toasted tamari seeds and topped with an optional drizzle of Tahini-Lemon Dressing (page 58) and a dab of chilli sauce.

BEETROOT, CARROT & POTATO RÖSTI

Serves 6–8 I Prep 30 minutes, plus draining the potatoes and leaving to rest before serving I Cook about 30 minutes
Dairy free I Gluten free I Nut-free option I Vegan

Rösti, a Swiss grated-potato favourite, is a versatile way to bring together new flavoursome combinations of root vegetables and potatoes. Here, my partner Brian and I have made it into one large, succulent cake, easy for slicing and serving, but the mixture also works well for individual rösti.

1kg/2lb 4oz/7 cups floury (Idaho or baking) potatoes, peeled and coarsely grated

500g/1lb 2oz/2¾ cups carrots, peeled and coarsely grated

1 large onion, finely chopped

500g/1lb 2oz/2¾ cups beetroot (beets), peeled and coarsely grated

2 tsp vegetable bouillon powder

4 tbsp olive oil or raw coconut oil

sea salt and freshly ground black pepper

a selection of any herbs and seasonal flowers, to garnish (optional)

1 quantity Lemon-Tahini Dressing (page 58), to serve (optional)

1. Put the grated potatoes, carrots and onion in a colander and toss with 2 tsp sea salt, then leave to drain for 10–15 minutes. Leave the beetroot to drain in a separate colander. Squeeze the liquid out of the potatoes, carrots and onion until they are as dry as possible. Do not squeeze the beetroot.

2. Mix the squeezed vegetables and beetroot with the bouillon powder and plenty of pepper.

3. Heat 2 tbsp of the oil in a heavy-based 23cm/9in frying pan, about 4cm/1½in deep and ideally with a tight-fitting lid, over a medium-high heat until it shimmers. Swirl the pan so the oil coats the sides as well.

4. Place handfuls of the rösti mixture around the edge of the pan, then fill the centre, packing it in until the pan is full to the brim and the surface is flat.

5. Cover the pan and turn down the heat to very low. Use a diffuser if you are cooking over a gas flame. If your pan doesn't have a lid, place a baking (cookie) sheet over the top.

Cook's notes:

Make thinner rösti by using more than one frying pan. You will need to use more oil and cook them for 8–10 minutes on each side. It isn't necessary to leave the rösti to rest before turning them over to finish cooking or before serving.

With potatoes, I like any combination of swede (rutabaga), celeriac (celery root), parsnips, turnips and Jerusalem artichokes. Just make sure you maintain the same proportion of potatoes to other vegetables, otherwise your rösti can fall apart.

VARIATIONS

Nut-free option
Use olive oil instead of raw coconut oil for cooking.

6. Cook for 12 minutes, or until the colour begins to fade a little at the edges and the rösti begins to steam a little. Make sure the bottom doesn't burn. Remove the pan from the heat and leave the rösti to rest for 10 minutes.

7. Use a spatula to loosen the edge, then, using a thick kitchen cloth to protect your hands, invert the pan onto a baking (cookie) sheet, so the rösti falls out. Detach any stuck pieces and smooth back into place.

8. Heat the remaining oil in the pan until it shimmers. Carefully, but firmly, slide the rösti back into the pan, cooked-side up.

9. Turn the heat down to medium, re-cover the pan and cook for 5 minutes. Turn heat down to low and finish cooking for another 10–12 minutes until the rösti is cooked through and golden brown on both sides. Allow it to rest for 6 minutes before turning out.

10. To serve, invert the rösti onto a warmed serving plate and garnish with herbs and flowers The rösti can be eaten cold with salads, and is especially good served with the Lemon-Tahini Dressing.

FARINATA WITH SPICY TOMATO SAUCE

Serves 6–8 | Prep 45 minutes, including roasting the tomatoes and leaving the batter to stand | Cook 40 minutes
Dairy-free option | Gluten free | Nut-free option | Vegan option

This is my amazing version of a thirteenth-century Genovese dish, which allegedly can be traced back to a storm-damaged cargo of chickpeas and olive oil. The resulting unappealing batter was served by the Genovese to their Pisa prisoners, who proudly refused to eat it and left it baking in the sun… the rest is food history.

175g/6oz cherry tomatoes, halved

6 tbsp olive oil or melted raw coconut oil

2 bay leaves, scrunched

175g/6oz/3 cups spinach, washed and chopped

175g/6oz/1½ cups red onions, sliced

175g/6oz/2 cups mixed (bell) peppers, de-seeded and sliced

175g/6oz/1½ cups courgettes (zucchini), sliced

3 tbsp freshly grated pecorino or Parmesan cheese (optional)

sea salt and freshly ground black pepper, to season

For the batter:

325g/11oz/3⅔ cups chickpea flour

2 garlic cloves, smashed

2 tsp sea salt

2 tbsp finely chopped mixed herbs

4 tbsp chopped spring onions (scallions)

500ml/18fl oz/2¼ cups beer, stout or water

6 tbsp olive oil

1–2 tsp hot paprika or harissa paste, to taste (optional)

1. Preheat the oven to Fan 200°C/Fan 400°F/Gas 7. Rub the tomatoes with a little of the oil and season to taste. Place on a baking tray (baking sheet) lined with a silicone mat and roast for about 30 minutes until they are blackened around the edges. Remove from the oven.

2. Meanwhile, put all the ingredients for the batter, including the paprika, if using, into a blender or food processor and blend until a thick batter forms. Leave the batter to sit at room temperature until required.

3. To make the sauce, heat 2 tbsp of the oil in a saucepan over a medium-high heat until it shimmers. Stir in the carrots, celery, onions, thyme and bay leaves and sweat (see opposite) until the onions are soft and translucent. Add the garlic and chilli powder and sweat for 1 more minute.

4. Pour in the remaining sauce ingredients and add pepper to taste. Cover and bring to the boil, then simmer, with the lid ajar, for 40 minutes, stirring occasionally, until thickened. Adjust the seasoning.

For the Spicy Tomato Sauce:

3 tbsp olive or sunflower oil or raw coconut oil

2 carrots, scrubbed and finely chopped

2 celery sticks, finely chopped

2 onions, finely chopped

3 thyme sprigs

2 bay leaves, scrunched

2 garlic cloves, smashed

1 tsp chilli powder

500ml/18fl oz/2¼ cups tomato passata (tomato puree)

150ml/5fl oz/⅔ cup dry red wine

2 tbsp tomato purée (tomato paste)

1½ tsp sea salt

1 tsp pomegranate molasses or sugar

2 tbsp tamari

1 tbsp balsamic vinegar

2 tsp vegetable bouillon powder

Cook's note: Sweating onions

Heat the oil in a heavy-based saucepan over a medium-high heat until it shimmers. Add the onions and immediately turn the heat down to medium low. Cover the pan and cook for 6 minutes, uncovering and stirring occasionally, until the onions are soft and translucent.

5. Meanwhile, blanch the spinach in a pan of boiling salted water for 2 minutes. Drain well and set aside.

6. Heat 4 tbsp oil in a 25cm/10in ovenproof, non-stick frying pan or a shallow, enamelled, cast-iron pan over a medium-high heat. Add the onions and sweat until they are soft and translucent. Add the (bell) peppers and cook for another 6 minutes. Stir in the courgettes (zucchini) and cook for a few more minutes until softened.

7. Raise the heat and throw in the blanched spinach. Stir and let the moisture evaporate, then add the cherry tomatoes.

8. Whisk the batter. Add 2 tbsp extra oil to the pan and heat until the oil sizzles. Pour the batter over the vegetables, which should be mostly covered, and smooth the top. Turn the heat down to very low and cook for about 15 minutes until the batter is set around the edge and towards the centre. Sprinkle the top with cheese, if using.

9. Place the frying pan in the middle of the oven and bake for 10–15 minutes until the centre is firm and the top is golden brown. Serve the farinata straight from the pan with the tomato sauce served separately.

VARIATIONS

Dairy-free and Vegan options
Replace the cheese, if using, with the same quantity of grated vegan-style Parmesan cheese.

Nut-free option
Use olive oil instead of the coconut oil option.

POLENTA, FENNEL CAPONATA & LENTIL SLICE

Serves 8–10 | Prep 50 minutes | Cook 25 minutes
Dairy free | Gluten free | Nut free | Vegan

This versatile polenta dish is made by filling a deep tart case with a flavoursome and nutritious fennel-flavoured caponata, the Sicilian version of ratatouille. Make sure the caponata vegetable dice are the same size so they cook in the same time. I add lentils to give the dish a nutritional boost.

For the Gluten-free Polenta Case (Shell):

225g/8oz bottled char-grilled (roasted bell) peppers, drained and finely chopped, with the liquid reserved

up to 600ml/1 pint/2½ cups Vegetable Bouillon (page 34) or vegetable stock, boiling

100g/3½oz/⅔ cup fine polenta

1 tsp smoked paprika

3 spring onions (scallions)

2 tbsp each chopped basil and flat-leaf parsley leaves

115g/4oz/1 cup courgettes (zucchini), grated

sea salt and freshly ground black pepper, to season

For the Fennel Caponata:

5 tbsp olive oil

1 aubergine (eggplant), diced

2 garlic cloves, smashed

1 large onion, diced

2 tsp turmeric

1 tsp chilli powder

leaves from 5 thyme or oregano sprigs

2 celery sticks, thinly sliced

2 carrots, scrubbed and diced

1. To make the polenta case (shell), add enough bouillon to make the pepper liquid up to 600ml/1 pint/2½ cups. Pour into a saucepan and bring to the boil. Add the smoked paprika, 5 grinds of black pepper and salt to taste.

2. Gradually add all the polenta in a steady stream and stir until the mixture comes back to the boil and thickens.

3. Turn the heat down to very low and use a diffuser if you are cooking over a gas flame. Cover the pan and simmer for 30–40 minutes, beating every 6 minutes or so, until the polenta forms a thick, smooth paste. (See Cook's Note, page 93.)

4. Meanwhile, blitz the spring onions, basil and parsley in a food processor until they are finely chopped, then stir them into the polenta, along with the courgettes (zucchini) and (bell) peppers. Adjust the seasoning to taste.

5. Pour the polenta mixture into a 23cm/9in loose-bottomed tart tin (tart pan with removable bottom). Wait for 5 minutes, then push the

½ fennel bulb, finely chopped

115g/4oz/heaped ½ cup green lentils

300ml/10fl oz/1¼ cups Vegetable Bouillon (page 34), plus extra, if needed

300ml/10fl oz/1¼ cups tomato passata (tomato puree)

7 tbsp dry white wine

2 tsp pomegranate molasses or sugar

4 tsp tomato purée (tomato paste)

2 bay leaves, scrunched

For the topping:

1 garlic clove, crushed

300ml/10fl oz/1¼ cups passata (tomato puree)

1 tbsp olive oil

2 tbsp tomato purée (tomato paste)

2 tsp vegetable bouillon powder

1 tsp sugar or pomegranate molasses

5 tbsp soya (soy) or rice cream

55g/2oz vegan Parmesan-style cheese

sea salt and freshly ground black pepper, to season

polenta up the side to form a high crust. Do not worry about the crust sticking, because it will easily come out of the tin when it is cool. Set aside until ready to fill.

6. To make the caponata, heat 3 tbsp of the oil in a large saucepan until it is very hot. Throw in the aubergine (eggplant) and toss to coat with oil, then cover the pan and cook for 5 minutes, stirring twice, or until the aubergines are well coloured and soft. Transfer them to a bowl.

7. Add the remaining oil and heat until it shimmers. Add the garlic and cook briefly until it is pale golden. Add onion and sweat (page 83) until soft and translucent. Stir in the turmeric, chilli powder, herbs, celery, carrots and fennel. Cover and sweat for 5 more minutes.

8. Stir in the lentils. Add the bouillon, passata (tomato purée), wine, pomegranate molasses, tomato purée (tomato paste) and bay leaves. The liquid should just cover the lentils, so top up with stock, if necessary. Bring to the boil. Stir well, cover and simmer for 35 minutes, stirring occasionally, over a very low heat until the liquid is almost absorbed, but add a little more stock if the mixture becomes too dry. Spoon into the polenta shell and smooth the top.

9. Meanwhile, preheat the grill (broiler) to high. To make the topping, blitz all the ingredients in a blender or food processor and season.

10. Spoon the topping over the lentil mixture. Place the polenta case under the grill until small, blackened patches appear. Leave to cool slightly before unmoulding and serving. Serve warm or cold.

GIANT DOLMADA CAKE

Serves 8–10 | Prep 50 minutes, including roasting the cucumbers, plus making the sauce and 4 hours chilling
Cook 20 minutes | Dairy-free option | Gluten free | Nut-free option | Vegan option

This is my multicultural take on the Middle Eastern classic snack. I make a colourful cabbage case, layering it with a spiced Japanese paste, za'atar, risotto, chickpeas and piquant baked cucumber. This is then turned out like a cake, ready to slice. A giant roll (see page 88) also looks spectacular.

2 cucumbers, de-seeded and cut into 1cm/½in pieces

3 tbsp olive oil or melted raw coconut oil

1 tbsp pomegranate molasses or sugar

1 tbsp tamari

5 or 6 whole leaves *each* from a green and a red cabbage, spines removed

55g/2oz/4 tbsp butter

3 large onions, thinly sliced

4 thyme sprigs

2 bay leaves, scrunched

225g/8oz/heaped 1 cup arborio or other risotto rice

900ml/1½ pints/4 cups Vegetable Bouillon (page 34) or vegetable stock, boiling

4 tsp za'atar

freshly grated zest and juice of 2 lemons

250g/9oz/1¼ cups canned chickpeas, drained

2 tbsp chopped mint leaves

sea salt and freshly ground black pepper, to season

1 quantity Lemon-Tahini Dressing (page 58), to serve

sweetcorn kernels and sugar-snap peas, to garnish (optional)

For the Japanese paste:

3 tsp Japanese umeboshi paste

1 tsp harissa paste

1 tbsp miso paste

2 tbsp tamari sauce

freshly squeezed juice of 2 lemons

2 tbsp toasted sesame oil

1. Preheat the oven to Fan 200°C/Fan 400°F/Gas 7. Line a 23cm/9in springform tin, 4cm/1½in deep, with clingfilm (plastic wrap), making sure there is a generous overhang so you can wrap up the whole dish later.

2. Place the cucumbers on a baking tray (baking sheet), drizzle with 1 tbsp of the olive oil, the pomegranate molasses and tamari and mix together until coated. Roast for 40 minutes, turning the cucumber halfway through.

3. Meanwhile, bring a saucepan of salted water to the boil and fill a bowl with iced water.

4. Add the cabbage leaves to the boiling water and blanch for 4–6 minutes, or until tender but not soggy. Immediately drain, then transfer them into a bowl of iced water, then drain them on kitchen paper (paper towels).

5. Use the cabbage leaves to line the springform tin, making an attractive contrasting colour design, with a generous overhang. Set aside the remaining leaves.

6. Melt the remaining olive oil with the butter in a wide, heavy-based saucepan over a medium-high heat until the butter stops sizzling. Add the onions and immediately turn the heat to medium-low, cover and cook for 6 minutes, uncovering and stirring occasionally, or until they are soft and translucent. Add the thyme, bay leaves and lemon zest and cook for 1 minute.

7. Stir in rice, coating it thoroughly with the butter and oil. Continue stirring the rice until the edges have become translucent but the centres are still opaque. You should be able to smell the aroma of the toasting grains.

8. Add a ladleful of the bouillon and stir until it is absorbed. Repeat, then add the za'atar and the lemon juice.

9. Continue adding bouillon, a few tbsp at a time, until all the stock is used and the risotto is creamy. There should be a slight crunch left in the rice, so start testing after 12 minutes. The finished consistency should resemble thick porridge (oatmeal). Stir in the chickpeas and check the seasoning. Leave to cool a little.

10. Whisk all the ingredients for the paste together, then brush the surface of the leaf-lined tin with half the mixture. Fill the tin with half of the risotto mixture, then arrange the cucumbers over the top and scatter with the mint.

11. Top with the remaining risotto, smooth the surface and brush with the rest of the sauce. Cover with the remainder of the cabbage leaves and tuck them neatly down the inside of the tin. Cover with clingfilm (plastic wrap) and chill for at least 4 hours.

12. Unmould the stuffed leaves onto a plate and brush with olive oil. Cut into slices and serve with the Lemon-Tahini Dressing.

BUTTERNUT SQUASH, APPLE & SMOKED ALMOND ROULADE

Serves 6–8 I Prep 1 hour, including roasting the vegetables, plus at least 1 hour chilling I Bake 15–20 minutes
Dairy-free option I Gluten free I Lower-sugar option I Nut-free option

This is a special cold buffet or wedding dish. Don't be put off by the length of preparation and cooking times, half of which is taken up by gentle cooking, so enjoy taking your time. A tasty, slow-cooked rice sauce replaces the gluten you would expect to find in a roulade.

sunflower oil, for brushing

6 eggs, separated

1 tbsp brown rice flour

1 tsp gluten-free baking powder

1 tsp smoked paprika, for dusting

For the Soubise Sauce:

55g/2oz/¼ cup arborio rice

55g/2oz/4 tbsp butter

500g/1lb 2oz/3 cups onions, sliced

1 tsp sea salt

2 thyme sprigs

1 bay leaf, scrunched

1 quantity Lemon-Tahini Dressing (page 58), to serve

For the filling:

450g/1lb/3 cups butternut squash, peeled and chopped

6 unpeeled garlic cloves

1 tsp harissa paste

2 tbsp olive or melted coconut oil

1 tbsp balsamic vinegar

freshly grated zest and juice of 1 lime

1 tbsp tamari

1 tsp sugar or agave syrup

1. Preheat the oven to Fan 180°C/Fan 350°F/Gas 6. Bring a saucepan of salted water to the boil.

2. To make the filling, put the squash and garlic cloves in a roasting tin (roasting pan) lined with a silicone mat. Whisk together the harissa paste, oil, vinegar, lime juice, tamari and sugar, then pour it over the squash and garlic, tossing to coat. Roast for 15 minutes. Remove the garlic and return the vegetables to the oven for 15 more minutes, or until the squash is soft. When the garlic is cool enough to handle, peel and set aside.

3. Meanwhile, to make the sauce, stir the rice into the saucepan of boiling water. Boil for 5 minutes from the time the water returns to the boil, then drain and set aside.

4. Melt the butter in a saucepan over a medium heat. Add the onions, coat with the butter and season with salt and pepper. Stir in the rice, thyme and bay leaf and fry, stirring, for 5 minutes.

5. Cover the pan, reduce the heat to very low and cook for 40 minutes, uncovering and stirring

250g/9oz/1 cup cream cheese or soft goat's cheese

½ tsp ground mace

2 tsp vegetable bouillon powder

4 tbsp unsweetened apple sauce

115g/4oz/¾ cup smoked almonds or toasted blanched hazelnuts

sea salt and freshly ground black pepper, to season

Cook's note: Beating egg whites

The wonderful light texture of savoury and sweet roulades and so many other baked goods comes from beating the egg whites properly to incorporate as much air as possible. Make sure you use a clean, dry bowl and that the beaters are clean and dry, too. This is especially important if you have just beaten egg yolks or other ingredients. If you leave any trace of yolk in the egg whites they will fail to increase in volume. To avoid this, break each white into a cup before adding it to the rest of the whites, so you can isolate accidents without contaminating the rest.

Beat egg whites with an electric mixer on a slow speed until they are frothy. Increase the speed to medium and continue beating until the volume quadruples. Increase the speed to high and continue beating until glossy, stiff peaks form.

every 10 minutes, or until the rice is very tender but not browned. If it does begin to brown, add 1–2 tbsp water. Thoroughly purée the onion and rice mixture in a blender or food processor to obliterate the grains as much as possible, then transfer to a large bowl and set aside.

6. Meanwhile, line a 40×30cm/16×12in Swiss roll (jelly roll) tin with parchment paper, extending 4cm/1½in above the rim, then set aside.

7. Beat the egg whites (see Cook's Note, left) with a pinch of salt with an electric mixer in a large, clean bowl until stiff peaks form.

8. Quickly beat the egg yolks, rice flour and baking powder into the cooled rice mixture. Stir 2 tbsp of egg whites into the rice mixture to lighten. Using a whisk, fold in the rest of the whites, making a figure-of-eight motion and rotating the bowl a quarter turn with each fold. Do not over-work or your roulade will be rubbery.

9. Pour the mixture (batter) into the prepared tin and smooth it into the corners. Bake for 20–25 minutes until the roulade is well risen and golden but not shrinking from the edges. Leave the roulade to cool in the tin on a wire rack.

10. Meanwhile, finish the filling. Beat the cheese, mace and bouillon powder in a large bowl. Purée the roasted butternut squash and garlic with the apple sauce and lime zest. Add the purée to the cheese mixture and beat together. Stir in the nuts and season to taste.

11. Invert the cooled roulade onto a sheet of greaseproof (waxed) paper and peel off the parchment. Cover with the filling, spreading it right to the edges. Use the paper to help roll up the roulade from a long side. Don't worry if it cracks. Trim the ends. Twist the ends of the paper to secure, then chill for at least 1 hour or up to 24 hours.

12. Dust the top with smoked paprika, slice with a serrated knife and serve with a jug of Lemon-Tahini Dressing.

CHAR-GRILLED PEPPER POLENTA CAKE WITH TOMATO & OLIVE TAPENADE

Serves 6–8 I Prep 30 minutes, including optional char-grilling peppers, plus making the onion marmalade and 1 hour setting
Cook 30 minutes I Dairy free I Gluten free I Nut free I Vegan

This savoury cake was inspired by griddled Italian polenta slabs that are often served bubbling with Gorgonzola cheese. There are endless imaginative variations using chopped herbs, roasted or puréed vegetables, seeds and assorted cheeses. Just make sure you add strong flavours and interesting textural layers to complement the bland polenta.

2.4 litres/4 pints/10⅔ cups Vegetable Bouillon (page 34) or vegetable stock, boiling

400g/14oz/2½ cups fine polenta

1 quantity Red Onion Marmalade (page 136)

225g/8oz/2½ cups red or yellow (bell) peppers, quartered, de-seeded and char-grilled (page 137), or use bottled char-grilled peppers, drained and sliced

5 tbsp finely chopped herbs, such as basil, chives and flat-leaf parsley

sea salt and freshly ground black pepper

chopped chives, herb sprigs and seasonal flowers, to garnish

sweetcorn kernels and sugar-snap peas (snow peas), to serve (optional)

For the Tomato & Olive Tapenade:

225g/8oz/1⅔ cups pitted black olives

115g/4oz sun-dried tomatoes soaked in olive oil, drained

2 garlic cloves, peeled

2 spring onions (scallions), chopped

4 tbsp olive oil

2 tbsp capers, rinsed

2 tsp Piri-piri Spice Mix (page 220), or to taste

1. Bring the stock and 1 tsp salt to the boil in a large saucepan. Add the polenta in a steady stream and stir until the mixture comes back to the boil and thickens. Turn down the heat to very low, and use a diffuser if you are cooking over a gas flame. Cover the pan and leave the polenta to cook for 30–40 minutes, uncovering and beating every 6 minutes or so, until it forms a smooth, thick paste. (See Cook's Note, opposite.)

2. Place all the tapenade ingredients and 6 grinds of black pepper into a blender or food processor and blend until you have a smooth paste. Stir in the red onion marmalade and chill until required.

3. As soon as the polenta is ready, stir in the peppers and herbs. Season with salt and pepper to taste.

4. Immediately pour the polenta into two 23cm/9in fluted or plain loose-bottomed tart tins (tart pans with removable bottoms), 4cm/1½in deep, and smooth the surface. Leave to cool for 1 hour, or until the polenta is set.

For the topping:

200ml/7fl oz/¾ cup plus 2 tbsp tomato passata (tomato puree)

1 tbsp tomato purée (tomato paste)

1 tbsp olive oil

1 tsp vegetable bouillon powder

2 tbsp rice or soya (soy) cream

1 tsp sugar or pomegranate molasses

Cook's note:

It might be considered by some sacrilegious, but my observation is that constant stirring of the polenta during cooking, *come mamma*, is not mandatory to ensure near-perfect results! Just stir *until* the mixture thickens, then leave covered, over a *very low* heat, beating every 6 minutes or so, for 30–40 minutes until a smooth, thick paste forms.

5. Meanwhile, mix all the topping ingredients, except the cream, together and season with 5 grinds of black pepper.

6. When the polenta has set, reheat the grill (broiler) to its highest setting. Spread the topping mixture over one of the polenta cakes. Drizzle the cream in concentric circles, then use a cocktail stick (toothpick) to drag through the circles to make a web effect.

7. Grill for 8–10 minutes until blackened patches begin to appear.

8. Immediately remove the tin from the grill, and allow the polenta cake to cool. Un-mould the plain cake and place it on a serving dish and spread with tapenade.

9. Remove the grilled cake from its tin and slide it off the metal base, which should come off easily. Place it on top, grilled side up. Garnish with herbs and flowers and serve with a sweetcorn and sugar-snap pea (snow pea) salad, if you like.

DOUBLE MAIZE BAKE WITH SPICY TOMATO SAUCE

Serves 6–8 | Prep 10 minutes, plus making the sauce | Cook 30–40 minutes
Dairy-free option | Gluten free | Nut free | Vegan option

Here's a quick, tasty, homely supper dish, especially good on chilly September evenings, when basil and fresh corn are still to be had from the land and the nights are beginning to draw in. Serve this with green beans straight from the garden and savour the last glowing embers of summer.

2 litres/3½ pints/9 cups Vegetable Bouillon (page 34) or vegetable stock

350g/12oz/2 cups plus 2½ tbsp fine polenta

225g/8oz/1¼ cups sweetcorn kernels, defrosted if frozen

30g/1oz/2 tbsp butter, plus extra for greasing the dish

1 tbsp rubbed thyme leaves (see Cook's Note, page 95)

1 red onion, grated

55g/2oz/½ cup freshly grated Parmesan cheese

30g/1oz/¼ cup freshly grated Cheddar cheese

sea salt and freshly ground black pepper

1 quantity Spicy Tomato Sauce (page 83), hot, to serve

green beans, to garnish (optional)

1. Bring the bouillon and 1 tsp salt to the boil in a large saucepan. Add the polenta in a steady stream and stir until the mixture comes back to the boil and thickens.

2. Turn down the heat to very low, and use a diffuser if you are cooking over a gas flame. Cover the pan and leave the polenta to cook for 30–40 minutes, uncovering and beating every 6 minutes or so, until it is a smooth, thick paste. (See Cook's Note, page 93.)

3. Meanwhile, blitz the sweetcorn in a food processor or blender until very well chopped. Add the corn mixture, butter and thyme to the polenta and adjust the seasoning.

4. Preheat the grill (broiler) to high and butter a shallow flameproof serving dish. Pour the polenta into the dish, smooth the top with a wet metal spatula and top with the grated onion and the two cheeses.

Cook's notes:

For the best flavour, strip the thyme leaves from their twigs, then rub them briskly together between your thumb and fingers to release the fragrant esters.

For an authentic Italian style of service, try pouring the cooked polenta directly onto an oiled wooden board and top with the sauced vegetables. Everyone can plunge in and serve themselves!

5.   Grill for about 6 minutes until the top is golden brown and bubbling. Serve with the hot sauce alongside and with green beans to garnish.

BAKED RICOTTA RING

Serves 6–8 | Prep 45 minutes | Bake 50 minutes
Dairy-free option | Gluten free | Nut-free option | Vegan option

This simple upside-down dish is enjoyable to make and spectacular to serve! Here is a tomato and cheese mixture that is delicious served with a fresh tomato sauce. I like to include sautéed mushrooms sprinkled with tamari or an avocado salad in the centre. Try sheep or goat's ricotta for a change of flavour.

20 cherry tomatoes, halved

1 tsp olive oil, plus extra for greasing the mould

1 tsp chopped rosemary leaves, or ½ tsp dried

½ tsp sugar

1kg/2lb 4oz/4 cups ricotta cheese or soft goat's cheese

6 eggs

30g/1oz/½ cup chopped flat-leaf parsley leaves

4 spring onions (scallions), finely chopped

2½ tbsp brown rice flour

½ tsp ground mace

225g/8oz/2 cups courgettes (zucchini), grated

sea salt and freshly ground black pepper

For the base:

55g/2oz/4 tbsp butter

115g/4oz/heaped 1 cup dried gluten-free breadcrumbs

4 tbsp ground almonds

4 spring onions (scallions), finely chopped

1. Preheat the oven to Fan 200°C/Fan 400°F/Gas 7. Lightly grease a 23cm/9in ring mould and set aside.

2. Line a baking tray (baking sheet) with a silicone mat. Add the tomatoes, oil, rosemary, sugar and salt and pepper to taste and toss together. Roast for 20–30 minutes until they are juicy and blackened in places. Remove from the oven and set aside.

3. Lower the oven temperature to Fan 160°C/Fan 325°F/Gas 4.

4. Meanwhile, to make the base, melt the butter in a frying pan until the sizzling stops. Add the breadcrumbs and fry, stirring, for 6 minutes, or until they are golden brown and crisp. Add the ground almonds, spring onions, garlic, pine nuts, thyme and lemon zest and fry, stirring, for 5 more minutes until the crumbs are toasty. Add the lemon juice and continue cooking until the liquid evaporates. Season to taste and leave to cool.

2 garlic cloves, chopped

1 tbsp toasted pine nuts, finely chopped

1 tbsp chopped thyme leaves, or ½ tsp dried

freshly grated zest and juice of 1 lemon

55g/2oz/½ cup Parmesan cheese, freshly grated

Cook's note:

The ideal summer accompaniment is a fresh tomato and basil coulis. Simply core, skin and de-seed 4 large tomatoes. Put them in a food processor or blender with 6 tbsp olive oil, 2 tbsp balsamic vinegar, 2 tbsp tamari, 1 tsp pomegranate molasses or a pinch of sugar and a handful of basil leaves and blitz. Season to taste. This is best made as close to serving as possible.

5. Blitz the ricotta cheese, eggs, parsley, spring onions, rice flour and mace together until smooth. Pour into a bowl, stir in the courgettes and season to taste.

6. Arrange the tomatoes around the base of the mould, cut-side up. Pour in the cheese mixture and smooth the surface. Sprinkle the crumbs over the top, then sprinkle with the Parmesan cheese.

7. Place the mould on a baking (cookie) sheet and bake for 50 minutes, or until slightly puffy. Leave to stand for 5 minutes before un-moulding.

8. To serve, run a metal spatula around the inner and outer rims. Place your serving plate on top and invert the ricotta ring, giving a sharp shake. Lift off the mould. Serve warm or chilled and fill the centre with whatever you fancy. If you make the coulis (see Cook's Note), serve it separately.

VARIATIONS

Dairy-free option
Replace the butter in the base with the same quantity of raw coconut oil or olive oil. Replace the ricotta cheese with the same quantity of vegan herbed cream cheese and replace the Parmesan cheese in the base with vegan-style Parmesan cheese.

Nut-free option
Replace the ground almonds in the base with the same quantity of finely ground sunflower seeds. Replace the pine nuts with the same quantity pumpkin seeds.

Vegan option
Follow the dairy-free option. Omit the eggs and replace them with 55g/2oz/3½ tbsp light tahini, and 115g/4oz/½ cup soya (soy) yogurt.

VEGETABLE QUINOA PIZZA

Makes two 25cm/10in pizzas | Prep 20 minutes, plus at least 8 hours soaking | Bake 40 minutes
Dairy-free option | Gluten free | Nut free | Vegan option

You might never eat a conventional wheat-based pizza again after you try this gluten-free version! The bases crisp up fantastically and can be used for both savoury and sweet pizzas. Remember to soak your quinoa for at least 8 hours. If you're in a hurry, replace the tomato sauce with pesto sauce.

1 tbsp olive oil

400g/14oz/2⅓ cups quinoa, soaked for 8 hours in cold water to cover, then drained

1 tsp sea salt

1 tbsp chopped fresh basil, marjoram or oregano, or 1½ tsp dried or 1 tsp chopped rosemary

2 garlic cloves, smashed

500ml/18fl oz/2¼ cups water

sea salt and freshly ground black pepper

sliced mozzarella cheese, ricotta or soft goat's cheese, for topping

olive oil or truffle oil, or a mixture, for drizzling

1. To begin the sauce, heat the oil in a heavy-based saucepan over a medium-high heat until it shimmers. Add the onions and sweat (page 83) until they are soft and translucent. Add the garlic and fry for 2 more minutes.

2. Add the thyme, bay leaves, basil, passata (tomato puree) and remaining ingredients with salt and pepper to taste. Cover and bring to the boil.

3. Turn down the heat and simmer for 20 minutes, with the lid slightly ajar. You should have a fragrant, thick sauce. Adjust the seasoning and set aside.

For the Tomato Pizza Sauce:

2 tbsp olive oil

450g/1lb/2¾ cups onions, chopped

3 garlic cloves, smashed

3 thyme sprigs

2 bay leaves, scrunched

2 tbsp chopped basil leaves

500ml/18fl oz/2¼ cups tomato passata
(tomato puree)

1 tbsp balsamic vinegar

1 tbsp tamari

1 tbsp tomato purée (tomato paste)

1 tsp sugar, pomegranate molasses or
unsweetened apple juice concentrate

1 tsp vegetable bouillon powder

For the optional toppings:

artichoke hearts, fresh or bottled, char-
grilled and sliced

aubergine (eggplant) slices, greased, char-
grilled and seasoned

courgette strips, greased, char-grilled and
seasoned

mushrooms, wiped, trimmed and sliced

red onions, sliced

mixed (bell) peppers, de-seeded and sliced

wild rocket (arugula)

4. Meanwhile, preheat the oven to 200°C/400°F/Gas 7. Brush two 25cm/10in loose-bottomed cake tins or cast-iron ovenproof frying pans with the oil, remembering to coat the sides as well. Place the cake tins or frying pans in the oven for 10 minutes.

5. Rinse the quinoa in a metal sieve, rubbing to remove the bitter outer coating.

6. Transfer it to a food processor with the salt, herbs and garlic and purée, adding the water via the feed tube until you get a thick batter. Season to taste.

7. Remove the hot tins or frying pans from the oven and pour in the batter, smoothing the surface with a metal spatula. Return to the oven and bake for 30 minutes.

8. Remove the bases from the tins and transfer to a baking (cookie) sheet lined with a silicone mat. Spread with the sauce and toppings of your choice, then lightly drizzle with oil.

9. Sprinkle the pizzas with the cheese and return them to the oven for 10–12 minutes until crusty and golden.

VARIATIONS

Dairy-free option
Replace the dairy cheese with vegan herbed cream cheese or vegan Parmesan-style cheese.

Vegan option
Use the dairy-free option. Do not use the truffle oil.

Sweet Quinoa Pizza
Add 1 tsp Madagascan vanilla extract and 2 tbsp maple syrup to the batter in step 6. Use melted raw coconut oil instead of olive oil or sunflower oil when brushing the cake tins or frying pans. After baking, remove from the oven and leave the bases to cool, then remove from the tins. Transfer to a baking (cookie) sheet lined with a silicone mat. Spread with a sweetened avocado and lime juice purée and top with pineapple or papaya chunks tossed with fresh lime juice, or use soft fruit slices. Sprinkle with icing (confectioners') sugar or drizzle with sweet syrup, then place under a hot grill (broiler) until brown speckles appear. Serve with soya (soy) yogurt, or, for a non-vegan version, Greek yogurt, crème fraîche, sorbet or ice cream.

Curries, Stews & Noodle Dishes

Carefully selected for their *chutzpah*, the following dishes from around the globe are chock-full of tangy pastes and powders guaranteed to kick-start you into finding a fruitful solution to the mind-boggling issue of family menus. Spicy, zesty, sweet and sour, you will find something to tickle everyone's taste buds. Pungent caraway dumplings bake atop a smoky goulash, and authentic German spätzle come smothered with a zingy artichoke salsa verde. At least once a week, have a go at making something to lift your soul beyond the contents of the kitchen sink! May you cruise in on the perfumed wafts.

I've included a couple of recipes that use tempeh – a soy-based meat substitute which originated in Indonesia. Tempeh has an earthy taste and a firm, chewy texture, and is very digestible owing to its special fermentation process. It is a welcome whole-food alternative to tofu, and you will find it, often frozen, in good health food stores.

SWEET-AND-SOUR EGG & TOFU CURRY

Serves 6–8 | Prep 1 hour, including marinating the tofu, soaking the saffron and making the sauce | Cook 30 minutes
Dairy-free option | Gluten free | Nut-free option | Vegan option

Here is an unusual, fruity, fresh, sharp, crunchy and nutritious sweet-and-sour curry. There are lots of ingredients and many steps for this curry, so I make it in stages with the final assembly just before serving. This dish is perfect for a curry night at home with friends.

1kg/2lb 4oz plain or smoked firm tofu, cut into thick matchsticks

1½ tsp ground aniseed

125g/4½oz/½ cup ghee

85g/3oz/¾ cup cucumber, peeled and cut into matchsticks

140g/5oz/1 cup beetroot (beets) or carrots, peeled and cut into thick matchsticks

140g/5oz/¾ cup cooked white beans, drained and rinsed, if canned

2 garlic cloves, finely chopped

2 shallots or 1 onion, finely grated

140g/5oz/2½ cups shredded chard or chopped spinach

225g/8oz/2 cups sprouted mung beans or sprouted lentils

175g/6oz/1 cup fresh mango, pitted and cut into bite-sized pieces, or pineapple, peeled, cored and cut into bite-sized pieces

1–2 red onions, thinly sliced into rings

6–8 hard-boiled eggs, allow one per serving, shelled, halved and each half studded with a blanched almond

sea salt and freshly ground black pepper

1. Coat the tofu matchsticks thoroughly with the aniseed, 1 tsp salt and ¾ tsp freshly ground black pepper. Melt 6 tbsp of the ghee, then pour it over the tofu and gently stir to coat. Leave to one side for at least 30 minutes.

2. Put the cucumber in a colander, sprinkle with salt and leave to drain for 15 minutes. Rinse well, drain again, then set aside.

3. Meanwhile, bring a saucepan of water to the boil. Put the saffron for the sweet-and-sour sauce in a small bowl, pour about 6 tbsp of boiling water over the top and leave to soak for 20 minutes.

4. Preheat the grill (broiler) to high and line the grill tray with a silicone mat. Place the marinated tofu on the mat and grill for 6–8 minutes until browned on each side. Set aside.

5. To make the sauce, combine the stock, lime juice and pomegranate molasses in a heavy-

For the Sweet-and-Sour Sauce:

a good pinch of saffron threads

600ml/1 pint/2½ cups vegetable stock, boiling

4 tbsp freshly squeezed lime juice or tamarind paste

4 tbsp pomegranate molasses or unsweetened apple juice concentrate

2 bay leaves, or 8 dried curry leaves, scrunched

1 tbsp coriander seeds

1 tsp ground cardamom

1 tsp ground cloves

1 tsp ground cinnamon

1 tsp sea salt

¾ tsp freshly ground black pepper

½ tsp ground aniseed

2 tbsp cornflour (cornstarch), blended with 4 tbsp water

VARIATIONS

Dairy-free option
Replace the ghee with raw coconut oil or sunflower oil.

Nut-free option
Replace the almonds with toasted pumpkin seeds.

Vegan option
Use the dairy-free option. Omit the eggs and replace them with 12–16 scrubbed small new potatoes, cooked in the curry until tender. Add the blanched almonds to the curry when you add the beetroot.

based saucepan over a medium heat, then add the remaining ingredients except the cornflour (cornstarch) mixture. Drain the saffron and add to the pan.

6. Bring the sauce to the boil. Add the beetroot (beets), then turn the heat to medium-low, cover and simmer for 15 minutes. Remove the bay leaves, whisk in the cornflour (cornstarch) mixture, add the beans, re-cover and leave over a low heat until needed.

7. Meanwhile, melt the remaining ghee in a wok or deep frying pan until it is hot. Stir-fry the garlic and shallots until they are tender. Add the chard and continue stir-frying until it wilts and all the liquid evaporates.

8. Pour the sauce and vegetables into the wok. Stir in the sprouts, mango chunks, cucumbers, red onions and tofu, and add salt and pepper to taste. Simmer for 8 minutes, stirring occasionally, or until all the vegetables are heated through. Place the hard-boiled eggs on top and serve.

CHICKPEA & TOFU THAI GREEN CURRY

Serves 6–8 | Prep 25 minutes | Cook 70 minutes
Dairy free | Gluten free | Nut-free option | Vegan

We serve huge vats of this aromatic, spicy recipe every year at the Totnes Christmas market, together with brown basmati rice and a sprinkling of fresh coriander. This is a fairly mild dish, but just double the quantity of curry paste for a fierier finish.

4 tbsp raw coconut oil

2 bay leaves, scrunched

2 large onions, chopped

2 tbsp Thai Curry Paste (page 219)

5 carrots, scrubbed and cut into 2cm/¾in dice

3 parsnips, peeled and cut into 2cm/¾in dice

500g/1lb 2oz plain firm tofu, cut into 2cm/¾in dice

1 tsp vegetable bouillon powder

225ml/8fl oz/1 cup coconut cream

4 courgettes (zucchini), cut into 3cm/1¼in dice

500g/1lb 2oz/2¼ cups freshly cooked or canned chickpeas, drained and rinsed

4 tbsp cornflour (cornstarch) blended with 4 tbsp cold water

225ml/8fl oz/1 cup soya (soy) or rice cream

sea salt and freshly ground black pepper

2 tbsp chopped coriander (cilantro), to garnish

brown basmati rice, pickles and flatbreads, to serve (optional)

VARIATIONS

Nut-free option
Replace the coconut oil with the same quantity of sunflower oil. Omit the coconut cream and increase the quantity of rice or soya (soy) cream to 450ml/16floz/2 cups.

1. Heat the oil in a heavy-based saucepan over a medium-high heat until it is shimmering. Add the bay leaves and onions, then immediately turn down the heat to medium-low, cover and fry, uncovering and stirring occasionally, for 6 minutes. Stir in the curry paste and cook for 3 more minutes.

2. Stir in the carrots, parsnips and tofu, cover and cook for 6 more minutes.

3. Add enough water to cover all the vegetables and tofu by 5cm/2in. Add the bouillon powder, coconut cream and salt and pepper to taste. Cover with a lid and simmer for 50 minutes, stirring occasionally.

4. Add the courgettes (zucchini) and chickpeas, and simmer for 12 more minutes. Stir in the cornflour (cornstarch) mix, stirring vigorously to avoid lumps, and simmer for 5 minutes. Do not boil.

5. Remove the pan from heat and add salt and pepper to taste. Add the soya (soy) cream and sprinkle with chopped coriander. Serve with rice, pickles and flatbreads, if you like.

TEMPEH GOULASH WITH CARAWAY DUMPLINGS

Serves 8 | Prep 40 minutes | Cook 1 hour
Dairy free | Gluten free | Nut-free option | Vegan

Sitting down to this warming, glowing, mildly spicy stew makes light work of even the most miserable winter evenings. Tempeh is a fermented soyabean product that originated in Indonesia. It has a firm texture and makes a tasty alternative to tofu. Dumplings are on my top-10 list of favourite comfort foods.

2 tbsp chickpea flour

sea salt and freshly ground black pepper

450g/1lb tempeh, defrosted if necessary, drained and cut into 1cm/½in cubes

raw coconut or olive oil for frying

5 garlic cloves, smashed

4 floury (Idaho or baking) potatoes, scrubbed and diced

3 carrots, scrubbed and diced

2 celery sticks, including leaves, finely chopped

2 leeks, chopped and washed

2 large onions, chopped

2 parsnips, peeled and diced

3 bay leaves, scrunched

3 thyme sprigs

1 tbsp caraway seeds, freshly ground

1 tsp smoked paprika

2 tbsp sweet paprika

350ml/12fl oz/1½ cups tomato passata (tomato puree)

900ml/1½ pints/4 cups Vegetable Bouillon (page 34) or vegetable stock

1 green (bell) pepper, de-seeded and diced

chopped fresh flat-leaf parsley, to garnish

chopped de-seeded tomatoes and soya (soy) yogurt, to serve

1. Preheat the oven to Fan 180°C/Fan 350°F/Gas 6.

2. In a large bowl, mix the chickpea flour with 1 tsp sea salt and 1 tsp black pepper. Add the tempeh and toss, making sure all the chunks are well coated.

3. Melt 1 tbsp coconut oil in a heavy-based frying pan over a medium-high heat until it shimmers. Brown the tempeh in small batches. Remove each batch before adding a touch more oil and letting the heat regain its original temperature and then adding the next batch. You want browned, not stewed, tempeh. Set aside until required.

4. Heat 2 tbsp of the oil in a large flameproof casserole (Dutch oven) over a medium-high heat until it shimmers. Add the garlic, potatoes, carrots, celery, leeks, onions, parsnips, bay leaves and thyme, then stir briskly for a few minutes until everything is beginning to brown a little.

5. Add the ground caraway and the smoked and sweet paprika and stir well. Turn down the heat to medium-low, cover and fry for 10 minutes, uncovering and stirring twice.

For the Caraway Dumplings

100g/3½oz/1 cup plus 1½ tbsp chickpea flour, plus extra for dusting

100g/3½oz/⅔ cup brown rice flour

100g/3½oz/7 tbsp gluten-free vegetarian chopped suet or raw coconut oil, finely chopped

2 tbsp chopped fresh flat-leaf parsley, plus extra to garnish

1 tsp bicarbonate of soda (baking soda)

1 tsp ground caraway seeds

sea salt and freshly ground black pepper, to season

1 tsp cider vinegar

a little soya (soy) milk

VARIATIONS

Nut-free option
Replace the coconut oil with the same quantity of sunflower or olive oil.

---

6. Add the tempeh and passata (tomato puree), stir well and then add the bouillon and salt and pepper to taste. Cover and place in the oven for 30 minutes.

7. Meanwhile, make the dumplings by mixing the chickpea flour, brown rice flour, suet, parsley, bicarbonate of soda (baking soda) and caraway seeds together. Season to taste. Add the cider vinegar and just enough soya (soy) milk to make a stiff dough.

8. Flour your hands and shape into 12 dumplings.

9. Remove the casserole from the oven. Stir in the green (bell) pepper, then drop the dumplings into the stew and re-cover.

10. Return to the oven for 30 more minutes, or until the dumplings are risen and fluffy. Serve in bowls and top with chopped parsley. Separately hand round the bowl of chopped tomatoes and a bowl of soya (soy) yogurt.

TEMPEH TAGINE

Serves 8 | Prep 30 minutes, including the saffron, plus 24 hours marinating and making the curry paste | Cook 1 hour
Dairy free | Gluten free | Nut-free option | Vegan

This fragrant tagine is served with quinoa, instead of the more traditional couscous, to make it a gluten-free meal. Tempeh is well suited to the marinating process so begin this recipe 24 hours in advance. If you're using frozen tempeh, allow 24 hours for it to defrost in the fridge.

450g/1lb tempeh or smoked tofu, drained, if necessary, and cut into 2.5cm/1in cubes

raw coconut oil, as needed

3 large onions, finely chopped

6 garlic cloves, smashed

2 tbsp Ras-el-Hanout Paste (page 218) or bought paste or powder

500g/1lb 2oz/2¾ cups large tomatoes, skinned, de-seeded and chopped

500ml/18fl oz/2¼ cups tomato passata (tomato puree)

115g/4oz/heaped ¾ cup whole blanched almonds

225g/8oz baby potatoes, scrubbed

225g/8oz/1⅔ cups sweet potatoes, peeled and cut into 2.5cm/1in cubes

100g/3oz/scant 1 cup unsulphured dried apricots

4 tbsp pomegranate molasses

3 aubergines (eggplants), pricked all over with a fork

sea salt and freshly ground black pepper, to season

1. Twenty-four hours in advance, whisk all the marinade ingredients together. Add the tempeh and coat well, then place in an airtight, non-metallic container in the fridge for 24 hours, turning once.

2. The next day, remove the tempeh and pat it dry. Reserve any leftover marinade.

3. Heat 7.5cm/3in oil in a flameproof casserole (Dutch oven) over a medium-high heat until it is shimmering. Fry the tempeh in batches until it is golden brown and crisp, then drain on kitchen paper (paper towels).

4. Pour out all but 2 tablespoons of the oil and re-heat until it is shimmering. Add the onions and sweat (page 83) until they are soft and translucent. Stir in the garlic, the remaining marinade and the spice paste.

6 spring onions (scallions), chopped

400g/14oz/2⅓ cups quinoa, rinsed and drained well, then rubbed in a sieve to remove the coating

500ml/18floz/2¼ cups Vegetable Bouillon (page 34) or vegetable stock, hot

freshly grated zest and juice of 1 lime

2 tbsp chopped mint leaves

2 tbsp chopped coriander (cilantro), to garnish

For the marinade:

1 tbsp Ras-el-Hanout Paste (page 218) or bought paste or powder

2 garlic cloves, smashed

1½ tsp sea salt

freshly grated zest and juice of 2 lemons

a pinch of saffron threads soaked in boiling water for 20 minutes, then drained

VARIATIONS

Nut-free option
Replace the coconut oil with the same quantity of olive or sunflower oil. Replace the blanched almonds with the same quantity of pumpkin seeds.

5. Add the tomatoes, passata (tomato puree), almonds, baby potatoes, sweet potatoes, apricots and the pomegranate molasses, then add the tempeh. Bring to the boil and simmer for 35 minutes with the lid ajar, allowing the liquid to reduce and thicken.

6. If the sauce is too runny, transfer the solid ingredients to a bowl and boil the liquid until it reduces to the desired consistency. Take care not to splash yourself with the sputtering sauce.

7. Meanwhile, place the aubergines (eggplants) under a hot grill (broiler) or over a low gas flame, using tongs to give quarter turns when they become charred and squidgy. Continue until the whole aubergines are soft. This will take about 25 minutes.

8. Leave the aubergines to cool a little, then peel under running water. Don't worry about any black bits left on the aubergines. Drain and roughly chop them into small chunks; they will be quite mushy. Season to taste.

9. Heat 1 tbsp coconut oil in a saucepan over a medium heat. Add the spring onions (scallions) and fry for a few minutes until they are tender. Add the rinsed quinoa and fry until it is toasty.

10. Pour in the bouillon and bring to the boil. Turn down the heat to its lowest setting and simmer for 15 minutes, with the lid ajar. Cover and leave for 5 minutes. Fluff up the quinoa with a fork, then mix in the chopped aubergines, lime zest and juice and mint. Adjust the seasoning. Pile in a pretty serving dish and spoon the tagine over the top. Scatter with the coriander (cilantro) and serve.

SPÄTZLE WITH ARTICHOKE SALSA VERDE & THAI GREENS

Serves 4–6 | Prep 25 minutes | Cook 30 minutes
Dairy free | Gluten free | Nut-free option

This is a fabulous cross-cultural dish. The spätzle noodles are German in origin but go beautifully with an artichoke and herb sauce sharpened with lemon and some Asian-style greens steamed with chilli, tamari and sesame. You can buy a spätzle press, which resembles a potato ricer, but a colander is a simple alternative that works just as well.

400g/14oz/2½ cups brown rice flour

140g/5oz/¾ cup plus 1 tbsp sweet rice flour (grind your own from glutinous rice if you can't find the flour)

115g/4oz/scant 1 cup cornflour (cornstarch)

115g/4oz/scant 1 cup tapioca flour

2 tsp xanthan gum

1 tsp sea salt

freshly ground black pepper, to taste

a pinch of freshly grated nutmeg

4 eggs, beaten

about 225ml/8fl oz/1 cup water

olive oil, for coating

fried onion rings and shredded sun-dried tomatoes in oil, to garnish (optional)

Cook's note:

The salsa verde is also wonderful served with freshly cooked whole artichokes. Dip the leaves into the salsa. Allow one large artichoke per person.

1. Bring a saucepan of salted water to the boil, then reduce the heat to a steady simmer.

2. Meanwhile, to make the salsa verde, put all the ingredients in a food processor or blender and blend together. Cover and chill until required.

3. To make the spätzle, whisk all the dry ingredients together. Beat in the eggs, adding just enough water to make a thick paste.

4. Put a large spoonful of the paste at a time into a spätzel press, potato ricer or colander and quickly press it firmly through into the simmering water. Use a knife to cut the noodles off underneath, as necessary. If you are using a colander or ricer, make sure it doesn't get too close to the water or your spätzle will cook before they hit the water, clogging up the colander or ricer.

5. Cook for 3 minutes, or until they rise to the surface. Remove with a slotted spoon and put in a warm serving dish with a little olive oil.

For the Salsa Verde:

125ml/4fl oz/½ cup olive oil

2 bottled artichoke hearts, drained

1 garlic clove

3 tbsp mixed chopped basil, coriander (cilantro), marjoram and mint

2 tbsp chopped flat-leaf parsley

1 tbsp cashew nuts

1 tbsp freshly squeezed lemon juice or red wine vinegar

1 tsp wholegrain mustard

1 tsp capers, rinsed

For the Steamed Thai Greens:

1 tbsp coconut oil

675g/1½lb/5 cups greens, such as Swiss chard, rinsed and chopped

1 tsp de-seeded, very finely chopped red chilli

2 garlic cloves, smashed

2 tbsp tamari

1 tbsp toasted sesame oil

6. Repeat the procedure until you have used all the mixture. Cover with foil and keep warm in the oven, with the door ajar, until ready to serve.

7. To cook the greens, heat the oil in a wok over a high heat until it shimmers. Add the greens and stir-fry for 2–3 minutes until brown bits appear. Lower the heat to medium, add the garlic and chilli, if using, and stir-fry for 2 more minutes.

8. Add 2 tbsp water, cover and steam for 4 minutes, or until the greens are just tender. Add the tamari and sesame oil and stir well.

9. Serve the spätzle with the greens alongside and the salsa verde for spooning over. Garnish with fried onion rings and sun-dried tomatoes, if you like.

VARIATIONS

Nut-free option
Replace the coconut oil with sunflower oil. Replace the cashew nuts with sunflower seeds.

SEAWEED RICE NOODLE & TOFU STIR-FRY WITH SATAY SAUCE

Serves 6–8 | Prep 50 minutes, plus making the curry paste | Cook 20 minutes
Dairy free | Gluten free | Nut-free option | Vegan

I display this dish cold at the market so people can take it home for supper, but I also reheat at the stall for anyone who can't wait that long. I use the wok as a mould and the resulting mountain resembles an over-sized spaghetti cake, which always excites interest. I serve it with the spicy satay sauce.

400g/14oz firm tofu, cut into 1cm/½in cubes

250g/9oz dried brown rice and seaweed noodles, or plain brown rice noodles

1 tbsp toasted sesame oil

4 tbsp raw coconut oil, for stir-frying

3 large onions, chopped

55g/2oz/⅔ cup shiitake mushrooms, thinly sliced

115g/4oz/1 cup carrots, peeled and cut into matchsticks

115g/4oz/1 cup sweet red ramiro peppers, de-seeded and cut into matchsticks

115g/4oz broccoli, stalks cut into matchsticks and florets separated

115g/4oz/scant 1 cup courgettes (zucchini), cut into matchsticks

115g/4oz/1 cup cavolo nero, shredded

115g/4oz/heaped 1 cup mixed sugar-snap peas (snow peas) and green beans, cut into small pieces

55g/2oz/⅓ cup sweetcorn kernels, defrosted if frozen

1. To make the satay sauce, heat the coconut oil in a heavy-based saucepan over a medium heat. Add the spring onions (scallions) and stir-fry for 3 minutes. Add the curry paste and stir for another minute.

2. Add all the remaining ingredients with just enough water to dissolve the creamed coconut. Beat until the sauce is smooth. Gently simmer for 10 minutes over a low heat, stirring occasionally, and adding water as necessary (the sauce will thicken as it cooks). Do not boil.

3. To make the marinade, blitz all the marinade ingredients in a blender or food processor until a smooth paste forms. Place in a non-metallic bowl and add the tofu, making sure it is well coated, then set aside.

4. Meanwhile, fill a large bowl with cold water and set aside. Bring a large pan of salted water to the boil. Add the seaweed noodles and boil for no more than 3 minutes, or according to the packet instructions.

For the Satay Sauce:

2 tbsp raw coconut oil

8 spring onions (scallions), finely chopped

1–2 tbsp Thai Curry Paste (page 219)

2 tbsp crunchy peanut butter

2 tbsp tamarind paste or freshly squeezed lime juice

1 tbsp tamari

1 tbsp bottled sweet chilli sauce

1 very finely chopped fresh green chilli (optional)

175ml/6fl oz/¾ cup creamed coconut

For the tofu marinade:

2 garlic cloves, smashed

2 spring onions, roughly chopped

1 or 2 fresh red or green chillies, de-seeded and chopped

1cm/½in piece root ginger (gingerroot)

4 tbsp tamari, plus extra to taste

4 tbsp rice or balsamic vinegar

4 tbsp toasted sesame oil

VARIATIONS

Nut-free option
Replace the coconut oil with the same quantity of sunflower oil. Replace the peanut butter with a seed butter.

5. Drain the noodles in a colander, then immediately plunge them into the bowl of cold water and leave until cool. Drain again, put them in a bowl, mix with the sesame oil and set aside.

6. Preheat grill (broiler) to high and line the grill rack with a silicone mat. Put the tofu and marinade on the rack and grill, turning occasionally for about 5 minutes until it is well browned on both sides.

7. Meanwhile, heat the wok over a high heat. Melt 2 tbsp coconut oil until it shimmers. Add the onions and stir for about 8 minutes until they are lightly browned and soft. Add the mushrooms and stir-fry for a few more minutes until browned. Transfer the vegetables to a bowl and set aside.

8. Heat the remaining 2 tbsp coconut oil. Add the carrots and peppers and stir to mix. Cover the wok with a large lid or baking (cookie) sheet and steam for 4 minutes.

9. Add all the green vegetables and stir-fry for 5 more minutes, or until the vegetables are bright green, but still crunchy. Add the sweetcorn kernels.

10. Stir in the tofu and the onion mixture, scraping in all the marinade from the grill pan. Add the noodles and re-heat thoroughly. Add extra tamari to taste. Serve the satay sauce separately.

KASHMIRI BUTTER BEAN & VEGETABLE CURRY

Serves 6–8 | Prep 30 minutes, including soaking the saffron and making the spice mix | Cook 40 minutes
Dairy-free option | Gluten free | Nut-free option | Vegan option

This is a rich, sweet, thick-sauced golden curry that satisfies on several counts. It's straightforward to make and long on flavour. I serve this with brown basmati rice at my food stall from November to March, where nobody seems to tire of it! At home I serve this with poppadoms and chutneys.

2 tbsp raw coconut oil

3 red onions, chopped

250g/9oz/1¾ cups butternut squash, peeled, de-seeded and chopped

115g/4oz/1 cup parsnip, scrubbed and chopped

115g/4oz/heaped ¾ cup swede (rutabaga), peeled and chopped

1 yellow (bell) pepper, de-seeded and diced

400ml/14fl oz/1¾ cups unsweetened coconut milk

½ tsp saffron threads, simmered in 6 tbsp water for 20 minutes, then drained

20 blanched almonds

250g/9oz/1¼ cups cooked butter beans, drained and rinsed if canned

225g/8oz/1 cup plain yogurt

2 tbsp tamarind paste

sea salt and freshly ground black pepper, to season

115g/4oz/heaped ¾ cup toasted coconut flakes, to garnish

a handful of chopped coriander (cilantro) leaves, to garnish

1. To make the curry paste, place all the ingredients in a blender or food processor and blend until a fine paste forms. Set aside.

2. Heat the coconut oil in a heavy-based saucepan over a medium heat until it shimmers. Add the onion and stir-fry for 5 minutes, until the onion has turned translucent. Reduce the heat to medium-low and continue cooking for about 10 minutes until the onion is very tender and golden brown.

3. Stir in the spice paste and cook for 3 more minutes. Stir in the vegetables and coat them well with the spice paste. Cover and cook for 3 more minutes until heated through.

4. Add the coconut milk, saffron, almonds and salt to taste. Bring to the boil, then lower the heat and simmer for 30 minutes.

5. Add the butter beans, yogurt and tamarind and simmer for 10 more minutes. Do not boil. Adjust the seasoning. Scatter with toasted coconut flakes and coriander (cilantro), and serve.

For the Kashmiri Curry Paste:

2.5cm/1in piece of root ginger (gingerroot)

5 garlic cloves

2 tomatoes, coarsely chopped

2 fresh green chillies, de-seeded

1 fresh red chilli, de-seeded

2 tbsp Kashmiri Spice Mix (page 219) or garam masala

1 tsp turmeric

a pinch of sugar

VARIATIONS

Dairy-free and Vegan options
Replace the plain yogurt with the same quantity of soya (soy) yogurt.

Nut-free option
Replace the coconut oil with sunflower oil and replace the coconut milk with soya (soy) milk. Replace the blanched almonds with pumpkin seeds and omit the toasted coconut flakes.

Pastry, Tarts, Quiches & Savoury Cheesecakes

One small step for the cook, yet a giant leap of culinary faith for others, is required to dispel the myth that you can't make gluten-free pastry look and taste good.

The not-so-secret cypher of free-from pastry-making lies in the pages ahead, waiting for you to dabble, salivate and slurp your way to baking heaven. Classic recipes with exciting new twists line up to be visited at your leisure, including a cheesecake with dolcelatte and cucumber and the ravishing Butternut, Berry & Goat's Cheesecake.

Jazz up jaded palates using herbed, nutty or cheesy quiche shells, pies or tarts filled with imaginative ingredients. Even leftover stir-fry succumbs deliciously well to the quiche treatment. Just one note of caution: make sure you carefully follow the blind-baking (prebaking) instructions to avoid a soggy base.

HOW TO MASTER PERFECT PASTRY

Delicious dry, crisp pastry provides the perfect base for the range of tarts, quiches and pies in this chapter. It's quick and easy to make pastry in a food processor, but if you don't have one, don't worry – just use the technique described below. Legendary French chef Auguste Escoffier believed *legerdemain*, or 'lightness of hand', was a prerequisite for successful pastry-making. This will come with practice!

Making Pastry by Hand

1. Mix the flour(s) and salt in a large bowl. Cut in the fat(s) with a broad-bladed knife, then use your fingertips to rub in until you have a coarse breadcrumb consistency.

2. Slowly add the liquid and blend in, using the broad-bladed knife, until you have a loose ball.

3. Turn out the ball onto a floured surface and knead quickly. Flatten the pastry into a disc, wrap in clingfilm (plastic wrap) and leave to rest in the refrigerator for at least 2 hours, or for the time specified in the recipe.

Cook's note
If any of my pastries are chilled for 6 hours or longer, they should be removed from the fridge 30 minutes before rolling out.

Rolling Out Pastry

1. Use a lightly floured rolling pin to roll out the pastry (dough) on a lightly floured surface until it is 4mm/⅛in thick and slightly wider than the diameter of the tin you are using.

2. Keep an even thickness by using a well-floured surface and giving the pastry a quarter turn each time you roll it. If the pastry shows signs of sticking, use just enough extra flour to make rolling easy. Brush off any excess flour when you have finished rolling out.

Lining a Quiche or Tart Tin

1. Roll up the pastry over a lightly floured rolling pin and gently unroll it over the tin, easing the pastry onto the base and up the side. Take care not to stretch it. Press any overlapping pastry downwards to reinforce the thickness of the side. Do not trim off the overhang.

2. Prick the base all over with a fork. Cover and chill the pastry case (shell) for 15–30 minutes before filling and baking. This helps to prevent it shrinking in the oven.

3. Remove the pastry case from the fridge. If you are making a single-crust pie, boldly roll the rolling pin over the rim of the tin, creating a neat edge. Pinch the pastry all round the edge to make a slight rim.If you are making a two-crust pie, leave the excess pastry hanging over the edge until after the pie is filled.

4. When you have filled the case, brush the edge with beaten egg. Position the pastry lid (top crust), then crimp the 2 layers together to seal. Chill for 15–30 minutes, then cut off the excess pastry and bake.

Blind-baking a Pastry Case

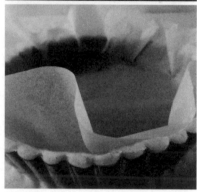

1. Preheat the oven to Fan 200°C/Fan 400°F/Gas 7. Line the tin as instructed in steps 1–3 on page 119.

2. Cut a piece of parchment paper large enough to cover the inside of the pastry-lined tin and extend 5cm/2in above the rim. Add enough dried chickpeas or baking beans (pie weights) to fill the tin to the rim.

3. Place the tin on a baking (cookie) sheet and bake for 10 minutes. Turn the tin 180-degrees to ensure even colouring, then continue baking for a further 8–10 minutes, or until golden brown.

4. Take the pastry case (shell) out of oven and remove the paper and chickpeas together by lifting each corner of the paper. Return the tin to the oven for 5 minutes to dry out the pastry and until it turns golden brown. Either fill the pastry case immediately and continue with your recipe, or leave it in the tin set on a wire rack before using. (The chickpeas and paper can be put aside to use again.)

Pastry Know-how

During preparation

1. My bottom-line tips for perfect pastry are: use chilled fat; use minimum liquid; use a firm but light touch.

2. Be aware that the room temperature and absorbency of your flour will affect the amount of liquid you need. Always add the liquid slowly and stop when the crumbs form.

3. In hot weather, butter is more difficult to manage, so return it to the fridge if it becomes sticky.

4.   For shortening, I use organic raw coconut oil, hard GMO-free margarine or non-hydrogenated white vegetable shortening.

Working with and baking pastry

1.   If your pastry (dough) tears while you are lining a tart or quiche tin, use your fingers to patch the damaged area with a small piece of excess pastry. Fix by brushing the surface with beaten egg or water, and smooth the patch firmly into place.

2.   If cracks appear in a pastry case (shell) during blind-baking (prebaking), repair them with leftover scraps of pastry fixed by brushing one surface with beaten egg or water.

3.   I use chickpeas when blind-baking, but you can use any dried pulses (legumes), or you can buy specific ceramic baking beans (pie weights) from cookware suppliers. Both can be re-used indefinitely.

4.   If your pastry is stuck to the base of the tin, use a long, sharp knife or metal spatula to 'saw' between the pastry and the tin.

 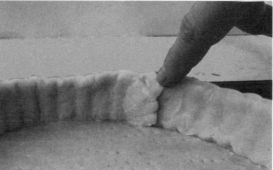

Storing pastry for later use

1.   Wrap any leftover pastry in clingfilm (plastic wrap) and freeze for up to 2 months. Defrost at room temperature before use.

2.   Unbaked pastry cases (shells) can be wrapped in clingfilm and frozen for up to 2 months. They can then be blind-baked from frozen in an oven preheated to Fan 180°C/Fan 350°F/Gas 6 for 8 minutes longer than specified in the recipe.

SPELT PASTRY

Makes enough for two 20cm/8in tarts or quiches, one 2-crust pie or 6 pasties I Prep 10 minutes, plus at least 2 hours chilling I Bake according to your recipe I Dairy-free option I Lower-sugar option I Nut free I Vegan option

This is my all-purpose shortcrust pastry (piecrust dough). It is rich, light and tasty, and I use it to make pasties, pies, quiches and tarts. I use 30 per cent white spelt flour and 70 per cent wholegrain spelt flour for lightness, but you can use all wholegrain flour, if you'd rather.

280g/10oz/2¼ cups wholegrain spelt flour

85g/3oz/⅔ cup white spelt flour, plus extra for dusting

1 tsp sea salt

200g/7oz/¾ cup plus 2 tbsp butter, chilled and cut into 1cm/½in cubes

3 tbsp non-hydrogenated white vegetable shortening, chilled and cut into 1cm/½in cubes

1 egg, mixed with enough chilled water to make 90ml/3floz/6 tbsp

1. Whizz the flours and salt together in a food processor. Add the chilled butter and shortening, and pulse just until you have a fine breadcrumb consistency.

2. Gradually add the egg mixture through the feed tube, pulsing just until the pastry (dough) comes together. You might not need all the egg mixture. The exact amount of liquid will vary depending on the weather and the absorbency of the flours you have used. Take care not to overwork at this stage or the pastry will be tough.

3. Tip the pastry onto a lightly floured surface and knead quickly but thoroughly into a thick disc. Wrap in clingfilm (plastic wrap) and chill for at least 2 hours, or up to 2 days.

4. If the pastry has chilled for more than 6 hours, remove it from the fridge 30 minutes before rolling out and using as specified in your recipe.

VARIATIONS

Dairy-free option
Replace the butter with the same quantity of chilled raw coconut oil, hard margarine or white vegetable shortening. Or, you can make up the quantity of butter with a mixture of these fats.

Lower-sugar option
Replace the sugar with 7 tbsp xylitol.

Vegan option
Replace the butter with the same quantity of chilled raw coconut oil, hard margarine or white vegetable shortening. Omit the eggs and use 90ml/3floz/6 tbsp chilled water instead.

Sweet Spelt Pastry
Omit the wholegrain spelt flour and use 380g/12½oz/2¾ cups all white spelt flour instead. Use chilled unsalted butter. Add 7 tbsp granulated sugar to the flour and salt in step 1 and beat the egg with 1½ tsp Madagascan vanilla extract and enough chilled water to make 90ml/3floz/6 tbsp liquid. Continue with the recipe above. When you're ready to roll out the pastry, unwrap and knead it briefly on a well-floured surface until pliable. If the pastry becomes sticky, re-form it into a ball, re-wrap and refrigerate for 10 minutes, otherwise proceed with your recipe.

Dairy-free Sweet Spelt Pastry
Replace the butter with the same quantity of chilled raw coconut oil, hard margarine or white vegetable shortening. Add 7 tbsp granulated sugar to the flour and salt in step 1 and beat the egg with 1½ tsp Madagascan vanilla extract and enough chilled water to make 90ml/3floz/6 tbsp liquid.

GLUTEN-FREE PASTRY

Makes enough for two 20cm/8in tarts or quiches, one 2-crust pie or 6 pasties I Prep 10 minutes, plus at least 2 hours chilling I Bake according to your recipe I Dairy-free option I Gluten free I Lower-sugar option I Nut free I Vegan option

Nobody will guess this isn't a wheat-based pastry, because the flavour and texture mimic that of a conventional shortcrust pastry. It is rich and crisp when baked, and very versatile. If it splits or cracks while being rolled out, just press it together and it re-seals itself!

85g/3oz/scant ¾ cup wholegrain buckwheat flour

85g/3oz/½ cup brown rice flour, plus extra for rolling out

85g/3oz/½ cup potato flour

85g/3oz/¾ cup maize flour (masa harina)

½ tsp sea salt

200g/7oz/¾ cup plus 2 tbsp butter, chilled and cut into 1cm/½in cubes

1 egg, beaten with enough chilled water to make 75ml/2½floz/5 tbsp, plus extra, if necessary

1. Whizz the flours and salt together in a food processor to mix. Add the chilled butter and pulse just until you have a fine breadcrumb consistency.

2. Gradually add the egg mixture through the feed tube, pulsing just until the pastry (dough) comes together. You might not need all the liquid. The exact amount of water will vary depending on the weather and the absorbency of the flours you have used.

3. Turn out onto a surface generously dusted with rice flour and knead quickly until smooth. Take care not to over-work at this stage or the pastry will be tough.

4. Wrap the pastry in clingfilm (plastic wrap) and chill for at least 2 hours, or up to 2 days.

5. If the pastry has chilled for more than 6 hours, remove it from the fridge 30 minutes before rolling out and using as specified in your recipe.

VARIATIONS

Dairy-free option

Replace the butter with the same quantity of chilled raw coconut oil, hard margarine or white vegetable shortening instead.

Vegan option

Replace the butter with the same quantity of chilled raw coconut oil, hard margarine or white vegetable shortening instead. Omit the egg and use 75ml/2½floz/5 tbsp chilled water instead.

Sweet Gluten-free Pastry

Add 7 tbsp granulated sugar to the flours and omit salt in step 1. Use chilled unsalted butter. Mix the egg with 1 tsp Madagascan vanilla extract and enough chilled water to make 75ml/2½floz/5 tbsp liquid.

Lower-sugar, Sweet, Gluten-free Pastry

Add 7 tbsp xylitol to the flours and salt in step 1. Use chilled unsalted butter. Mix the egg with 1 tsp Madagascan vanilla extract and enough chilled water to make 75ml/2½floz/5 tbsp liquid.

Vegan, Sweet Gluten-free Pastry

Add 7 tbsp granulated sugar to the flours and omit salt in step 1. Replace the butter with the same quantity of chilled raw coconut oil, hard margarine or white vegetable shortening instead. Omit the egg and use 75ml/2½floz/5 tbsp chilled water instead.

Gluten-free Polenta Pastry

Good polenta makes wonderful gluten-free cases (shells) for tarts and quiches. Use 100g/3½oz/⅔ cup fine polenta, 600ml/1 pint/2½ cups boiling Vegetable Bouillon (page 34) or stock and 1 tsp sea salt to make the polenta, following steps 1–2 in the Polenta, Fennel Caponata & Lentil Slice recipe (page 84). Meanwhile, preheat the oven to Fan 200°C/Fan 400°F/Gas 7 and lightly grease a 20cm/8in loose-bottomed tart tin (tart pan with removable bottom), 4cm/1½in deep, with olive oil.

When the polenta has become a smooth, thick paste, stir in 2 tbsp finely chopped herbs and salt and freshly ground black pepper to taste. Pour the hot polenta into the tin and leave for 5 minutes. Use damp fingers to mould it up the side of the tin to make a case, then brush with olive oil. Bake for 20–30 minutes, or until it is golden and slightly crispy. If the side has shrunk a little, gently push it up while the polenta is still hot. Continue with your recipe immediately, or leave the polenta case to cool on a wire rack.

GRUYÈRE, ALMOND & THYME PASTRY

Makes enough for one 23cm/9in Tatin or two 20cm/8in tarts | Prep 15 minutes, plus at least 2 hours chilling
Dairy-free option | Gluten-free option | Nut-free option | Vegan option

175g/6oz/1¼ cups plus 2 tbsp wholegrain
spelt flour

115g/4oz/1¼ cups chickpea flour

115g/4oz/1 cup Gruyère cheese, grated

85g/3oz/6 tbsp butter, chilled and cut into
1cm/½in cubes

6 tbsp ground almonds

½ tsp sea salt

2 tsp prepared Dijon mustard or wasabi
powder

2 eggs, beaten with enough chilled water
to make 125ml/4fl oz/½ cup

leaves from 6 thyme sprigs

1. Put all the ingredients, except the egg mixture, mustard and thyme leaves, in a food processor and just pulse until you have a fine breadcrumb-like mixture. If you are using wasabi powder, add it in this step.

2. Add the thyme leaves and quickly whizz. Gradually add the egg mixture and mustard through the feed tube and pulse just until the pastry (dough) comes together and forms a ball.

3. Remove the dough from the food processor. Flatten it into a disc, wrap in clingfilm (plastic wrap) and leave to rest in the refrigerator for at least 2 hours before rolling out and using as instructed in your recipe.

VARIATIONS

Dairy-free option (Cheese, Almond & Thyme Pastry)
Omit the butter and use the same quantity of chilled raw coconut oil, hard margarine or white vegetable shortening instead. Replace the Gruyère cheese with the same quantity of grated vegan hard cheese or vegan Parmesan-style cheese.

Gluten-free option
Replace the wholegrain spelt flour with 175g/6oz/1 cup plus 1½ tbsp brown rice flour, and use brown rice flour for rolling out.

Nut-free option (Gruyère, Sunflower & Thyme Pastry)
Replace the ground almonds with the same quantity of finely ground sunflower seeds.

Vegan option (Cheese, Almond & Thyme Pastry)
Use 175g/6oz/1¼ cups plus 2 tbsp wholegrain spelt flour, or 175g/6oz/1 cup plus 1½ tbsp brown rice flour, along with the chickpea flour. Omit the butter and replace it with the same quantity of chilled raw coconut oil, hard margarine or white vegetable shortening. Replace the Gruyère cheese with the same quantity of grated hard vegan cheese or vegan Parmesan-style cheese. Replace the eggs with 125ml/4fl oz/½ cup chilled water.

HAZELNUT PASTRY

Makes enough for one 23cm/9in Tatin, two 20cm/8in tarts or one 2-crust pie | Prep 15 minutes, plus at least 1 hour chilling
Dairy-free option | Gluten-free option | Lower-sugar option | Nut-free option | Vegan option

225g/8oz/1⅔ cups white spelt flour

115g/4oz/heaped ¾ cup toasted blanched hazelnuts, finely ground

6 tbsp granulated sugar

140g/5oz/¾ cup unsalted butter, chilled and cut into 1cm/½in cubes

1 egg, beaten with 1 tsp Madagascan vanilla extract plus enough chilled water to make 55ml/2floz/4 tbsp

1. Whizz the flour, sugar and ground hazelnuts in a food processor. Add the butter and pulse just until a fine breadcrumb-like mixture forms.

2. Gradually dribble the egg mixture through the feed tube and pulse just until the pastry (dough) comes together.

3. Turn out onto a lightly floured surface and quickly knead. Form the pastry into a flattened ball and wrap in cling film (plastic wrap). Chill for at least 2 hours before rolling out and using as instructed in your recipe.

VARIATIONS

Dairy-free option
Replace the butter with the same quantity of chilled raw coconut oil, hard margarine or white vegetable shortening.

Gluten-free option
Replace the white spelt flour with 85g/3oz/½ cup brown rice flour, 85g/3oz/⅔ cup tapioca flour and 55g/2oz/⅓ cup potato flour, sifted together.

Lower-sugar option
Replace the sugar with 6 tbsp xylitol.

Nut-free option (Sesame Pastry)
Replace the ground hazelnuts with the same quantity of sesame seeds, finely ground.

Vegan option
Omit the butter and replace it with the same quantity of chilled raw coconut oil, hard margarine or white vegetable shortening. Omit the egg and replace it with 1 tsp Madagascan vanilla extract mixed with enough chilled water to make 55ml/2fl oz/4 tbsp.

BEETROOT & BUTTERNUT TATIN

Serves 6–8 | Prep 20 minutes, plus making the pastry (dough) and at least 2 hours chilling | Bake 30–40 minutes
Dairy-free option | Gluten-free option | Nut-free option | Vegan option

This stunning savoury variation of the classic French apple tart glistens with ruby and amber translucent succulence on a rich cheese base. The pastry is thicker than usual so you get a good balance with the tender vegetables. I particularly like to serve this with Mixed Bean Salad (page 76).

6 large unpeeled garlic cloves

6 tbsp olive oil

4 tbsp balsamic or fruit vinegar

2 tbsp tamari

40g/1½ oz/3 tbsp butter or raw coconut oil

1½ tbsp dark brown sugar or pomegranate molasses

600g/1lb 5oz/4½ cups cooked beetroot (beets), peeled and cut into 1cm/½in slices, then quartered

600g/1lb 5oz/4¼ cups butternut squash, peeled, de-seeded and cut into 1cm/½in half-moon slices

1 quantity Gruyère, Almond & Thyme Pastry (page 126), prepared and chilled for at least 2 hours

white spelt flour, or flour of choice, for rolling out

sea salt and freshly ground black pepper, to season

1. If the pastry has chilled for 6 hours or longer, remove it from the fridge 30 minutes before rolling out. Preheat the oven to Fan 180°C/Fan 350°F/Gas 6.

2. Toss the garlic with 1 tbsp of the olive oil and roast for 12 minutes, or until soft.

3. Leave the garlic to cool. Peel, then blend the garlic with 2 tbsp olive oil, the balsamic vinegar and tamari, and set aside.

4. Melt the butter and remaining olive oil with the sugar in a 23cm/9in Tatin tin or a heavy-based, deep ovenproof frying pan over a low heat, stirring until the sugar dissolves.

5. Remove the tin from the heat and arrange a pleasing pattern of beetroot (beets) and squash – this will form the top when the tart is turned out. Top with layers of the remaining vegetables, brushing each layer with the garlic mixture and seasoning to taste. The subsequent layers need not be so neat. Cook in the oven for 10 minutes.

6. Meanwhile, roll out the pastry dough on a lightly floured surface until it is 1cm/½in thick and as wide as your tin. Remove the tin from the oven, then gently drape the pastry over the floured rolling pin, and unroll it over the hot tin. Loosely tuck the edge inside the rim of the tin.

7. Bake the tart for 30–40 minutes until golden brown and the vegetables are tender. Cover the top with foil if it browns too much.

8. Remove tin from the oven. Loosen the edge of the pastry with a rubber spatula, then using a thick oven cloth, invert the tart onto a warmed serving dish, giving it a sharp shake to dislodge. Re-arrange any stuck pieces of vegetable and serve hot or at room temperature.

MUSHROOM, CHARD & CHEDDAR QUICHE

Serves 4–6 | Prep 20 minutes, plus making the pastry (dough), at least 2 hours chilling and blind-baking (prebaking) the pastry case (shell) | Bake 20–30 minutes | Dairy-free option | Gluten-free option | Vegan option

A well-executed quiche is a delight to all the senses and due homage should be paid to this culinary brainwave, which provides such a perfect container for nature's bounty. Use this as a master recipe and you'll be on your way to baking endless combinations. I never tire of creating new quiches.

30g/1oz/2 tbsp butter

2 tbsp olive, sunflower or raw coconut oil

225g/8oz/3⅓ cups chestnut (cremini) mushrooms, trimmed and sliced

225g/8oz/4 cups chard or spinach leaves, chopped and washed and squeezed dry

freshly squeezed juice of 1 lemon, or 2 tbsp bottled juice

4 eggs

125ml/4fl oz/½ cup full-fat (whole) milk

6 tbsp single (light) cream

a pinch of freshly grated nutmeg

one 20cm/8in blind-baked (prebaked) pastry case (shell) (page 120), 4cm/1½in deep, made with ½ quantity Spelt Pastry (page 122)

140g/5oz/1⅓ cups Cheddar or Gruyère cheese, grated

sea salt and freshly ground black pepper, to season

1. Preheat the oven to Fan 180°C/Fan 350°F/Gas 6.

2. Melt half the butter and half the olive oil in a frying pan over a medium-high heat. Add the mushrooms and fry for about 8 minutes, turning them over occasionally, until they are well browned. Season to taste, then remove from the pan and set aside.

3. Add the remaining butter, oil and chard and stir-fry for a few minutes until the chard has wilted. Add the lemon juice and season to taste.

4. Blend together the eggs, milk, cream, nutmeg, ½ tsp salt and pepper to taste, then pour into a jug and set aside.

5. Place the pastry case (shell) in its tin on a baking (cookie) sheet. Spread the chard and mushrooms over the base. Fill the pastry case (shell) three-quarters full with the egg mixture. Sprinkle the cheese over the top.

Cook's notes:

A good test to see if a quiche is baked through is to plunge a metal skewer into the centre and then pass it across your bottom lip, noting if the heat is evenly distributed. If not, put the quiche back in the oven for 5 minutes, then retest.

For all quiche fillings, I find organic eggs, as opposed to simply free range, have a superior flavour and richer colour.

Any dairy ingredients in all my quiche recipes can be replaced with an equal quantity of vegan options, such as silken tofu, vegan cream cheese beaten with 2 tbsp brown rice flour, rice or soya (soy) cream and almond, rice or soya (soy) milk.

6. Place the baking sheet in the oven and fill the pastry case to the brim with the remaining egg mixture.

7. Bake for 20–30 minutes until the centre is firm and the top is golden brown.

8. Allow the tart to cool slightly, then remove it from the tin. Use a long knife to slide it from the metal base onto a warmed serving plate. Serve warm.

VARIATIONS

Dairy-free option
Use ½ quantity Dairy-free Spelt Pastry (page 123) to make the pastry case (shell). Replace the butter with an equal quantity raw coconut oil, hard margarine or white vegetable shortening. Replace the milk with an equal quantity of rice or soya (soy) milk and the single cream with an equal quantity of rice or soya (soy) cream. Replace the cheese with an equal quantity of grated vegan hard cheese.

Gluten-free option
Use ½ quantity Gluten-free Pastry (page 124) to make the pastry case (shell), or Gluten-free Polenta Pastry (page 125).

Vegan option
Use ½ quantity Vegan Gluten-free Pastry (page 125) to make the pastry case (shell), or a Gluten-free Polenta Pastry Case (page 125), made with vegan Parmesan-style cheese and olive oil. Replace the butter with an equal quantity of raw coconut oil, hard margarine or white vegetable shortening. Replace the milk with an equal quantity of rice or soya (soy) milk and the single cream with an equal quantity of rice or soya (soy) cream. Omit the eggs and replace them with 225g/8oz/1 cup vegan cream cheese beaten with 2 tsp brown rice flour and 1 tsp vegetable bouillon powder or yeast flakes (nutritional yeast) until smooth. Replace the Cheddar cheese with an equal quantity of grated vegan hard cheese or vegan Parmesan-style cheese.

FENNEL & ADZUKI BEAN PIE

Serves 6–8 I Prep 20 minutes, plus making the pastry (dough) and at least 2 hours chilling and 20 minutes soaking the sun-dried tomatoes I Bake 40–50 minutes I Dairy-free option I Gluten-free option I Nut-free option I Vegan option

This is a chunky and nutritious addition to any buffet table. The braised beans are heartily satisfying without being at all stodgy. The pie makes an unusual picnic choice, and any leftovers will be devoured. Home-cooked beans are definitely best here, so remember to soak them the night before.

1 quantity Spelt Pastry (page 122), prepared and chilled for at least 2 hours

3 tbsp olive, sunflower or raw coconut oil

2 large onions, finely chopped

2 garlic cloves, chopped

2 large carrots, scrubbed and diced

1 large fennel bulb, diced

1 bay leaf, scrunched

500ml/18fl oz/2¼ cups tomato passata (tomato puree)

150ml/5fl oz/⅔ cup dry red wine

5 sun-dried tomatoes, soaked for at least 20 minutes, drained and chopped

1 tsp smoked paprika

1 tbsp tomato purée (tomato paste)

2 tsp vegetable bouillon powder

sea salt and freshly ground black pepper, to season

350g/12oz/1½ cups cooked adzuki beans, drained and rinsed if canned

white spelt flour, for rolling out

2 egg yolks, beaten with 2 tsp olive oil

black onion seeds, to garnish

pink peppercorns, to garnish (optional)

1. If the pastry has been chilled for 6 hours or longer, remove it from the fridge 30 minutes before rolling out.

2. Heat the oil in saucepan over a medium-high heat. Add the onions and sweat them (page 83) until they are translucent. Add the garlic and fry for 1 more minute.

3. Add the carrots, fennel and bay leaf, re-cover and fry for 6 minutes, stirring occasionally.

4. Add the passata (tomato puree), wine, tomatoes, paprika, tomato purée (tomato paste), bouillon powder and seasoning to taste. Bring to the boil, stirring.

5. Simmer, with the lid ajar, for 30 minutes, stirring occasionally. The mixture should be fairly thick but not dry. Add more water, if necessary, or reduce by raising the heat and removing the lid.

6. Stir in the beans, then leave to cool.

7. Follow the instructions on page 119 for rolling out two-thirds of the pastry. Line a 23cm/9in

VARIATIONS

Dairy-free option
Use 1 quantity Dairy-free Spelt
Pastry (page 123).

Gluten-free option
Use 1 quantity Gluten-free Pastry
(page 124) and roll it out with
brown rice flour.

Nut-free option
Use butter in the pastry, and olive
or sunflower oil in the main recipe.

Vegan option
Use 1 quantity Vegan Spelt Pastry
(page 123) and omit the eggs for
glazing. Instead, brush the pie with
2 tsp olive oil beaten with 2 tsp rice
or soya (soy) cream.

loose-bottomed tin (pan with removable bottom) with a rim and 4cm/1½in deep, leaving the excess pastry as overhang.

8. Roll out the remaining pastry until it is the size of the top of the quiche tin.

9. Spoon the cool bean mixture into the pastry case (shell). Brush the edge of the pastry with the egg mixture, then cover with the pastry lid (top crust) and crimp to seal, but leave the overhang. Place in the fridge for at least 15 minutes.

10. Meanwhile, preheat the oven to Fan 180°C/Fan 350°F/Gas 6. Remove the pie from the fridge. Trim the excess pastry. Brush the pastry lid with the egg mixture, then garnish with onion seeds and pink peppercorns. Cut a steam hole in the centre.

11. Bake for 40–50 minutes until golden brown. Cover with foil, if necessary, to prevent crust from burning. Leave to cool slightly, then remove the outer ring. Serve hot, warm or at room temperature.

HERBED POTATO PIE

Serves 6–8 | Prep 20 minutes, plus making the pastry (dough) and at least 2 hours chilling | Bake 1 hour
Dairy-free option | Gluten-free option | Nut free | Vegan option

This is a delicious creamy potato, herb and egg pastry-covered pie. It is the perfect vegetarian choice for a stylish picnic or a summer evening buffet, and will keep for up to 24 hours in the fridge, while the flavours develop. It is also very good eaten straight from the oven.

1 quantity Spelt Pastry (page 122), prepared and chilled for at least 2 hours

white spelt flour, for rolling out

400g/14oz/2⅔ cups waxy potatoes, peeled and very thinly sliced

55g/2oz/4 tbsp butter, melted

1 egg yolk, beaten with 1 tsp olive oil and 1 tsp water, for egg wash

1 tsp black onion seeds

225ml/8fl oz/1 cup single (light) cream

2 egg yolks

1 tbsp finely chopped basil leaves

1 tbsp finely chopped chives

1 tbsp finely chopped flat-leaf parsley

sea salt and freshly ground black pepper

Cook's note:

Any leftover pastry can be rolled into berry and/or leaf shapes to decorate the top crust. Attach them with a little beaten egg, then glaze the whole surface again.

1. If the pastry has been chilled for 6 hours or longer, remove it from the fridge 30 minutes before rolling out.

2. Follow the instruction on page 119 for rolling out two-thirds the pastry. Line a 23cm/9in loose-bottomed tin (pan with removable bottom) with a rim and 4cm/1½in deep, with the pastry, leaving the overhang.

3. Roll out the remaining one-third of the pastry until it is the size of the top of the quiche tin.

4. Bring a medium pan of salted water to the boil and add the sliced potatoes. Boil for 5 minutes, then drain and plunge them into cold water. Drain and pat dry with kitchen paper (paper towels).

5. Beat the cream with the eggs and season well with salt and pepper. Layer the potatoes to the top of the lined tin, brushing each layer with butter, salt, pepper and a sprinkling of herbs. Pour the egg mixture over the top.

6. Brush the pastry edge with the egg wash. Roll up the pastry lid (top crust) over a floured rolling pin and unroll it over the top of the pie. Crimp the edges to seal, but do not trim the overhang. Place in the fridge for at least 15 minutes.

7. Meanwhile, preheat the oven to Fan 180°C/Fan 350°F/Gas 6. Remove the pie from the fridge and cut off the excess pastry. Brush the pastry lid with the eggwash mixture, then scatter with the onion seeds. Cut a steam hole in the centre and insert a 2.5cm/1in-wide foil funnel.

8. Place the pie on a baking (cookie) sheet and bake for 50 minutes–1 hour, or until the top is golden brown and the potatoes are soft.

ROASTED PEPPER & GOAT'S CHEESE QUICHE

Serves 4–6 | Prep about 1 hour 40 minutes, including making the marmalade, plus making the pastry (dough), chilling for at least 2 hours and blind-baking (prebaking) | Bake 20–30 minutes
Dairy-free option | Gluten-free option | Lower-sugar option | Nut free | Vegan option

A classic combination for good reasons – the sweet onion marmalade is cut by the sharp balsamic vinegar note, and the Mediterranean warmth glows through. Make the effort to char-grill the peppers, as they add to the succulence. Use a mixture of red and yellow peppers, if you can find them.

125ml/4fl oz/½ cup full-fat (whole) milk or goat's milk

6 tbsp single (light) cream

4 eggs

one 20cm/8in blind-baked (prebaked) pastry case (shell) (page 120), 4cm/1½in deep, made with ½ quantity Spelt Pastry (page 122)

2 large red or yellow (bell) peppers, de-seeded, quartered and char-grilled (see Cook's note, page 137), or 175g/6oz/1¾ cup bottled char-grilled peppers, drained and thinly sliced

140g/5oz/⅔ cup soft goat's cheese with a runny middle, rinded and diced

For the Red Onion Marmalade:

2 tbsp olive oil

3 large red onions, thinly sliced

1 bay leaf, scrunched

½ tsp chopped thyme leaves

½ tsp chopped marjoram leaves

3 tbsp rapadura sugar

2 tbsp balsamic vinegar

sea salt and freshly ground black pepper, to season

1. To make the red onion marmalade, heat the oil in a saucepan over a medium-high heat until it shimmers. Add the onions and sweat (page 83) for 6 minutes. Add the herbs, re-cover and continue to cook over a low heat for 5 more minutes.

2. Raise the heat and add the sugar, stirring only to prevent burning; you are aiming for the sugar to caramelize. After about 6 minutes stir in the balsamic vinegar and season to taste.

3. Cover the pan and cook over a very low heat for about 40 minutes, uncovering and stirring occasionally, or until the onion marmalade is thick, dark and fragrant.

4. Meanwhile, preheat the oven to Fan 180°C/Fan 350°F/Gas 6.

Cook's notes:

To char-grill the peppers, heat the grill (broiler) to high. Place the de-seeded and quartered peppers on the grill rack, skin-side up, and grill, turning them occasionally, until charred. Wrap immediately in clingfilm (plastic wrap) and leave until cool. Peel off skins and thinly slice, then set aside.

Rapadura is an unrefined sugar that you can buy in health food stores or online.

5. Beat the milk, cream and eggs together and season with salt to taste. Place the tart tin with the pastry case (shell) on a baking (cookie) sheet.

6. Spread the onion marmalade over the pastry case, then scatter with the pepper strips and season with black pepper. Pour in the egg mixture and sprinkle the goat's cheese over the surface.

7. Carefully place into the oven and top up with extra milk, if necessary, until the filling comes to the top of the pastry case's rim.

8. Bake for 20–30 minutes until firm and golden brown. (See skewer tip on page 131.) Leave to cool slightly in the tin set on a wire rack, then remove from the tin and transfer to a serving dish. Serve hot, warm or at room temperature.

VARIATIONS

Dairy-free option
Use ½ quantity Dairy-free Spelt Pastry (page 123) to make the pastry case (shell). Replace the dairy or goat's milk with an equal quantity of rice or soya (soy) milk and replace the single cream with an equal quantity of rice or soya (soy) cream. Replace the goat's cheese with an equal quantity of vegan herbed cream cheese.

Gluten-free option
Use ½ quantity Gluten-free Pastry (page 124) to make the pastry case (shell), or a Gluten-free Polenta Pastry Case (page 125).

Lower-sugar option
Replace the sugar in the onion marmalade with the same quantity of pomegranate molasses.

Vegan option
Use ½ quantity Vegan Gluten-free Pastry (page 125) to make the pastry case (shell), or a Gluten-free Polenta Pastry Case (page 125), made with vegan Parmesan-style cheese and olive oil. Follow the dairy-free option above. Omit the eggs and replace them with 225g/8oz/1 cup vegan herbed cream cheese, 2 tbsp light tahini and 1 tsp vegetable bouillon powder or yeast flakes (nutritional yeast), beaten until smooth.

VEGAN COURGETTE & CASHEW QUICHE

Serves 4–6 | Prep 20 minutes, plus making the pastry and at least 2 hours chilling | Bake 40–50 minutes
Dairy free | Gluten-free option | Vegan

This is my master recipe for making vegan quiches, so you can replace the courgettes with any cooked vegetable of your choice, and replace the seeds with nuts. Just use your imagination. The vegan ingredients give a slightly grainier texture to the classic egg filling, but your family will love it.

one 20cm/8in blind-baked (prebaked) pastry case (shell) (page 120), 4cm/1½in deep, made with ½ quantity Vegan Spelt Pastry (page 123), or ½ quantity Vegan Gluten-free Pastry (page 125), or ½ quantity Vegan Cheese, Almond & Thyme Pastry (page 126) or a Gluten-free Polenta Pastry Case (page 125), made with vegan Parmesan-style cheese and olive oil

4 tbsp olive oil

2 garlic cloves, finely chopped

450g/1lb/4 cups courgettes (zucchini), coarsely grated

freshly grated zest and juice of 1 lemon

225g/8oz/1 cup vegan garlic-and-herb cream cheese or smoked tofu, chopped

125ml/4fl oz/½ cup rice or soya (soy) milk, plus extra, if necessary

6 tbsp rice or soya (soy) cream

2 tbsp light tahini

1 tbsp brown rice flour

1 tsp vegetable bouillon powder

½ tsp turmeric

4 tbsp chopped cashew nuts or sunflower seeds

2 tsp black onion seeds (optional)

sea salt and freshly ground black pepper

1. Preheat the oven to Fan 180°C/Fan 350°F/Gas 6.

2. Heat the oil in a heavy-based saucepan over a medium-high heat until it shimmers. Add the garlic and fry for barely a minute.

3. Add the courgettes (zucchini) and stir-fry for 8 minutes, or until all the moisture has evaporated. Add the lemon zest and juice and cook for 2 more minutes.

4. Remove the pan from heat. Add ½ tsp salt and 5 grinds of pepper, then spread the mixture over the pastry case (shell) base and set aside.

5. Put the garlic cream cheese, soya (soy) milk, rice cream, tahini, rice flour, bouillon powder and turmeric in a blender or food processor and blend until very smooth. Season with salt and pepper to taste.

VARIATIONS

Chestnut, Cranberry, & Caramelized Onion Quiche
Make the pastry case (shell), as left. Make 1 quantity Onion Marmalade (page 136) and stir in 1 tbsp chopped sage, then spread onto the pastry case. Sprinkle with 4 tbsp chopped cooked chestnuts. Pour over the cream cheese mixture from step 5, left, and sprinkle with 4 tbsp cranberries or redcurrants, defrosted if frozen. Bake as in the main recipe, step 7.

Mushroom, Butter Bean & Seed Quiche
Make the pastry case (shell), as left. Prepare the Mushroom, Butter Bean & Seed Salad (page 68). Spread the salad over the pastry case, then top with the cream cheese mixture from step 5, left. Bake the quiche as in the main recipe, step 7.

6. Put the pastry case in its tin on a baking (cookie) sheet. Pour the cream-cheese mixture over the courgettes. Carefully transfer to the oven and add extra rice milk, if necessary, so the topping reaches the rim. Scatter the surface with cashews and black onion seeds, if you like.

7. Bake for 40–50 minutes until the filling has set. It will have a fairly wobbly consistency until it cools. Leave the quiche to cool in its tin set on a wire rack. Remove from the tin and serve.

BUTTERNUT, BERRY & GOAT'S CHEESECAKE

Serves 4–6 | Prep 40 minutes | Bake 40–50 minutes | Dairy-free option | Gluten free | Nut-free option | Vegan option

I created this signature dish for my many customers who only eat goat's-milk products, and it has been a bestseller ever since. Don't be put off by the thought of strong tasting, goaty flavours. This is a mild, unusually good-looking and tasty savoury reworking of the popular American baked cheesecake.

8 unpeeled garlic cloves

500g/1lb 2oz/2¼ cups soft goat's cheese or mascarpone

250g/9oz/1 cup plus 2 tbsp goat's or dairy ricotta cheese

150ml/5fl oz/⅔ cup goat's yogurt or crème fraîche

30g/1oz/½ cup basil leaves, or 2 tbsp vegan pesto

3 spring onions (scallions), coarsely chopped

3 eggs

2 tsp vegetable bouillon powder or yeast flakes (nutritional yeast)

115g/4oz/1 cup sour berries, such as cranberries or redcurrants, defrosted if frozen

sea salt and freshly ground black pepper, to season

For the topping:

450g/1lb/3½ cups butternut squash, peeled and cut into 4cm/1½in cubes

1 tbsp tamari or liquid aminos

1 tbsp balsamic vinegar

2 tsp rapadura sugar

a small pinch of Piri-piri Spice Mix (page 220) or chilli flakes

1 tbsp raw, melted coconut or olive oil

1. Preheat the oven to Fan 200°C/Fan 400°F/Gas 7. Line the base and side of a 20cm/8in springform tin, 5cm/2in deep, with parchment paper, leaving a 5cm/2in collar above the rim.

2. To make the topping, put the butternut squash, vinegar, tamari, sugar, Piri-piri and oil in a roasting tray (baking sheet) lined with a silicone mat. Add the garlic from the filling ingredients, and toss so everything is well coated.

3. Roast for 12 minutes, then remove the garlic, which should be soft, and set it aside to cool. Turn the squash over and roast for 10 more minutes, or until soft. Leave to cool.

4. Turn the oven temperature down to Fan 160°C/Fan 325°F/Gas 4.

5. Meanwhile, to make the base, heat the oil in a frying pan over a medium-high heat until it shimmers. Turn the heat down, add the spring onions and stir for 5 minutes.

6. Stir the buckwheat and rice flakes to amalgamate thoroughly and continue stirring until toasty

For the base:

4 tbsp raw coconut or olive oil

4 spring onions, chopped, or ½ leek, finely chopped and washed

55g/2oz/½ cup buckwheat flakes

55g/2oz/⅔ cup brown rice flakes

4 tbsp toasted blanched hazelnuts, chopped

1 tbsp chopped rosemary, or 1½ tsp dried

freshly grated zest and juice of 1 lemon

brown spots appear. Stir in the nuts, rosemary and lemon zest. Cook for a couple more minutes, then add the lemon juice and cook until the liquid evaporates, stirring occasionally. Season with salt and pepper, then set aside to cool.

7. Sprinkle three-quarters of the base mixture in an even layer over the bottom of the tin and press down; reserve the remainder.

8. To make the filling, peel the roasted garlic and put it in a blender or food processor with the goat's cheese, goat's yogurt, basil, spring onions (scallions), eggs and bouillon powder. Blend until smooth, then season to taste.

9. Carefully pour the cheese mixture over the base. Arrange the squash on top in a central mound. Sprinkle the berries in a ring around the squash, then scatter the remaining lemon-flake base mixture around the edge of the tin, leaving a band of cheese mixture peeping through.

10. Place the tin on a baking (cookie) sheet and bake for 40–50 minutes until the cheesecake is wobbly, but set. Do not over-cook. Set the tin on a wire rack and leave to cool completely. Carefully unclip the side, invert onto a large, flat plate or tray and peel off the metal base and paper. Replace the metal base, cover the cheesecake with your serving dish and re-invert. Chill and serve.

DOLCELATTE & CUCUMBER CHEESECAKE

Serves 4–6 | Prep 20 minutes, plus at least 4 hours chilling and marinating the tempeh or tofu (optional) | Bake 45 minutes
Dairy-free option | Gluten free | Vegan option

A sweet, sour and salty tang contrasts well with the creamy blue cheese in this unique treat. Few of my customers had ever tried baked cucumbers before I started selling this. The crunchy, unexpected topping made it an instant success, and the tempeh provides a tasty, fermented tone.

250g/9oz dolcelatte or other soft blue cheese

500g/1lb 2oz/2 cups soft goat's cheese or mascarpone

150ml/5floz/⅔ cup goat's yogurt or crème fraîche

30g/1oz/½ cup basil leaves, or 2 tbsp vegan pesto

3 spring onions (scallions), coarsely chopped

3 eggs

1 tbsp yeast flakes (nutritional yeast) or vegetable bouillon powder

sea salt and freshly ground black pepper

ingredients for one base from the Butternut, Berry & Goat's Cheesecake recipe (page 141)

For the topping:
1 cucumber, cut into 4cm/1½ in cubes

350g/12oz tempeh, defrosted if frozen and marinated, or smoked tofu, marinated (see opposite)

8 unpeeled garlic cloves

1 tbsp olive oil

1 tbsp unsweetened apple juice

1. Preheat the oven to Fan 200°C/Fan 400°F/Gas 7. Line the base and side of a 20cm/8in springform tin, 5cm/2in deep, with parchment paper, leaving a 5cm/2in collar above the rim.

2. To make the topping, put the cucumber, oil, apple juice concentrate, tamari, vinegar and thyme in a roasting tray (baking sheet) lined with a silicone mat and toss well so everything is coated in oil. Add the garlic.

3. Roast for 12 minutes, then remove the garlic, which should be soft, and set it aside to cool. Turn the cucumber over and roast for 10 more minutes until soft, then set aside to cool.

4. Marinate the tempeh (opposite).

5. Turn down the oven temperature to Fan 160°C/Fan 325°F/Gas 4. To make the base, follow steps 5–6, pages 140–141.

6. To make the cheesecake mixture, peel the roasted garlic cloves and put them in a blender or food processor with the dolcelatte, goat's cheese, goat's yoghurt, basil leaves, spring onions (scallions),

concentrate or 1 tsp sugar

1 tbsp tamari

1 tbsp balsamic vinegar

leaves from 5 thyme sprigs

10 gooseberries

15 black grapes, halved and seeded

10 black Greek olives, pitted

eggs and yeast flakes (nutritional yeast), and blend until smooth. Season to taste.

7. Sprinkle three-quarters of the lemon-flake base mixture in an even layer over the bottom of the lined tin and press it down; reserve the remainder.

8. Carefully pour the cheese mixture over the base. Arrange the roasted cucumber and the tempeh on top in a central mound. Sprinkle the gooseberries, grapes and olives in a ring around the cucumber, then scatter the remaining lemon-flake mixture around the edge, leaving a band of cheese mixture peeping through.

9. Bake as in step 10 on page 141 for 40–50 minutes until the cheesecake is wobbly, but set. Do not over-bake. Leave to cool and chill for 4 hours.

VARIATIONS

Dairy-free option
Replace mascarpone or soft goat's cheese in the cheesecake mixture with the same quantity of vegan herbed cream cheese, replace the dolcelatte or other dairy cheese with vegan blue cheese and replace the goat's yogurt or crème fraîche with the same quantity of soya (soy) yogurt.

Vegan option
For the cheesecake mixture, follow the dairy-free option above. Omit the eggs and replace them with 115g/4oz/ scant ½ cup light tahini plus 2 tbsp brown rice flour, beaten until smooth.

MARINATED TEMPEH OR TOFU

250g/9oz tempeh, defrosted if frozen, or smoked tofu

For the marinade:

2 garlic cloves

1 spring onion, coarsely chopped

2 tbsp liquid aminos

2 tbsp pomegranate molasses or maple syrup

2 tbsp balsamic vinegar

1cm/½ in piece fresh ginger

1 tsp yeast flakes (nutritional yeast)

1. Blend all the marinade ingredients in a blender or food processor until smooth. Pour the marinade over the tempeh and leave for at least 15 minutes.

2. Meanwhile, preheat the grill (broiler) and place the tempeh and any remaining marinade on a silicone mat.

3. Grill the tempeh for 8–10 minutes on either side, or until it is well browned.

Sweet
Recipes

Sweetheart Tarts

For many, nothing can replace the uniquely satisfying experience of a freshly baked homemade slice of melting, buttery pastry filled with ingenious, classic combinations of eggs, cream and fruit. The following recipes include vegan, lower-sugar and dairy-free alternatives, all of which are equally satisfying for those on a restricted diet.

Amongst the following popular desserts you will spot a revamped caramel apple tart, a tutti-frutti tatin and a mango and cider mincemeat streusel tart. As with the previous savoury versions, a blind-baked (prebaked) pastry case always sets off your tempting creations to their best advantage.

If you don't have time to make everything from scratch, prepare your pastry or base in advance. Line your tart tin with the dough, and either freeze it unbaked, or blind-bake and then freeze it, ready to complete the recipe nearer the time of serving.

TARTE AU CITRON VERT

Serves 4–6 | Prep 10 minutes, plus making and chilling the pastry (dough) and blind-baking (prebaking) the pastry case
Bake 30 minutes | Dairy-free option | Gluten-free option | Lower-sugar option | Nut free | Vegan option

This classic recipe can be varied by changing the citrus fruit, using mandarin, lemon, lime or blood oranges. Strewing with handful of pomegranate seeds or berries just before serving adds visual and flavour interest. I like to serve this with pouring cream and a bowl of raspberries or strawberries.

4 eggs

400ml/14fl oz/1¾ cups double (heavy) cream

115g/4oz/½ cup plus 1 tbsp sugar

1 tsp Madagascan vanilla extract

freshly grated zest and juice of 5 limes

one 20cm/8in blind-baked (prebaked) pastry case (page 120) made with ½ quantity Sweet Spelt Pastry (page 123)

1. Preheat the oven to Fan 160°C/Fan 325°F/Gas 4.

2. Beat the eggs, cream, sugar, vanilla and lime zest and juice together until smooth.

3. Place the pastry case on a baking (cookie) sheet and pour in half the egg mixture. Put the baking sheet in the oven and add the remaining mixture. Bake for 30 minutes, or until the filling is just set, but still slightly wobbly. Leave to cool in the tin on a wire rack for at least 10 minutes.

VARIATIONS

Dairy-free option
Use ½ quantity Dairy-free Spelt Pastry (page 123) to make the pastry case. When making the pastry (dough), add 6 tbsp granulated sugar to the flours and salt and add ½ tsp vanilla extract to the liquid. Replace the double cream in the filling with the same quantity of rice or soya (soy) cream.

Gluten-free option
Use ½ quantity Sweet Gluten-free Pastry (page 125) to make the pastry case and use rice flour for rolling out.

Lower-sugar option
Use ½ quantity Lower-sugar, Sweet Gluten-free Pastry (page 125). Replace the sugar in the filling with 125ml/4fl oz/½ cup agave or rice syrup.

Vegan option
Use ½ quantity Vegan Sweet Gluten-free Pastry (page 125) to make the pastry case. In step 2 of the main recipe above, replace the eggs with 225g/8oz/1 cup vegan cream cheese plus 1 tbsp brown rice flour, and replace the dairy cream with the same quantity of rice or soya (soy) cream.

CARAMEL APPLE TART

Serves 4–6 | Prep 35 minutes, plus making and chilling the pastry (dough) and blind-baking (prebaking) the pastry case
Bake 25 minutes | Dairy-free option | Gluten free | Nut free

This delicious tart is inspired by a Roux brothers' recipe, which I have simplified. It combines caramel, apples, eggs and cream to produce an exquisite winter variation on a classic theme. Golden toffee mouthfuls nestle beneath the gleaming golden custard surface. Enjoy this warm with vanilla-speckled ice cream or Chantilly cream.

2 large cooking apples

2 tbsp freshly squeezed lemon juice

115g/4oz/½ cup unsalted butter, chopped

140g/5oz/¾ cup sugar

½ tsp ground cinnamon

4 grinds of freshly ground black pepper

one blind-baked (prebaked) 20cm/8in pastry case made with ½ quantity Sweet Gluten-free Pastry (page 125)

400ml/14fl oz/1¾ cups double (heavy) cream

2 eggs

1. Preheat the oven to Fan 200°C/Fan 400°F/Gas 7.

2. Peel and core the apples. Cut each into 8 slices, then brush with lemon juice; set aside.

3. Melt the butter over a medium heat until it shimmers. Add the sugar and cook, swirling the mixture in the pan, until it turns a caramel colour, but is not too dark. Add the cinnamon, then the apple slices and black pepper. Continue cooking for 4 minutes, turning once, or until the apples are *just* softening and the juices are beginning to run.

4. Remove the apples from the pan with a slotted spoon and set aside the caramel juices. Arrange the apples in the pastry case and set the tin on a baking (cookie) sheet.

5. Beat together the cream, the reserved caramel juices and the eggs until blended, then pour the mixture over the apples.

6. Bake for 25 minutes, or until just set, so it's not runny but is still slightly wobbly. Cool until just warm, then serve.

VARIATIONS

Dairy-free option
Use Dairy-free, Gluten-free Pastry (page 125) to make the pastry case. When making the pastry (dough), add 6 tbsp granulated sugar to the flours and salt and add ½ tsp Madagascan vanilla extract to the liquid.

In the main recipe replace the butter with the same quantity of raw coconut oil and replace the double cream with the same quantity of rice or soya (soy) cream.

BANOFFEE PIE

Serves 4–6 | Prep 30 minutes, plus optional boiling of the condensed milk, chilling the crumb base and chilling before serving | No baking | Dairy-free option | Gluten-free option | Nut free | Vegan option

This is a Christmas market special, and each year we sell more portions. I think the rum and lemon raise the sweetness to new heights, and the slightly bitter coffee notes in the cream, coupled with a generous sprinkling of raw cacao nibs, takes this to a sophisticated level.

225ml/8fl oz/¾ cup canned caramel condensed milk (dulce de leche)

3 large bananas

1 tbsp freshly squeezed lemon or lime juice

2 tbsp dark rum (optional)

600ml/1 pint/2½ cups double (heavy) cream

4 tbsp sugar or xylitol

1 tsp Madagascan vanilla extract

2½ tsp espresso coffee powder dissolved in 1 tbsp boiling water, at room temperature

2 tbsp brandy (optional)

grated 70 per cent dark chocolate, to decorate

For the digestive crumb base:

115g/4oz/½ cup butter

2 tbsp sugar or xylitol

225g/8oz/3 cups digestive biscuits (Graham crackers), finely crushed (about 18 biscuits)

1. If you can't find caramel condensed milk (dulce de leche), simmer an unopened can of plain sweetened condensed milk in an uncovered saucepan, with water coming just to the top of the pan, for 2 hours. Leave to cool.

2. To make the base, melt the butter, then add the sugar and stir until it dissolves.

3. Stir the butter into the biscuit (cracker) crumbs. Tip into a 20cm/8in loose-bottomed tart tin (tart pan with removable bottom), 4cm/1½in deep, and use an empty glass jar to press the crumbs evenly over the base and up the side. Cover with clingfilm (plastic wrap) and chill for at least 30 minutes.

4. Meanwhile, peel and slice the bananas and toss them in the lemon juice and rum, if using. Spread the caramel condensed milk over the chilled crumb base and top with a layer of bananas.

5. Whip the cream with the sugar until it is just becoming stiff, then fold in the vanilla, espresso and brandy, if using. Pipe or spread the cream over the bananas and sprinkle with the grated chocolate. Cover and chill for at least 4 hours.

Dairy-free option

Replace the caramel condensed milk (dulce de leche) with ½ quantity Vegan Caramel (below) and replace the butter in the crumb base with the same quantity of hard margarine or raw coconut oil. Replace the double cream in the topping with 1 quantity Vegan Cream (below). If using dark chocolate, use a dairy-free variety.

Gluten-free option

Replace the crumb base with 1 Caramel Rice Flake Base (steps 2–6, page 184), made with all the crumb mixture, but omitting the cinnamon and orange flower water.

Vegan option

Replace the butter in the digestive crumb base with the same quantity of raw coconut oil, or use 1 Caramel Rice Flake Base (steps 2–6, page 184), made with the entire crumb mixture, but omitting the cinnamon and orange flower water. Replace the caramel condensed milk (dulce de leche) with ½ quantity Vegan Caramel (below) and replace the double cream with the Vegan Cream (below). If using dark chocolate, use a dairy-free variety.

VEGAN CARAMEL

400g/14oz/2 cups sugar

125ml/4floz/½ cup water

2½ tbsp agave or rice syrup

2 tbsp raw coconut oil or hard margarine, chopped

125ml/4fl oz/½ cup full-fat coconut cream

a pinch of salt

1. Put the sugar, water and agave syrup in a saucepan over a low heat and stir until the sugar dissolves. Turn the heat up and leave to boil, swirling but not stirring, for up to 10 minutes until the liquid turns a rich, golden amber colour.

2. Immediately remove the pan from the heat and cover your hand with a thick cloth. Swirl in the coconut oil and add the coconut cream. The mixture will spit.

3. Leave to cool until the caramel begins to thicken, then pour immediately over the chilled crumb base.

VEGAN CREAM

600ml/1 pint/2½ cup full-fat (whole) coconut cream or vegan whipping cream

1. The day before, put the coconut or whipping cream in the fridge along with the electric beaters.

2. Drain the coconut cream in a fine sieve to remove any excess coconut water.

3. Beat the creamy coconut or whipping cream with an electric mixer, using chilled beaters, slowly at first and then faster, making sure you incorporate as much air as possible, until the cream doubles in volume.

MANGO & CIDER MINCEMEAT STREUSEL TART

Serves 4–6 I Prep 40 minutes, plus overnight macerating the mincemeat, making and chilling the pastry (dough) and blind-baking (prebaking) the pastry case I Bake 40–50 minutes I Dairy-free option I Gluten-free option I Lower-sugar option

The mango chunks bring an intense sour-sweet surprise to this no-added-sugar favourite, which is delicious any time of the year. This quantity of mincemeat is more than you need for a single tart, but it keeps for up to two months in a sealed sterilized jar in the fridge.

one 20cm/8in blind-baked (prebaked) pastry case, baked in a tin 5cm/2in deep, made with ½ quantity Sweet Spelt Pastry (page 123)

icing (confectioners') sugar, for dusting

For the Lower-sugar Mango & Cider Mincemeat:

900g/2lb mixed unsulphured dried fruit, such as apricots, cranberries, currants, dates, figs, mixed peel, pitted prunes and sultanas (golden raisins), finely chopped, if large

225g/8oz dried mango pieces

freshly grated zest and juice of 2 limes

freshly grated zest and juice of 2 oranges

2 tsp ground mixed spice (apple pie spice)

1 tsp freshly grated nutmeg

500ml/18floz/2¼ cups (hard) cider or unsweetened apple juice

225g/8oz/2 cups grated vegetable suet or raw coconut oil, chilled and grated

1. To make the mincemeat, mix together all the ingredients, except the suet, and leave overnight at room temperature in a covered bowl or saucepan.

2. The next day, simmer over a medium-low heat in a covered pan for 20 minutes, uncovering and stirring occasionally so the mixture does not catch on the base. Allow to cool, then stir in the suet. Use at once or store.

3. To make the crème pâtissière, scrape the seeds from the vanilla pod (bean) into a saucepan with the milk and orange zest, then add the pod. Gently bring to the boil. Remove from the heat and leave to infuse for 10 minutes.

4. Meanwhile, preheat the oven to Fan 160°C/Fan 325°F/Gas 4.

5. Beat the egg yolks with the sugar until thick and creamy, then stir in cornflour (cornstarch) mixture and the orange juice.

For the Orange Crème Pâtissière:

½ vanilla pod (bean), split lengthways

250ml/9fl oz/1 cup plus 2 tbsp full-fat milk

freshly grated zest and juice of 1 large orange

3 egg yolks

4 tbsp sugar

2 tbsp cornflour (cornstarch), slaked (mixed) with 1 tbsp orange flower water and 4 tbsp water

For the streusel topping:

115g/4oz/½ cup butter, chilled

115g/4oz/¾ cup plus 1 tbsp white spelt flour

2½ tbsp caster (superfine) sugar

½ tsp ground cinnamon

6. Whisk the infused milk into the egg mixture and beat until smooth. Return the mixture to the pan and slowly bring to the boil, stirring. Boil for 2 minutes, then pour into a bowl and cover with clingfilm (plastic wrap) placed directly on to the surface. Leave to cool until tepid.

7. To make the streusel topping, cut the butter into the flour, sugar and cinnamon until the mixture resembles coarse crumbs, then set aside.

8. Pour the custard over the base of the pastry case to make a 2cm/¾in layer. Drop spoonfuls of the mincemeat over the surface until it is covered (reserve the leftover for another recipe), then sprinkle with the streusel topping.

9. Bake for 30–40 minutes until the topping is golden brown. Leave to cool in the tin for at least 10 minutes on a wire rack. Serve warm or tepid, dusted with icing (confectioners') sugar.

VARIATIONS

Dairy-free option
Use ½ quantity Dairy-free Sweet Spelt Pastry (page 123) to make the pastry case. Replace the dairy milk in the crème pâtissière with the same quantity of coconut milk. Replace the butter in the streusel topping with the same quantity of chilled hard margarine or raw coconut oil.

Gluten-free option
Use ½ quantity Sweet Gluten-free Pastry (page 125) to make the pastry case. Replace the spelt flour in the streusel topping with 115g/4oz/¾ cup brown rice flour.

Lower-sugar option
Use ½ quantity Lower-sugar, Sweet Gluten-free Pastry (page 125) to make the pastry case. Replace the sugar in the crème pâtissière and the streusel topping with the same quantities of xylitol. Dust the baked tart with powdered xylitol.

PEAR & CHOCOLATE TART

Serves 8 | Prep 30 minutes, plus making and chilling the pastry (dough) and blind-baking (prebaking) the pastry case
Bake 20–30 minutes | Dairy-free option | Gluten-free option | Lower-sugar option | Nut free | Vegan option

Like the Caramel & Apple Tart, this is another delicious Sunday-lunch-with-friends tart. Pears and chocolate go so well together that to combine them with sweet pastry, eggs and cream is sublime, to say the least! The vegan version is yummy, too, especially when served with soya custard mixed with espresso.

175ml/6fl oz/¾ cup double (heavy) cream

85g/3oz 70 per cent dark chocolate, roughly chopped

2 ripe pears

one 20cm/8in blind-baked (prebaked) pastry case (page 120) made with ½ quantity Sweet Spelt Pastry (page 123)

2 eggs

85g/3oz/½ cup sugar

1 tsp Madagascan vanilla extract

double (heavy) cream, whipped cream or ice cream, to serve (optional)

1. Preheat the oven to Fan 160°C/Fan 325°F/Gas 4.

2. Meanwhile, heat the cream until it is simmering, not boiling. Add the chocolate and stir until it melts, then leave to cool slightly.

3. Peel the pears, then quarter and core them. Arrange the pears, cut-side down, over the base of the pastry shell, then set the tin on a baking (cookie) sheet.

4. Beat the eggs, sugar and vanilla together, then beat into the chocolate-flavoured cream.

5. Pour the cream mixture over the pears. Bake for 20–30 minutes until the filling is set. Cover with kitchen foil if the pears start over-browning.

6. Leave the tart in the tin to cool completely on a wire rack. Serve with pouring cream, custard, whipped cream or ice cream, if you like.

Cook's note

For a change, try substituting the pears for fresh figs macerated in Armagnac, or stoned, halved greengages. You can also replace the dark chocolate with white instead.

TARTE TATIN WITH HAZELNUT PASTRY

Serves 4–6 | Prep 25 minutes, plus making and chilling the pastry (dough) | Bake 30–40 minutes
Dairy-free option | Gluten-free option | Lower-sugar option | Nut-free option | Vegan option

Nowadays, *la tarte des demoiselles Tatin* is a very popular dessert; however, I remember eating this upside-down apple dessert, all glistening with caramelized buttery juices, in an Antibes restaurant long before it made the mainstream Channel crossing. My twist is to use a variety of fruit on rich, crisp hazelnut pastry.

1 quantity Hazelnut Pastry (page 127), chilled for at least 2 hours

1kg/2lb 4oz apples, bananas, pears or pineapple

freshly squeezed lemon juice, for tossing

115g/4oz/½ cup plus 1 tbsp sugar, mixed with 1 tsp ground cinnamon, cardamom or star anise, if you like

115g/4oz/½ cup unsalted butter, chilled

brown rice flour, for rolling out

about 10 naturally coloured glacé (candied) cherries or unsulphured pitted prunes or dried apricots (optional)

4 tbsp Calvados, Poire William liqueur, kirsch or brandy (optional)

1. If the pastry has been chilled for 6 hours or longer, remove it from the fridge 1 hour before rolling out. Preheat the oven to Fan 180°C/Fan 350°F/Gas 6.

2. Meanwhile, peel, core and cut the fruit as follows: for apples, quarter and cut into 1cm/½in slices; for bananas, slice lengthways; for pears, quarter lengthways; for pineapple, slice into rings. Toss the apples, bananas and pears with lemon juice to prevent browning; set aside.

3. Heat a 23cm/9in Tatin tin or heavy-based, deep ovenproof frying pan over a medium heat. Sprinkle in the sugar and slowly heat until it melts and turns pale golden. Do not stir.

4. Turn up the heat and leave until the sugar syrup turns dark golden brown. Watch closely so it does not burn. Do not stir or shake the pan until the sugar has caramelized. Swirl in the butter and vigorously shake the pan until it is well mixed.

5. Remove the pan from the heat and arrange a layer of fruit in an attractive pattern. If you've used pineapple, fill the holes with glacé (candied) cherries.

6. Add the rest of the fruit. You can flambé the fruit with your chosen alcohol for a sophisticated flavour, if you want. Leave to cook over a medium heat whilst rolling out the pastry (dough).

7. Roll out the pastry on a lightly floured surface until it is 1cm/½in thick and the same width as your tin. Gently drape the pastry over the floured rolling pin, then unroll it over the hot tin. Loosely tuck the pastry edge inside the rim, and prick the surface with a fork.

8. Bake for 30–40 minutes until the pastry is crisp and evenly browned.

9. Remove the tin from oven and allow the tart to cool for 10 minutes in the tin set on a wire rack. If there is too much juice, pour it off into a small pan, then boil until it reduces to a syrup. You can then use this to glaze the top of the un-moulded tart.

10. Run a broad-bladed spatula around the rim of the tin to loosen the tart. Using a thick oven cloth, cover the tin with a warmed 30cm/12in serving dish, turned upside down, and invert the two, giving the tin a sharp shake to dislodge the tart. Re-arrange any stuck-on pieces of fruit, brush with any reduced syrup and serve warm.

Tarte Tatin with Hazelnut Pastry | 157

Roulades, Dessert Cakes & Cheesecakes

All recipes in this chapter have been designed as gluten free, and they range from 3–10 on the naughty scale! The hazelnut meringue is layered with a perfumed apricot purée and accompanied with a fresh raspberry coulis – alchemy in action! Tender, fruity baked cheesecakes sit on a caramel, almond and rice-flake crumb, and the moist, lower-sugar vegan nectarine cake will be gratefully received by those with detoxing on their mind... but who still want to have their cake and eat it!

Always a bit special, the roulades make any occasion a celebration. Also on offer are two elegant, rich dessert cakes set on easy-to-serve sponge bases, and a tasty Christmas cake made with chunky mango mincemeat.

You can successfully freeze all of the cakes in this chapter – except the cheesecakes – leaving off the decorations. Defrost in the fridge and finish according to the recipe.

MASTER ROULADE RECIPE

Serves 6–8 | Prep 20 minutes, plus at least 1 hour cooling | Bake 15 minutes
Dairy-free option | Gluten free | Lower-sugar option | Nut-free option

Always a bit special, a roulade turns any occasion into a celebration. You can freeze all the roulades in this chapter before decorating for up to two months, ready for special occasions. Simply defrost in the fridge, then decorate as instructed in your recipe. Follow this master recipe and use your imagination for endless flavours.

115g/4oz/heaped 1 cup ground almonds

55g/2oz/⅓ cup potato or rice flour

6 eggs

175g/6oz/¾ cup plus 1 tbsp caster (superfine) sugar

55g/2oz/4 tbsp unsalted butter, melted and cooled

icing (confectioners') sugar and/or unsweetened cocoa powder, for dusting and decorating (optional)

filling of your choice (see opposite)

1. Preheat the oven to Fan 180°C/Fan 350°F/Gas 6. Line a 40×30cm/16×12in Swiss roll (jelly roll) tin with parchment paper extending 4cm/1½in above the rim, then set aside.

2. Combine the ground almonds and flour and set aside.

3. Beat the eggs and sugar together in a large bowl with an electric mixer for about 10 minutes until they form a pale yellow mousse.

4. Use a large balloon whisk to rapidly fold in the butter, followed by the almond mixture. Use a figure-of-eight motion, giving the bowl a quarter turn with each fold.

5. Quickly pour the mixture (batter) into the prepared tin, smoothing it into the corners.

6. Bake the roulade for 15 minutes, or until it is pale golden and firm. Remove from the oven and leave it to cool in the tin on a wire rack.

Cook's notes:

A wide-bladed metal spatula is the best choice for spreading mixtures (batters) and covering the roulades. Dip it in boiling water and wipe frequently to keep it clean for easier, smoother spreading.

Simple roulade fillings:

Rich, indulgent whipped cream, studded with fresh fruit, is the classic roulade filling. At its most basic, simply fold fruit into whipped cream – try chopped mango or papaya sprinkled with lime juice, pitted cherries, cinnamon-spiced apple or orange-flavoured cranberries, chopped strawberries or raspberries.

A well-reduced fruit purée, such as apricot (page 176), is another delicious option. Spread 280g/10oz/1¼ cups purée over the un-rolled roulade and top with 300ml/10fl oz/1¼ cups whipped cream, then re-roll. Or, for a less-rich roulade, use double the amount of purée and omit the cream. Dust the filled roulade with cinnamon- or cardamom-flavoured icing (confectioners') sugar or unsweetened cocoa powder.

All mascarpone fillings and icings in the Sweet Vegetable Cake chapter (pages 188–207) are suitable for filling roulades. If you want a lower-sugar filling, replace the sugar with xylitol or agave or rice syrup. If a filling sweetened with syrup is too sloppy to hold its shape, add up to 2 tbsp psyllium husks (page 22).

7. Meanwhile, lay a large sheet of greaseproof (waxed) paper on the work surface and sprinkle with sifted icing (confectioners') sugar or cocoa powder, depending on your recipe. When the roulade is cool, invert it onto the paper and peel off the parchment paper.

8. Cover with the filling in your recipe, spreading it to the edges.

9. Use the paper to help roll up the roulade from a long side. Don't worry if it cracks. Trim the ends with a sharp knife. Twist the ends of the paper to secure the roll, then chill for at least 1 hour or up to 24 hours.

10. Up to 2 hours before you are ready to serve, decorate or simply dust with sifted icing sugar and/or unsweetened cocoa powder.

VARIATIONS

Dairy-free option
Replace the butter in the cake mixture with the same quantity of melted and cooled hard margarine or raw coconut oil. Replace the double cream with the same quantity of vegan whipping cream.

Lower-sugar option
Replace the sugar in the cake mixture with the same quantity of xylitol and use powdered xylitol for dusting. Use a sugar-free filling, such as apricot purée (page 176).

Nut-free option
Replace the ground almonds in the cake mixture with the same quantity of finely ground sunflower seeds. Replace the butter with sunflower oil.

STRAWBERRY & LEMON ROULADE

Serves 6–8 | Prep 20 minutes, plus cooling and at least 1 hour chilling | Bake 15 minutes
Gluten free | Nut-free option (page 161)

Here's a classic, cool summer combination that adds a real sense of occasion to any afternoon tea party, or a stylish ending to a family meal. For variety, replace the strawberries in the filling with raspberries, dust the rolled roulade with icing (confectioners') sugar and decorate with extra raspberries and mint sprigs.

ingredients for 1 quantity Master Roulade Recipe (page 160)

For the filling and decoration:
900ml/1½ pints/3½ cups double (heavy) cream
115g/4oz/½ cup caster (superfine) sugar
freshly grated zest and juice of 2 lemons

1 tsp Madagascan vanilla extract
280g/10oz strawberries, hulled and finely chopped, plus extra, thinly sliced strawberries, to decorate
strawberry vegetarian gelling agent – enough to set 300ml/10fl oz/1¼ cups liquid according the packet instructions
pomegranate seeds

1. Follow steps 1–7 of the Master Roulade Recipe (page 160).

2. Meanwhile, to make the filling, whip the cream until soft peaks form. Fold in the sugar, then the lemon juice, vanilla and strawberries. Chill until required.

3. Fill, roll and wrap as in steps 8–9 (page 161).

4. When ready to decorate, make up the jelly in a measuring jug with boiling water, following the packet instructions, then set aside until it is just becoming syrupy.

5. Unwrap and roll the roulade onto a wire rack set over a tray. Cover with thinly sliced strawberries and press pomegranate seeds into any gaps. Quickly pour and then gently brush the syrup over the surface and leave to set before slicing.

TIRAMISU ROULADE

Serves 6–8 | Prep 20 minutes, plus cooling and at least 1 hour chilling | Bake 15 minutes
Dairy-free option | Gluten free | Lower-sugar option | Nut-free option (page 161)

Such a fabulous combo, this has to be test-driven at least once. It's very rich, so serve it in thin slices. It will keep for up to 24 hours in the fridge, so any leftovers are extra yummy with your mid-morning coffee. I can never resist a slice the next morning!

ingredients for 1 quantity Master Roulade Recipe (page 160)

For the filling and decoration:
2½ tsp espresso coffee powder dissolved in 1 tbsp boiling water

4 tbsp Marsala or brandy

4 eggs, separated

115g/4oz/½ cup caster (superfine) sugar

1 tsp Madagascan vanilla extract

250g/9oz/1 cup plus 2 tbsp mascarpone

unsweetened cocoa powder sifted with finely ground coffee beans

---

VARIATIONS

Dairy-free option
Use the dairy-free option with the Master Roulade Recipe on page 160. Replace the mascarpone in the filling with the same quantity of vegan cream cheese.

Lower-sugar option
Use the lower-sugar option with the Master Roulade Recipe on page 160. Replace the sugar in the filling with 125ml/4fl oz/½ cup agave or rice syrup or 8 tbsp xylitol. If the filling is too sloppy to hold its shape, add up to 2 tbsp psyllium husks (page 22).

Nut-free option
Use the nut-free option with Master Roulade Recipe on page 160.

---

1. Follow steps 1–7 of the Master Roulade Recipe (page 160).

2. To make the filling, combine the espresso and Marsala, then set aside. Beat the egg yolks, mascarpone and vanilla together until fluffy. In a separate bowl, beat the egg whites until soft peaks form. Add the sugar and continue beating until stiff.

3. Stir 2 tbsp of the egg whites into the yolk mixture, then fold in the remainder.

4. Fill, roll and wrap as in steps 8–9 (page 161), sprinkling with the espresso and using half the filling. Chill the remaining filling.

5. To serve, spread with the remaining filling and sift the coffee-flavoured cocoa powder onto the top.

VERONIQUE'S CHOCOLATE GANACHE ROULADE

Serves 6–8 | Prep 40 minutes, plus cooling and at least 2 hours chilling | Bake 15 minutes
Dairy-free option | Gluten free | Nut-free option

This very rich and wonderful chocoholics' feast makes an ultimate birthday or Christmas treat. I have such warm memories of my artist friend Veronique, who used to invite us impoverished singletons to her delightful soirees. These often culminated in platefuls of this sumptuous ganache-filled roulade smothered in a gleaming chocolate coat.

175g/6oz 70 per cent dark chocolate

6 eggs, separated

175g/6oz/¾ cup plus 1 tbsp caster (superfine) sugar

1 tsp Madagascan vanilla extract

1½ tbsp unsweetened cocoa powder, plus extra for dusting

1 tbsp potato flour

toasted and finely chopped hazelnuts or toasted almonds, or chopped dark bittermint chocolates (peppermint patties), to decorate (optional)

For the ganache filling and chocolate coating:

300ml/10fl oz/1¼ cups double (heavy) cream

225g/8oz 70 per cent dark chocolate, chopped

2 tsp Madagascan vanilla extract

4–5 tbsp dark rum, brandy or crème de menthe, to taste

1. Preheat the oven to Fan 180°C/Fan 350°F/Gas 6. Line a 40×30cm/16×12in Swiss roll (jelly roll) tin with greaseproof paper extending 4cm/1½in above the rim, then set aside.

2. Melt the chocolate in a bowl over a pan of simmering water, then set aside and cool slightly.

3. Beat the egg yolks and sugar together until they have tripled in volume and are pale and thick, and the beaters leave a trail when lifted. Add the vanilla.

4. In a separate, spotlessly clean bowl, with clean beaters, beat the egg whites until they are glossy and stiff.

5. Fold the melted chocolate into the yolks, using a balloon whisk in figure-of-eight motions and giving the bowl a quarter turn with each fold. Stop immediately when the yellow streaks become chocolate coloured. Stir in a large spoonful of the whites, then delicately fold in the remainder, using the figure-of-eight technique.

6. Sift the cocoa powder and potato flour together over the mixture, then quickly fold in. Immediately pour the mixture (batter) into the prepared tin, and quickly smooth it into the corners. Bake for 15 minutes, or until firm to the touch.

7. Meanwhile, to make the ganache and chocolate for coating, heat the cream in a small saucepan until it is scalding, but not boiling. Remove the pan from the heat and stir in the chocolate until the mixture is smooth. Add the vanilla.

8. Immediately pour half this mixture into a shallow bowl and chill until completely cool (about 10 minutes). Leave the remaining half in the pan off the heat; it needs to be kept runny. Remove the cool mixture from the fridge and beat vigorously for 4–6 minutes until it begins to thicken and turn pale and fluffy. Do not over-beat or it will become grainy.

9. Follow step 7 on page 161, covering the paper with sifted cocoa powder. Sprinkle the roulade with the alcohol and spread with the chocolate ganache, smoothing it to the edges. Use the paper to help roll up the roulade from a long side. Don't worry if it cracks. Trim the edges with a sharp knife.

10. Transfer the roulade to a wire rack over a tray. Ladle the runny chocolate over the cake, making sure the entire cake is covered. Scoop up the spills from the tray and re-apply them to the cake, using a metal spatula that has been dipped in boiling water and wiped. Do not worry if you don't completely coat it on the first attempt – just smooth more chocolate over the gaps. Immediately sprinkle with the nuts of your choice and/or bittermints (peppermint patties), if using. Chill for at least 2 hours before serving.

ZESTY LEMON POLENTA CAKE

Serves 12–16 | Prep 30 minutes, plus 2 hours cooling | Bake 50 minutes–1 hour
Dairy-free option | Gluten free | Lower-sugar option | Nut-free option

Here's a rich and satisfying lemon hit with a slightly granular almond finish. A little goes a long way, so serve thin slices, but don't worry because the cake keeps well and even matures over a few days. Not that it's likely to hang around that long!

350g/12oz/1½ cups unsalted butter, softened

350g/12oz/1¾ cups sugar

5 eggs

350g/12oz/3½ cups ground almonds

175g/6oz/1 cup plus 1½ tbsp fine polenta

freshly grated zest and juice of 4 lemons

2 tsp gluten-free baking powder

1½ tsp Madagascan vanilla extract

2 tbsp pine nuts

For the Almond Sponge Base:

3 eggs

5 tbsp sugar

55g/2oz/½ cup ground almonds

2½ tbsp potato or rice flour

30g/1oz/2 tbsp unsalted butter, melted and cooled

Cook's note:

Check the cake after 30 minutes' baking. If the surface is browning too much, loosely cover with foil, making sure the foil does not touch the cake's surface, then continue baking.

1. Preheat the oven to Fan 160°C/Fan 325°F/Gas 4. Line a 30cm/12in springform cake tin, 5cm/2in deep, with parchment paper, extending 5cm/2in above the rim.

2. First, make the base. Break the eggs into a bowl, add the sugar and beat for 8–10 minutes until a thick yellow mousse forms.

3. Mix the ground almonds with the potato flour, then gently fold into the egg mixture using figure-of-eight motions and giving the bowl a quarter turn with each fold.

4. Quickly add the butter in a spiral motion, immediately folding it in. Use a balloon whisk in a figure-of-eight motion until just amalgamated. Immediately pour the mixture (batter) into the prepared tin and smooth the surface. Bake for 10–12 minutes until the base is risen and pale golden brown. Leave the base in the tin on a wire rack.

5. Lower the oven temperature to Fan 150°C/Fan 300°F/Gas 3.

6. To make the cake, beat the butter and sugar together until fluffy and pale.

7. Beat in the eggs, one at a time. Mix together the ground almonds, polenta, baking powder and vanilla, then add to the mixture with the lemon zest and juice.

8. Spoon the mixture onto the sponge base, still in the tin, and smooth the surface. Sprinkle with the pine nuts.

9. Bake for 40–50 minutes until a skewer inserted in the centre comes out clean, the cake is firm in the centre and a deep golden brown colour. Cover the cake with a clean kitchen towel and leave to cool in the tin on a wire rack for 2 hours.

10. To un-mould the cake, remove the ring. Peel back the lining paper and place a baking (cookie) sheet on top. Use both hands to grasp the tin and baking sheet together, then firmly, quickly and carefully invert the cake upside-down. Lift off the metal base and peel off the paper. Top with your serving plate, then carefully invert the cake right-side up onto the plate and remove the baking sheet.

DOUBLE CHOCOLATE TRUFFLE TORTE

Serves 12–16; makes about 25 truffles I Prep 40 minutes, plus at least 2 hours chilling and making the truffles (optional)
Bake 50 minutes–1 hour I Dairy-free option I Gluten free I Lower-sugar option

Rich but still light, this delicious cake is set on an almond sponge base. For a simpler version, omit the ganache topping and nuts and dust the un-moulded cake with unsweetened cocoa powder. The alcoholic chocolate ganache icing can also be rolled into truffles for an indulgent end to any special meal.

For the Almond Sponge Base:

3 eggs

5 tbsp sugar

55g/2oz/½ cup ground almonds

2½ tbsp potato or rice flour

30g/1oz/2 tbsp unsalted butter, melted and cooled

For the cake mixture:

225g/8oz 70 per cent dark chocolate, chopped

225g/8oz/1 cup unsalted butter, softened and chopped

6 eggs, separated

1 tsp Madagascan vanilla extract

225g/8oz/1 cup caster (superfine) sugar

225g/8oz/heaped 2 cups very finely ground blanched almonds

unsweetened cocoa powder, for dusting

chopped toasted hazelnuts and/or blanched almonds, to decorate (optional)

For the ganache:

600ml/1 pint/2½ cups double (heavy) cream

600g/1lb4oz 70 per cent dark chocolate, chopped

1 tsp Madagascan vanilla extract

4 tbsp brandy, Grand Marnier or dark rum (optional)

Cook's note:

Check the cake after 30 minutes baking. If the surface is browning too much, loosely cover with foil, making sure the foil does not touch the cake's surface, then continue baking.

1. Preheat the oven to Fan 160°C/Fan 325°F/Gas 4. Line a 30cm/12in springform cake tin, 5cm/2in deep, with parchment paper, extending 5cm/2in above the rim.

2. First, make the base. Break the eggs into a bowl, add the sugar and beat for 8–10 minutes until a thick yellow mousse forms.

3. Mix the ground almonds with the potato flour, then gently fold into the egg mixture using figure-of-eight motions and giving the bowl a quarter turn with each fold.

4. Quickly add the butter in a spiral motion, immediately folding it in. Use a balloon whisk in a figure-of-eight motion until just amalgamated. Immediately pour the mixture (batter) into the prepared tin and smooth the surface. Bake for 10–12 minutes until the base is risen and pale golden brown. Leave the base in the tin on a wire rack.

5. Lower the oven temperature to Fan 150°C/Fan 300°F/Gas 3.

6. To make the cake, melt the chocolate in a bowl set over a pan of simmering water, stirring until smooth. Do not let the bottom of the bowl touch the water. Set aside to cool slightly.

7. Beat the butter, egg yolks and vanilla extract together until fluffy and pale. Beat in the cooled chocolate, then set aside.

8. In a separate bowl, beat the egg whites until stiff peaks form. Add the sugar, tablespoon by tablespoon, and continue beating for about 5 minutes until a stiff, glossy meringue forms.

9. Stir a couple tablespoonfuls of the meringue into the chocolate mixture to lighten it, then fold in the rest. Fold in the ground almonds, then spoon the mixture onto the sponge base, still in the tin, and smooth the surface.

10. Bake for 40–50 minutes until a skewer inserted in the centre comes out clean, and the cake is firm in the centre. Cover the cake with a clean kitchen towel and leave to cool in the tin on a wire rack for 2 hours.

11. Meanwhile, make the ganache. Heat the cream in a small saucepan until it is scalding, but not boiling. Remove the pan from the heat and stir in the chocolate until it melts and the mixture is smooth. Stir in the vanilla and alcohol, if using. Beat the mixture for a few minutes with a wooden spoon until it is slightly aerated.

12. Pour the ganache over the cake in the tin. Scatter with the hazelnuts and/or almonds, if you like. Place the tin on a wire rack and leave the cake to cool completely, then chill for at least 1 hour.

13. To un-mould the cake, remove the ring. Peel back the lining paper and place a baking (cookie) sheet on top. Use both hands to grasp the tin and baking sheet together, then firmly, quickly and carefully invert the cake upside-down. Lift off the metal base and peel off the paper. Top with your serving plate, then carefully invert the cake right side up onto the plate and remove the baking sheet. Sift with cocoa powder before serving.

LUCIA'S CHOCOLATE VEGAN CAKE

Serves 6–8 I Prep 20 minutes, plus making the icing and at least 2 hours chilling I Bake 1 hour
Dairy free I Gluten free I Lower sugar I Vegan

I acquired the inspiration for this recipe when I worked in Willow, the wonderful Totnes vegan and vegetarian wholefood restaurant, and it has proved very versatile. It is a winner because it is quick and simple to make, and reliably produces perfect results every time. You also don't have to be vegan to enjoy it!.

115g/4oz/¾ cup brown rice flour

115g/4oz/1⅓ cups soya (soy) flour, toasted

2 tsp gluten-free baking powder

¼ tsp sea salt

125ml/4fl oz/½ cup agave or rice syrup or unsweetened apple juice concentrate

115g/4oz no-added-sugar, dairy-free chocolate

125ml/4fl oz/½ cup unsweetened fruit juice of your choice or water

175g/6oz/¾ cup unsweetened apple sauce, chestnut purée or mashed banana

125ml/4fl oz/½ cup sunflower oil, or 115g/4oz/½ cup raw coconut oil

1 tsp bicarbonate of soda (baking soda)

1 quantity Lizi's Vegan Velvet Chocolate Icing (page 212), to decorate

1. Preheat the oven to Fan 160°C/Fan 325°F/Gas 4. Line the base and side of a 20cm/8in springform tin, 5cm/2in deep, with parchment paper.

2. Sift the flours, baking powder and salt into a bowl and set aside.

3. Combine the syrup, chocolate, fruit juice, oil and apple sauce in a large saucepan over a medium heat, stirring to dissolve the syrup. When the mixture is steaming hot, but not boiling, remove the pan from the heat and whisk in the bicarbonate of soda (baking soda). It will froth up.

4. Whisk in the flours and the mixture (batter) should become quite thick. Pour it into the prepared tin and smooth the surface. Bake for at least 1 hour until the top is cracked all over and the centre is springy to the touch. Leave to cool completely on a wire rack for at least 2 hours.

5. Invert the cake onto a large serving plate, then remove the base and peel off the paper. Invert it right-way up onto a serving plate and decorate with the chocolate icing.

Cook's note:

The basic cake mixture in this recipe can also be baked in two lined 15cm/6in cake tins. Reduce the baking time to 45 minutes.

VEGAN NECTARINE UPSIDE-DOWN CAKE WITH RASPBERRY TOPPING

Serves 12–16 | Prep 30 minutes, plus cooling | Bake 1¼ hours
Dairy free | Gluten free | Lower sugar | Vegan

This simple, popular and moist cake combines lush flavour with only a small addition of rice syrup; the remaining sweetness comes from the combination of fruit. This makes it an ideal choice for anyone on a restricted diet who still wants to have their cake and eat it!

6–8 ripe nectarines, stoned (pitted) and halved – you want enough to cover the bottom of the tin

225g/8oz/1¼ cups plus 2½ tbsp brown rice flour

225g/8oz/2⅔ cups soya (soy) flour, toasted

4 tsp gluten-free baking powder

1 tsp sea salt

1 tsp ground mace

1 tsp ground allspice

350ml/12fl oz/1½ cups unsweetened apple juice, (hard) cider or water

225ml/8fl oz/1 cup sunflower oil, or 225g/8oz/1 cup raw coconut oil, chopped

125ml/4fl oz/½ cup rice syrup

350g/12oz/1½ cups bananas or avocados, mashed

350g/12oz/2¾ cups cooking apples, peeled, cored and finely chopped

2 tsp bicarbonate of soda (baking soda)

soya (soy) or rice cream, to serve (optional)

1. Preheat the oven to Fan 160°C/Fan 325°F/Gas 4. Line the base and side of a 30cm/12in springform tin, 5cm/2in deep, with parchment paper.

2. Pop a raspberry from the topping ingredients into the hollow left by the stone (pit) of each nectarine, and arrange them, cut-side down, over the base of the tin. Set aside.

3. Mix the flours, salt, baking powder and ground spices in a bowl and set aside.

4. Combine the fruit juice, oil, syrup, bananas and apples in a large saucepan over a medium heat, stirring to dissolve the syrup, until steaming hot, but not boiling. Remove the pan from the heat and whisk in the bicarbonate of soda (baking soda). The mixture will froth up.

5. Whisk in the flours and the mixture (batter) should become quite thick. Pour it into the prepared tin over the fruit and smooth the surface. Bake for at least 1¼ hours, or until the surface is covered in small cracks and the centre is springy to the touch. Leave to cool completely on a wire rack.

For the raspberry topping:

225ml/8fl oz/1 cup apple or blackcurrant juice

unflavoured vegetarian gelling agent – enough to set 225ml/8fl oz/1 cup liquid according to the packet instructions

225g/8oz raspberries, defrosted and drained, if frozen

Cook's note:

Cover the cake with foil if it is browning too much before the surface looks evenly cracked. It is important it is baked all the way through or the result will be doughy.

6. Meanwhile, to make the topping, combine the fruit juice and gelling agent in a saucepan and make up according to the packet instructions. Do not boil. Leave to cool until just becoming syrupy.

7. When the cake is cool, remove the ring and peel back the paper. Place your serving dish on top, the invert the cake and dish. Remove the metal base and peel off the paper, keeping the nectarines on the top. Attractively arrange the remaining raspberries over the top and brush with the syrupy jelly.

8. Allow to set for at least 10 minutes, then serve with soya (soy) or rice cream to pour over, if you like.

STICKY GINGER & PRUNE PARKIN

Serves 12–16 | Prep 40 minutes, including making the topping, plus cooling the cake | Bake 1 hour
Dairy free | Gluten free | Lower-sugar option | Vegan

This rich, wheat-free vegan treat combines a luscious fruit purée topping with a ginger-studded cake. The three types of ginger included in this fantastic winter warmer will perk you up and tingle your taste buds. The gluten-free pinhead oatmeal provides a chewy texture, as well as conferring extra staying power.

225g/8oz/1¼ cup gluten-free pinhead oatmeal (steel-cut oats)

115g/4oz/¾ cup brown rice flour

115g/4oz/1⅓ cups soya (soy) flour, toasted

4 tsp gluten-free baking powder

⅛ tsp ground cloves

350g/12oz/scant 1½ cups unsweetened apple sauce, mashed avocado or mashed banana

175g/6oz/½ cup blackstrap molasses

4 tbsp finely chopped preserved ginger in syrup

3 tbsp agave or rice syrup

225ml/8fl oz/1 cup water

225ml/8fl oz/1 cup sunflower oil, or 225g/8oz/1 cup raw coconut oil, chopped

1cm/½in piece of fresh ginger, grated

2 tsp ground ginger

2 tsp bicarbonate of soda (baking soda)

seasonal fruit and mint sprigs, to decorate

chopped candied ginger, to decorate (optional)

Cook's note:

If you can't find pinhead oatmeal, finely grind porridge oats or oat groats in a coffee grinder.

1. Preheat the oven to Fan 160°C/Fan 325°F/Gas 4. Line the base and side of a 30cm/12in springform cake tin, 5cm/2in deep, with parchment paper.

2. Combine the oatmeal (steel-cut oats), both flours, baking powder and cloves in a bowl and set aside.

3. Heat the apple sauce, molasses, preserved ginger, syrup, water, oil and both forms of ginger in a saucepan over a medium heat, stirring to dissolve the syrup, until steaming but not boiling. Remove the pan from the heat, whisk in the bicarbonate of soda and watch the mixture rise in the pan.

4. Tip in the flours and stir them in to make a very thick mixture (batter). Work quickly so you don't deflate the mixture.

5. Immediately pour the mixture into the prepared tin and quickly smooth the surface and spread to the edges.

For the prune purée topping:

175g/6oz stoned (pitted) prunes

300ml/10fl oz/1¼ cups water

1 Earl Grey or Rooibos tea bag

2 tsp Madagascan vanilla extract

rice or agave syrup, to taste

wide sliver of lemon zest

175g/6oz/scant ½ cup canned chestnut purée

freshly grated zest and juice of 1 lime

VARIATIONS

Lower-sugar option
Replace the blackstrap molasses in the cake mixture with the same quantity of pomegranate molasses. Omit the preserved ginger in syrup from the cake mixture and the decoration.

6. Bake for 40–50 minutes, until the surface is covered with cracks. Transfer the tin to a wire rack and leave the cake to cool completely.

7. Meanwhile, put all the topping ingredients, except the chestnut purée, lime zest and chopped candied ginger, into a small saucepan over a low heat. Cover and cook for 30 minutes, or until the prunes are very soft.

8. Remove the teabag, then add the chestnut purée and lime zest. Purée in a blender or food processor until the topping is smooth.

9. When the cake is cool, remove the ring and peel back the paper. Place your serving dish on top, then invert the cake and dish. Remove the metal base and peel off the paper. Spread with the topping and decorate with herb sprigs, fruit and ginger, if you like.

HAZELNUT MERINGUE GÂTEAU WITH RASPBERRY SAUCE

Serves 6–8 | Prep 40 minutes, plus 24 hours chilling | Bake 30–40 minutes | Gluten free

After my mother's dinner parties, in the early hours, my sister Sarah and I would sneak downstairs to scoff most of the remains of this luscious dessert. You don't need the thrill of the illicit, however, to enjoy the alchemy of apricot, raspberry and hazelnuts. Make this 24 hours in advance.

For the meringue layers:

6 egg whites

a pinch of sea salt

350g/12oz/1½ cups caster (superfine) sugar

3 tbsp toasted chopped hazelnuts

2 tsp raspberry or white wine vinegar

For the filling:

175g/6oz/1½ cups unsulphured dried apricots

1 vanilla pod (bean)

1 Earl Grey or Rooibos tea bag

wide sliver of lemon zest

450ml/16fl oz/2 cups double (heavy) cream

For the raspberry sauce:

250g/9oz raspberries, defrosted if frozen

3 tbsp icing (confectioners') sugar, or 3 tbsp raspberry cordial

2 tbsp raspberry liqueur (optional)

1. Preheat the oven to Fan 150°C/Fan 300°F/Gas 3. Line the bases and sides of two 23cm/9in springform tins with parchment paper.

2. Using a spotlessly clean bowl and beaters, beat the egg whites on a slow speed until bubbles appear throughout. Increase the speed to medium and continue beating until the volume has quadrupled. Increase the speed to high and continue beating until stiff peaks form.

3. Immediately reduce the speed to medium and add the sugar, sprinkling it down the side of the bowl so as not to deflate the whites. Continue beating for 4–5 minutes until a stiff, glossy meringue forms.

4. Sprinkle the nuts and vinegar into the bowl. Use a balloon whisk to rapidly, but delicately, fold them in, using a figure-of-eight motion and giving the bowl a quarter turn with each fold. This technique ensures a light meringue.

5. Pile the meringue into the prepared tins and smooth the tops.

6. Bake for 30–40 minutes until the meringues are pale golden and crisp on the outside. The centres will have a softer texture. Allow both to cool in the tins on a wire rack. Invert the cooled meringue halves onto a baking sheet, peel off the paper and slide one half onto your serving plate.

7. Meanwhile, put the apricots, vanilla pod (bean), tea bag and lemon zest in a small covered saucepan with just enough water to cover and bring to the boil. Turn the heat down to low and poach for 20 minutes, or until they are very soft.

8. Leave the apricots to cool in the liquid. Remove the vanilla pod and tea bag, then transfer the apricots, lemon zest and the poaching liquid to a blender or food processor and purée. Chill until required.

9. When ready to assemble, whip the cream until soft peaks form. Spread the apricot purée on the bottom meringue and top with the whipped cream. Place the remaining meringue on top, cover lightly with clingfilm (plastic wrap) and chill, ideally up to 24 hours.

10. To make the sauce, put the raspberries in a blender or food processor, sift in the icing (confectioners') sugar and blend well. Sieve (strain), then add the liqueur and as much water as necessary to make a thick pouring sauce. Serve chilled in a jug and hand round separately.

QUICK CHRISTMAS CAKE

Serves 6–8 I Prep 35 minutes, plus making the mincemeat I Bake 2 hours
Dairy-free option I Gluten free I Lower-sugar option I Vegan option

If this is your first time making and decorating a Christmas cake, or you're looking for a new twist on the classic mix of spices, dried fruits and nuts, then this succulent offering with my mango and cider mincemeat could be the one for you. Make the cake in November and then lovingly 'feed' it with dark rum or brandy until December.

225g/8oz/1 cup butter, chopped and softened

115g/4oz/½ cup plus 1 tbsp rapadura sugar

1 tbsp blackstrap molasses

6 eggs, separated

1 tsp Madagascan vanilla extract

freshly grated zest of 2 oranges

freshly grated zest of 1 lemon

175g/6oz/1 cup plus 1½ tbsp brown rice flour

175g/6oz/2 cups soya (soy) flour, toasted, or 175g/6oz/scant 2 cups chestnut flour

2 tsp gluten-free baking powder

250ml/9floz/1 cup plus 2 tbsp fresh orange juice

500g/1lb 2oz/scant 1½ cups Lower-sugar Mango & Cider Mincemeat (page 152)

20 pecan nuts, shelled

4 tbsp dark rum or brandy for 'feeding'

Cook's note:

If you'd like a marzipan topping, roll out 450g/1lb marzipan on a surface dusted with icing (confectioners') sugar and cut to fit. Brush the cake's top with 2 tbsp apricot jam melted with 1 tbsp lemon juice, then unroll the marzipan onto the cake and crimp the edges.

1. Preheat the oven to Fan 150°C/Fan 300°F/Gas 3. Line the base and side of a 20–23cm/8–9in spring-form tin, 5cm/2in deep, with parchment paper.

2. Put the butter, sugar and molasses in a bowl and beat with an electric mixer until pale and fluffy.

3. Beat in the egg yolks, one at a time, until thoroughly blended, followed by the vanilla extract and orange and lemon zests.

4. Mix the flours and baking powder together, then gently sift into the egg mixture and fold in.

5. Combine the orange and lemon juices with the mincemeat, then add to the above mixture and fold in.

6. Beat the egg whites until stiff peaks form. Gently stir a few tablespoons into the cake mixture (batter) to loosen, then lightly fold in the remainder. Do not over-work the mixture or you will lose the airy quality.

7. Spoon into the prepared tin and smooth the surface. Stud the surface with pecans.

8. Bake for 2 hours, covering the top with kitchen foil if it is browning too much, until a skewer inserted in the centre comes out clean.

9. Leave the cake to cool in the tin on a wire rack. When it is completely cool, un-mould, prick the surface with a cocktail stick (toothpick) and sprinkle with a spoonful of the rum or brandy.

10. Re-wrap the cake in greaseproof (waxed) paper and store in an airtight container. Repeat the sprinkling process very couple of weeks until Christmas.

SPICED APPLE & SEVILLE MARMALADE CHEESECAKE

Serves 6–8 | Prep 20 minutes, plus baking the base, cooling and at least 4 hours chilling | Bake 40–50 minutes
Dairy-free option | Gluten free | Lower-sugar option | Vegan option

This is a moist and very light cheesecake set on a delicate almond sponge base, and is best eaten on the day it is baked. I often make batches of Seville marmalade in winter, but feel free to use a good-quality bought marmalade. The bitter orange flavour cuts through the creamy richness with ease.

ingredients for 1 quantity Almond Sponge Base (page 166)

sunflower oil, for greasing

For the filling:

500g/1lb 2oz/2¼ cups mascarpone

150ml/5fl oz/⅔ cup soured cream (sour cream)

4 tbsp Seville marmalade

2 eggs, separated

1 tbsp brown rice flour

1 tsp Madagascan vanilla extract

115g/4oz/½ cup plus 1 tbsp sugar

1. To make the almond sponge base, follow steps 1–5 in the Zesty Lemon Polenta Cake recipe, page 166, using a greased 20–23cm/8–9in springform tin, 5cm/2in deep, and lining the side with parchment paper. Leave the base in the tin on a wire rack after baking.

2. To make the filling, beat together the mascarpone, soured cream (sour cream), marmalade, egg yolks, rice flour and vanilla.

3. In a separate bowl, beat the egg whites with an electric mixer until soft peaks form. Sprinkle in the sugar and continue beating until stiff peaks form.

4. Fold the egg whites into the cheese mixture, using figure-of-eight motions and giving the bowl a quarter turn with each fold.

5. Spoon the cheesecake mixture on top of the base and smooth the surface. Bake for 40–50 minutes, or until wobbly but not runny. Do not over-bake or your cheesecake will be crumbly. It should have a creamy centre. Remove from the oven and leave to cool in the tin on a wire rack.

For the topping:

250ml/9fl oz/1 cup plus 2 tbsp unsweetened apple sauce

2 tbsp fresh or ready-to-eat dried cranberries

2 tbsp sugar

½ tsp ground cinnamon

unflavoured vegetarian gelling agent – enough to set 300ml/10fl oz/1¼ cups according to the packet instructions

125ml/4fl oz/½ cup unsweetened apple juice

6. To make the topping, put the apple sauce, cranberries, sugar, cinnamon and 2 tbsp water in a small saucepan over a medium heat. Cover and simmer for 10 minutes to cook the cranberries. Purée, then leave to cool.

7. Pour the apple juice into a small saucepan. Add the gelling agent and prepare according to the packet directions. Do not allow the mixture to boil. Stir in the apple sauce mixture.

8. Spread the topping over the cool cheesecake and refrigerate for at least 4 hours, but ideally overnight before serving.

VEGAN FRUITY TEASECAKE

Serves 8 | Prep 30 minutes, plus making the base, cooling and at least 6 hours chilling | Bake 40–50 minutes
Dairy free | Gluten free | Lower-sugar option | Vegan

Try this unexpected alternative to a dairy cheesecake and you'll find the taste difference is not at all apparent, hence the name – teasecake! So, if you're catering for a vegan friend, don't feel you have to make a separate dessert – your non-vegan guests will never know the difference!

ingredients for 1 Vegan Caramel Rice Flake Base (page 184), including raw coconut oil, not butter

For the teasecake mixture:

225g/8oz mixed berries of your choice, such as blackcurrants, blueberries, raspberries and strawberries, defrosted if frozen, hulled, if necessary, and halved if large

500g/1lb 2oz/2¼ cups vegan cream cheese or silken tofu

150ml/5fl oz/⅔ cup soya (soy) yogurt

115g/4oz/½ cup plus 1 tbsp sugar

55g/2oz/3½ tbsp light tahini

1 tbsp white rice flour

2 tsp Madagascan vanilla extract

For the blackcurrant topping:

125ml/4fl oz/½ cup Cassis or blackcurrant cordial, or a mixture

blackcurrant vegetarian gelling agent – you need enough to set 300ml/10fl oz/1¼ cups liquid according to the packet instructions

200g/7oz blackcurrants, defrosted, if frozen and patted dry

1. Make the Caramel Rice Flake Base, follow steps 1–6 in the Mincemeat, Orange & Saffron Cheesecake recipe (page 184), using the raw coconut oil and omitting the cinnamon and orange flower water. Leave the base to cool in the tin, and set aside the remaining crumbs.

2. Preheat the oven to Fan 160°C/Fan 325°F/Gas 4.

3. Arrange the fruit on top of the base.

4. Beat together all the filling ingredients until very smooth. Spoon the filling over the base, taking care not to dislodge the fruit, then smooth the surface. Sprinkle around the edge with the reserved crumbs.

5. Bake for 40–50 minutes, or until wobbly but not runny. It should have a creamy centre. Remove the cake from the oven and leave it to cool in the tin on a wire rack. Chill for at least 6 hours.

Cook's note:

Other fruits suitable for arranging on top of the base include stoned (pitted) and sliced mangoes, and stoned cherries, nectarines and plums. Just use the best in season.

VARIATIONS

Lower-sugar option
Use the lower-sugar option (page 185) to make the Caramel Rice Flake Base. Replace the sugar in the teasecake mixture with 125ml/4fl oz/½ cup agave or rice syrup. Omit the Cassis or cordial from the topping. Use a no-added-sugar gelling agent and 300ml/10fl oz/1¼ cups water.

6. To make the topping, make the Cassis or cordial up to 300ml/10fl oz/1¼ cups with water. Pour the liquid into a small saucepan with the blackcurrants and simmer for 5 minutes. Add the gelling agent and prepare according to the packet directions. Do not boil. Leave until just becoming syrupy.

7. Remove the outer ring from the tin and peel back the paper. Place a baking (cookie) sheet over the cheesecake, then grip the metal base and baking sheet with both your hands and invert. Remove the metal base and peel off the paper. Place your serving plate on top, and invert again so the cheesecake is right-side up.

8. Pour the blackcurrant jelly over the cheesecake, then chill for another 10 minutes before serving.

MINCEMEAT, ORANGE & SAFFRON CHEESECAKE

Serves 6–8 | Prep 20 minutes, plus making the mincemeat, baking the crumb base and chilling at least 6 hours
Bake 40 minutes | Dairy-free option | Gluten free | Lower-sugar option | Nut-free option | Vegan option

I created this festive cheesecake for the winter markets. The pungent, sour and bitter notes tune brilliantly with the fruity alcoholic sweetness of the mango mincemeat. The saffron lends subtle colour and style. The gluten-free base provides a caramel crunch. It's simple to make, despite the long list of ingredients!

a pinch of saffron threads, soaked in 6 tablespoons hot water for at least 20 minutes

500g/1lb 2oz/2¼ cups mascarpone

150ml/5fl oz/⅔ cup crème fraîche or goat's yogurt

140g/5oz/¾ cup sugar

3 eggs

1 tsp Madagascan vanilla extract

freshly grated zest and juice of 2 oranges, plus extra zest to decorate

2 tbsp Seville orange marmalade

2 tbsp pomegranate molasses or maple syrup

225g/8oz/⅔ cup Lower-sugar Cider & Mango Mincemeat (page 152)

55g/2oz/½ cup cranberries or redcurrants, defrosted if frozen

whipped cream flavoured with orange liqueur or orange flower water, to serve

Chinese gooseberries, to decorate (optional)

For the Caramel Rice Flake Base:

6 tbsp sugar

55g/2oz/4 tbsp butter

115g/4oz/1¼ cups brown rice flakes or gluten-free breadcrumbs

1. Preheat the oven to Fan 160°C/Fan 325°F/Gas 4. Line the base and side of a 20–23cm/8–9in springform tin, 4cm/1½in deep, with parchment paper, extending 5cm/2in above the rim.

2. To make the rice flake base, sprinkle the sugar in an even layer in a non-stick frying pan over a medium-high heat. Swirl the pan occasionally, but do not stir, until the sugar melts into a golden-brown caramel.

3. Swirl in the butter, which will separate but don't worry about it.

4. Lower the heat a little and stir in the ground almonds and cinnamon, then add the rice flakes. Stir the mixture constantly for 5 minutes, or until all it turns nicely golden brown. Fold in the orange zest and juice and cook gently until the moisture evaporates.

5. Quickly tip three-quarters of the crumbs into the pan and use a rubber spatula to spread it out evenly, pressing down firmly. The mixture will be hot and sticky, so take care.

55g/2oz/½ cup ground almonds

1 tsp ground cinnamon

freshly grated zest and juice of 1 orange

2 tbsp orange flower water

6. Sprinkle the base with orange flower water, then set aside. Reserve the remaining topping, breaking it into smallish pieces before it sets hard, then set the base aside.

7. Drain the saffron. Put the saffron liquid, the mascarpone cheese and all the remaining cheesecake ingredients, except the mincemeat and berries, in a blender or food processor and blend until smooth. Do not over-blend.

8. Carefully pour the mixture over the base and smooth the top. Neatly pile the mincemeat in the centre and ring with the berries.

9. Scatter the reserved crumbs around the edge, leaving a narrow border between the berries and the crumbs.

10. Bake for 40–50 minutes, or until the cheesecake is wobbly but not runny. Do not over-bake or your cheesecake will be crumbly. It should have a creamy centre.

11. Remove from the oven and leave to cool in the tin on a wire rack, then cover and chill for at least 6 hours.

12. Remove the outer ring from the tin and peel back the paper. Place a baking (cookie) sheet over the cheesecake, then grip the metal base and baking sheet with both your hands and invert. Remove the metal base and peel off the paper. Place your serving plate on top, and invert again so the cheesecake is right-side up.

13. Serve with the orange-flavoured whipped cream for an extra festive feel and decorate with Chinese gooseberries, if you like.

WHITE CHOCOLATE & RASPBERRY CHEESECAKE WITH POACHED PEARS

Serves 6–8 | Prep 20 minutes, plus baking the base, cooling and at least 6 hours chilling | Bake 40–50 minutes
Dairy-free option | Gluten free | Lower-sugar option | Nut-free option | Vegan option

This soft-centred cheesecake has a crunchy caramel base and is a real showstopper! It looks spectacular. The white chocolate enhances the creaminess, which perfectly complements the tart, glistening raspberry top and lemon-poached pears. The pears also make an excellent dessert served chilled with caramel ice cream.

ingredients for 1 quantity Caramel Rice Flake Base (pages 184–185), omitting the cinnamon and orange flower water, and replacing the orange zest and juice with the freshly grated zest and juice of 1 lemon

For the lemon-poached pears:

4 ripe dessert (Bosc) pears

1 tbsp sugar

thinly pared zest and juice of 2 lemons

1 vanilla bean (pod), split

For the cheesecake mixture:

225g/8oz white chocolate, chopped

125ml/4fl oz/½ cup crème fraîche

500g/1lb 2oz/2¼ cups mascarpone or mild soft goat's cheese

3 eggs

2 tsp vanilla bean paste or Madagascan vanilla extract

140g/5oz/¾ cup sugar

225g/8oz raspberries, defrosted and drained, if frozen

sugared gooseberries and cherries and unsprayed flowers, to decorate

1. Peel, core and quarter the pears. Place them in a small saucepan over a medium heat with the sugar, lemon zest and juice, vanilla and just enough water to cover them. Bring to the boil, then lower the heat to low and simmer for 15 minutes, or until the pears are tender.

2. Remove them and set aside. Strain the liquid to use as a glaze and reserve the zest. When the pears are cool, chill until required.

3. Make the Caramel Rice Flake Base, following steps 1–6 in the Mincemeat, Orange & Saffron Cheesecake recipe (page 184), omitting the cinnamon and replacing the orange with lemon zest and juice. Leave the base to cool in the tin and set aside the remaining crumbs.

4. Meanwhile, preheat the oven to Fan 160°C/Fan 325°F/Gas 4.

VARIATIONS

Dairy-free option
Use the dairy-free option for the rice flake base on page 185. Replace the mascarpone in the cheesecake mixture with vegan cream cheese or silken tofu and the crème fraîche with soya (soy) yogurt. Replace the white chocolate with the same quantity of grated dairy-free white chocolate, adding it to the other ingredients in step 5 without melting. If you make the cheesecake with silken tofu it will need to bake 5–10 minutes longer.

Lower-sugar option
Use the lower-sugar option (page 185) for the rice flake base. Replace the sugar in the cheesecake mixture with 150ml/5fl oz/⅔ cup agave or rice syrup. Use the same quantity of grated no-added-sugar white chocolate, adding it to the other ingredients without melting. Replace the sugar in the pear poaching liquid with the same quantity of xylitol. Use a no-added-sugar gelling agent.

Nut-free option
Replace the ground almonds in the rice flake base with finely ground sunflower seeds.

Vegan option
Follow the dairy-free option. Omit the eggs and replace them with 115g/4oz/scant ½ cup light tahini plus 2 tbsp brown rice flour, beaten until smooth.

5. To make the cheesecake mixture, melt the white chocolate in a small bowl over a pan of simmering water. Put the chocolate, reserved poached lemon zest and the remaining cheesecake ingredients, except the raspberries, in a blender or food processor and blend until smooth.

6. Pour this mixture over the base and smooth the surface. Scatter the raspberries over the top, then scatter the reserved crumbs from the base recipe around the edge.

7. Bake for 40–50 minutes, or until wobbly but not runny. Do not over-bake or your cheesecake will become grainy. Leave the cheesecake to cool completely in the tin on a wire rack, then chill for at least 6 hours.

8. When ready to serve, un-mould as in step 7 on page 183 and decorate.

All of our produce is organic, and locally sourced whenever possible....

Sweet Vegetable Cakes

These wonderful, healthier offerings have been evolving ever since the beetroot, chocolate, raspberry and hazelnut cake hit the street, which got me thinking about what other seasonal vegetables would yield to the cake treatment. Consuming one of your nine a day in a cake, I thought, might go down well with health-conscious parents as well.

Nothing was sacrosanct from experimentation – parsnip, courgette, sweet potato, Brussels sprout, sweet chilli and even the slightly exotic aubergine went into the mix. The results have to be experienced to be believed. I find that customers, after their initial surprise at finding half the veg patch in their cake, choose them according to their mood.

The fillings are customized and the textures vary, but are generally quite dense. A slice will keep you going for ages – satisfying but without the sickly penalty. Enjoy!

BEETROOT & CHOCOLATE CAKE

Serves 8 | Prep 35 minutes, plus at least 1 hour chilling | Bake 30–40 minutes
Dairy-free option | Gluten free | Lower-sugar option | Nut-free option | Vegan version (page 204)

Since I created this indulgent recipe I have barely been able to keep up with sales! The moist, earthy darkness of beetroot marries with the sophisticated bitter notes of dark chocolate, alongside the creamy filling of sharp raspberry and rich aroma of toasted hazelnuts. It's so irresistible some of the customers at my food stall simply refuse to buy anything else.

115g/4oz 70 per cent dark chocolate, chopped

250g/9oz/1 cup plus 2 tbsp unsalted butter, softened

225g/8oz/1 cup plus 2 tbsp sugar

1½ tbsp blackstrap molasses

4 eggs (total weight 225g/8oz in shells)

1 tsp Madagascan vanilla extract

500g/1lb 2oz/2¾ cups raw beetroot (beets), peeled and *finely* grated

115g/4oz/¾ cup brown rice flour, or 115g/4oz/1¼ cups chestnut flour

115g/4oz/1⅓ cups soya (soy) flour, toasted

4 tsp gluten-free baking powder

unsweetened cocoa powder, for dusting

raw cacao nibs, to decorate

dried, sugared or fresh unsprayed rose petals, to decorate (optional)

For the filling and icing:
500g/1lb 2oz/2¼ cups mascarpone

115g/4oz/½ cup plus 1 tbsp sugar

2 tbsp chopped toasted hazelnuts

1 tsp Madagascan vanilla extract

115g/4oz frozen raspberries, defrosted and drained, plus extra, to decorate

1. Preheat the oven to Fan 160°C/Fan 325°F/Gas 4. Line the bases and sides of two 23cm/9in springform tins, 4cm/1½in deep, with parchment paper, leaving a 5cm/2in rim.

2. Put the chocolate in a heatproof bowl over a pan of simmering water and stir until it melts. Do not let the bottom of the bowl touch the water. Set aside and leave to cool slightly.

3. Put the butter, sugar and molasses in a bowl and beat for at least 6 minutes until pale and fluffy. Add one egg at a time, constantly beating. Beat in the vanilla and melted chocolate, then set aside.

4. Put the grated beetroot (beets) in a large bowl. Add the rice and soya (soy) flours and baking powder and toss together, using your hands, until well mixed. Children love helping with this – just make sure their hands are clean.

5. Scoop the chocolate mixture on top and mix together thoroughly, using your hands again.

6. Divide the mixture (batter) between the tins and smooth the tops. Bake for 30–40 minutes until the surface is evenly cracked and the centre springy to the touch.

7. Leave the cakes to cool on wire racks, then un-mould and peel off the paper.

8. Meanwhile, to make the filling, beat together the mascarpone, sugar, hazelnuts and vanilla. Fold in the raspberries.

9. Use two-thirds of the filling to sandwich the cakes. Spread the rest on top of the cake, leaving a 5cm/2in outer border all round. Dust the edges liberally with cocoa powder, just catching the outer edge of the icing, and decorate with cacao nibs, raspberries and rose petals, if you like.

10. Chill for 1 hour, but no longer than 12 hours, before serving.

Cook's note:

In this chapter I've included a specific weight with each egg quantity since egg sizes vary and the liquid:dry ingredient ratio needs to be correct to ensure a successful bake.

SWEET POTATO, PECAN & CAPPUCCINO CAKE

Serves 8 | Prep 40 minutes, plus at least 1 hour chilling | Cook 30–40 minutes
Dairy-free option | Gluten free | Lower-sugar option | Vegan version (page 206)

This all-singing, all-dancing cake inspires purple prose, unless, of course, cappuccino isn't your thing, in which case both parties may be forgiven. Expect baked coffee velvet sandwiched with a punchy, creamy espresso and tamarind filling. Omit the topping powder and caramelized pecans for a simpler affair.

250g/9oz/1 cup plus 2 tbsp butter, softened

225g/8oz/1 cup caster (superfine) sugar

4 eggs (total weight 225g/8oz in shells)

1 tsp Madagascan vanilla extract

2½ tsp espresso coffee powder dissolved in 1 tbsp boiling water

500g/1lb2oz/2¾ cups sweet potatoes, peeled and finely grated

115g/4oz/1⅓ cups soya (soy) flour, toasted

115g/4oz/¾ cup brown rice flour

4 tsp gluten-free baking powder

1 tsp ground cardamom

½ tsp ground ginger

unsweetened cocoa powder, for dusting (optional)

raw cacao nibs, to decorate

For the filling and icing:

500g/1lb 2oz/2¼ cups mascarpone

125ml/4fl oz/⅓ cup maple syrup

3 tbsp tamarind paste or lemon juice

2½ tsp espresso coffee powder dissolved in 1 tbsp boiling water

1 tsp Madagascan vanilla extract

85g/3oz/scant ¾ cup pecan halves, toasted and roughly chopped

1. Follow steps 1 (lining tins) and 3 (batter mixing) of the Beetroot & Chocolate Cake recipe (page 190), omitting the molasses and adding the dissolved coffee in place of the melted chocolate.

2. Place the sweet potatoes in a large bowl. Add the soya (soy) and rice flours, baking powder, cardamom and ginger and toss together, using your hands, until mixed. Scoop the coffee-flavoured mixture on top and mix together thoroughly, using your hands again.

3. Divide the mixture (batter) between the lined tins and smooth the tops. Bake for 30–40 minutes until the surface is slightly cracked all over and the centre is springy to the touch.

4. Leave the cakes to cool on wire racks, then un-mould and peel off the paper.

5. Meanwhile, to make the filling, beat together the mascarpone, maple syrup, tamarind, coffee and vanilla. Fold in the pecans. Chill until required.

For the caramelized pecans (optional):

4 tbsp sugar

16 pecan nuts (halves)

For the topping powder (optional):

2 tsp maca powder

2 tsp caster (superfine) sugar

1 tsp raw cacao nibs

1 tsp ground coffee beans

Cook's notes:

All my sweet vegetable cakes serve 8. If you're catering for a larger crowd, double all the quantities and use two 30cm/12in tins, 5cm/2in deep, prepared as described (step 1, page 190) to serve 16 and increase the baking time to 40–50 minutes. Don't forget to double the ingredients for the fillings and toppings, too.

If, on the other hand, you want simpler, less creamy cakes, halve all the ingredients for the cake and bake in a single 20cm/8in springform tin, 5cm/2in deep, prepared as described (step 1, page 190), or in 12 muffin cases (cups). This way you can omit the filling and the choice of topping is up to you – sometimes a simple dusting of icing (confectioners') sugar and/or unsweetened cocoa powder is all that's required.

6. If you are making the caramelized pecans, melt the sugar in a small, heavy-based saucepan over a medium-high heat until it is dark golden brown. You can swirl the sugar syrup in the pan, but do not stir.

7. Immediately remove the pan from the heat. Use chopsticks or tweezers to dip the pecans into the syrup. Allow to cool on parchment paper.

8. Use two-thirds of the filling to sandwich the cakes. Spread the remaining filling on top to within 8cm/3¼in of the edge.

9. If you are making the topping powder, grind all the ingredients into a fine powder in a clean coffee grinder.

10. Sift the topping powder or cocoa powder liberally onto the plain outer border of the cake. Arrange the plain or caramelized pecans around the edge and sprinkle cacao nibs over the topping. Chill for about 1 hour, but no longer than 12 hours before serving.

VARIATIONS

Dairy-free option

Replace the butter in the cake mixture with the same quantity of margarine or raw coconut oil. Replace the mascarpone in the filling and icing with the same amount of vegan cream cheese.

Lower-sugar option

Replace the sugar in the cake mixture with the same quantity of xylitol or 225ml/8fl oz/1 cup agave or rice syrup. Replace the caster sugar with the same quantity of xylitol if making the topping powder. If the filling is too sloppy to hold its shape, add up to 2 tbsp ground psyllium husks (page 22).

TROPICAL PARSNIP & POLENTA CAKE

Serves 8 I Prep 40 minutes, plus at least 1 hour chilling I Cook 30–40 minutes
Dairy-free option I Gluten free I Lower-sugar option I Nut-free option I Vegan version (page 206)

This was the third vegetable cake to arrive at the stall, and it's now second in popularity! I knew I wanted something with a vibrant, golden summer glow, and the polenta and the passion jelly topping do the trick. You'd never guess there are parsnips in there, because the flavour is tangy, clean and uplifting.

250g/9oz/1 cup plus 2 tbsp butter, softened

225g/8oz/1 cup plus 2 tbsp sugar

4 eggs (total weight 225g/8oz in shells)

1 tsp Madagascan vanilla extract

freshly grated zest and juice of 1 lemon

500g/1lb 2oz/2¾ cups parsnips, peeled and *finely* grated

85g/3oz/½ cup brown rice flour

85g/3oz/1 cup soya (soy) flour, toasted

4 tsp gluten-free baking powder

30g/1oz/⅓ cup ground almonds

55g/2oz/⅓ cup fine polenta

2 tsp ground cardamom

½ tsp ground ginger

For the filling:

250g/9oz/1 cup plus 2 tbsp mascarpone

2½ tbsp sugar

finely grated zest and juice of 1 lime

1 tsp Madagascan vanilla extract

For the topping:

tropical or lime vegetarian jelly crystals – enough to set 300ml/10fl oz/1¼ cups liquid according to the packet instructions

2 passion fruit

blueberries, to decorate (optional)

1. Follow steps 1 (lining tins) and 3 (batter mixing) of the Chocolate & Beetroot Cake recipe (page 190), omitting the dark chocolate and molasses and adding the lemon juice in place of the melted chocolate.

2. Place the parsnips in a large bowl. Add the rice and soya (soy) flours, baking powder, ground almonds, polenta, cardamom, ginger and lemon zest to the parsnips and toss together, using your hands, until well mixed. Scoop the lemon-flavoured mixture on top and mix together thoroughly with your hands.

3. Divide the mixture (batter) between the tins and smooth the tops. Bake for 30–40 minutes until the surface is golden brown and slightly cracked, and the centre is springy. Leave the cakes to cool on wire racks, then un-mould and peel off the paper.

4. Meanwhile, to make the filling, beat together the mascarpone, sugar, lime zest and juice and vanilla.

5. Use the filling to sandwich the cakes together.

6. Cut the passion fruit in half, and scoop the seeds and juice into a heatproof measuring jug.

7. Sprinkle the jelly crystals into the jug and top up with boiling water to 300mls/10 fl oz. Stir to dissolve the crystals and leave to stand until just turning syrupy.

8. Place the filled cake on a rack over a sheet of greaseproof (waxed) paper. Ladle the syrupy jelly slowly over the cake, waiting until it sets before adding more. Transfer to a serving plate. Chill for at least 1 hour but no more than 12 hours before serving.

COURGETTE, WHITE CHOCOLATE & MINT CAKE

Serves 8 | Prep 40 minutes, plus at least 1 hour chilling | Bake 30–40 minutes
Dairy-free option | Gluten free | Lower-sugar option | Vegan version (page 206)

This isn't an in-your-face traditional mint-choc hit. Instead, it's a cooling slice of summer, with subtle hues and flavours that expand as you munch. Courgette and mint prettily fleck the sponge and the delicate green icing contains crunchy peppermint bursts.

115g/4oz white chocolate, chopped

freshly grated zest and juice of 1 lemon, kept separate

250g/9oz/1 cup plus 2 tbsp butter, softened

225g/8oz/1 cup plus 2 tbsp sugar

4 eggs (total weight 225g/8oz in shells)

1 tsp Madagascan vanilla extract

500g/1lb 2oz/4½ cups courgettes (zucchini), topped and tailed and coarsely grated (squeezed weight)

115g/4oz/¾ cup brown rice flour

115g/4oz/1⅓ cups soya (soy) flour, toasted

55g/2oz/⅓ cup fine polenta

4 tsp gluten-free baking powder

2 tbsp pine nuts, toasted

For the filling and icing:

55g/2oz/1 cup mint leaves

4 tbsp sugar

500g/1lb 2oz/2¼ cups mascarpone

2 tbsp freshly squeezed lime juice

2 tbsp crème de menthe or a few drops of peppermint extract, or to taste

1 tbsp spinach juice, or 1–2 tsp green superfood powder

1 tsp Madagascan vanilla extract

1. Follow steps 1 (lining tins), 2 (melting chocolate) and 3 (batter mixing) of the Beetroot & Chocolate Cake recipe (page 190), omitting the molasses and adding the lemon juice with the vanilla and melted white chocolate. Take care not to over-heat the white chocolate while melting because it is more sensitive than dark; set aside and cool slightly.

2. Place the courgettes (zucchini) in a large bowl. Add the rice and soya (soy) flours, polenta, baking powder and lemon zest to the courgettes and toss together, using your hands, until well mixed.

3. Scoop the white chocolate and egg mixture on top and mix together thoroughly, using your hands again.

4. Divide the mixture (batter) between the prepared tins and smooth the tops. Scatter the pine nuts around the outer edge of *one* of the cakes. Bake for 30–40 minutes until the surface is golden and evenly cracked, and the centre is springy to the touch. Leave the cakes to cool on wire racks, then un-mould and peel off the paper.

55g/2oz crunchy bittermint chocolates (peppermint patties), chopped into small pieces

ground psyllium husks, to thicken (optional)

For the topping:

2 tbsp unsalted pistachio kernels, chopped

chopped crystallized mint leaves (optional)

icing (confectioners') sugar, to decorate

5. Meanwhile, to make the filling, pulverize the mint and sugar in a pestle and mortar, then beat together with the mascarpone, lime juice, crème de menthe, spinach juice and vanilla. Fold in the chopped bittermint chocolate (peppermint patties).

6. Use two-thirds of the filling to sandwich the cakes together, placing the one with the pine nuts on top, nut-side up. Spread the remaining filling on top, up to the pine-nut border. Sprinkle with the chopped pistachios and crystallized mint in a band near the edge of the topping. Very lightly dust icing (confectioners') sugar over the pine nuts. Chill for at least 1 hour, but no more than 12 hours, before serving.

MOROCCAN AUBERGINE & ROSE CELEBRATION CAKE

Serves 8 | Prep 45 minutes | Bake 35–45 minutes
Dairy-free option | Gluten free | Lower-sugar option | Vegan version (page 207)

The idea for this perfumed, jewelled cake was in the back of my mind for six months, ever since one of my customers told me about how good her aubergine cake was. This is a magnificent celebration cake, and, thus, the decorative process is necessarily precise to guarantee a great-looking success!

250g/9oz/1 cup plus 2 tbsp butter, softened

225g/8oz/1 cup plus 2 tbsp sugar

4 eggs (total weight 225g/8oz in shells)

2 tsp Madagascan vanilla extract

freshly grated zest and juice of 1 lime

500g/1lb 2oz/4 cups aubergine (eggplant), topped and tailed and finely chopped

115g/4oz/1 cup wholegrain buckwheat flour

115g/4oz/1⅓ cups soya (soy) flour, toasted

85g/3oz/scant 1 cup pecan halves, toasted and chopped

¾ tsp ground ginger

½ tsp ground cardamom

½ tsp chilli powder

4 tsp gluten-free baking powder

1 tbsp pistachio kernels, toasted

4 tbsp rose water

For the filling and icing:

500g/9oz/1 cup plus 2 tbsp mascarpone

3 tbsp pomegranate molasses or lime juice

3 tbsp sugar

3 tbsp beetroot (beet) juice or a few drops of pink food colouring

2 tsp Madagascan vanilla extract

1. Follow steps 1 (lining tins) and 3 (batter mixing) of the Beetroot & Chocolate Cake recipe (page 190), omitting the molasses and adding the lime juice in place of the melted chocolate.

2. Place the aubergines (eggplants) in a large bowl. Add the buckwheat and soya (soy) flours, pecans, ground spices, lime zest and baking powder to the aubergines and toss together, using your hands, until well mixed.

3. Scoop the egg mixture on top of the aubergine mixture and mix together thoroughly, using your hands again.

4. Divide the mixture (batter) between the tins and smooth the tops. Scatter the pistachio nuts around the outer edge of *one* of the cakes. Bake for 30–40 minutes until the surface is evenly cracked and the centre springy to the touch.

5. Leave the cakes to cool on wire racks, then un-mould and peel off the paper.

3 drops rose oil

115g/4oz/½ cup fresh pomegranate seeds, no pith

For the topping:

300ml/10fl oz/1¼ cups pomegranate juice

2 tbsp rosewater

1 drop rose oil, to taste

unflavoured vegetarian gelling agent – you need enough to set 300ml/10fl oz/1¼ cups liquid according to the packet instructions

55g/2oz/4 tbsp fresh pomegranate seeds, no pith

For the decoration:

1 tbsp unsalted, raw pistachio kernels, very finely chopped

sliced triangles of rose-flavoured Turkish delight (optional)

fresh yellow, red and pink unsprayed rose petals, rolled up and finely shredded, to decorate (optional)

icing (confectioners') sugar

unsweetened cocoa powder

VARIATIONS

Dairy-free option
Replace the butter in the cake mixture with an equal quantity of hard margarine or raw coconut oil. Replace the mascarpone in the filling and icing with an equal quantity of vegan cream cheese.

Lower-sugar option
Replace the sugar in the cake mixture with 225ml/8fl oz/1 cup agave or rice syrup or apple juice concentrate. Replace the sugar in the filling and icing with the same quantity of xylitol or agave or rice syrup. If the filling is too sloppy to hold its shape, add up to 2 tbsp ground psyllium husks (page 22). Be sure to use a no-added-sugar vegetarian gelling agent.

6. While the cakes are cooling, make the filling and icing by beating all the ingredients, except the pomegranate seeds, together. Set aside one-third of the mixture, then stir the pomegranate seeds into the remainder.

7. To make the topping, put the pomegranate juice, rosewater and rose oil in a small saucepan with the gelling agent and make according to the packet instructions. Remove the pan from heat and leave until just becoming syrupy, then stir in the pomegranate seeds.

8. Invert the cake without the pistachios onto a serving plate and sprinkle with the rose water. Spread the filling studded with pomegranate seeds over this layer.

9. Top with the remaining cake, pistachio-side up. Spread the reserved icing on top, making an indentation, right up to where the pistachios are.

10. Carefully ladle the slightly cool, syrupy jelly into the indentation in the centre of the icing. Sprinkle with the reserved pomegranate seeds.

11. Decorate the cake with the chopped pistachios and Turkish delight pieces, if using, around the rim of the icing, then scatter the shredded rose petals, if using, over the top. Lightly sift icing (confectioners') sugar over the petals and a touch of cocoa over the pistachio nuts. Chill for at least 1 hour but no more than 12 before serving, then bask in the glory!

JUMPIN' JAMAICAN SWEET POTATO & ORANGE CAKE

Serves 8 | Prep 40 minutes, plus at least 1 hour chilling | Bake 30–40 minutes
Dairy-free option | Gluten free | Lower-sugar option | Vegan version (page 207)

Spicy and light, with citrus and several layers of ginger, this is one of the most interesting vegetable cakes I bake. The unexpected flavour of the caraway seeds is certain to make you sit up and take notice. With a cup of tea, it delivers a burst of Caribbean sunshine to brighten cold, grey afternoons.

250g/9oz/1 cup plus 2 tbsp butter, softened

225g/8oz/1 cup plus 2 tbsp sugar

1 tbsp blackstrap molasses

4 eggs (total weight 225g/8oz in shells)

1 tsp Madagascan vanilla extract

freshly grated zest and juice of 2 large oranges

500g/1lb 2oz/2¾ cups sweet potato, peeled and *finely* grated

115g/4oz/1¼ cups chestnut flour

115g/4oz/1⅓ cups soya (soy) flour, toasted

2 tbsp blue poppy seeds

4 tsp gluten-free baking powder

2 tsp finely grated fresh ginger

2 tsp ground ginger

1 heaped tbsp caraway seeds

1 tsp freshly grated nutmeg

½ tsp ground cinnamon

unsweetened cocoa powder, for dusting

2 tbsp raw cacao nibs or coarsely grated 70 per cent dark chocolate, to decorate (optional)

1. Follow steps 1 (lining tins) and 3 (batter mixing) of the Beetroot & Chocolate Cake recipe (page 190), adding the orange juice in place of the melted chocolate.

2. Place the sweet potatoes in a large bowl. Add the chestnut and soya (soy) flours, orange zest, poppy seeds, baking powder, fresh and ground ginger, caraway seeds, nutmeg and cinnamon to the sweet potatoes and toss together, using your hands, until well mixed

3. Scoop the orange-flavoured egg mixture on top and mix together using your hands again.

4. Divide the mixture (batter) between the prepared tins and smooth the tops. Bake for 30–40 minutes until the surface is golden brown, evenly cracked and the centre is springy to the touch. Leave the cakes to cool on wire racks, then un-mould and peel off the paper.

5. Meanwhile, to make the filling and icing, beat all the ingredients together. Cover and chill until required.

For the filling and icing:

500g/1lb 2oz/2¼ cups mascarpone

115g/4oz/½ cup plus 1 tbsp sugar

2 tbsp pomegranate molasses or tamarind paste

1 tsp ground mace

1 tbsp fresh ginger juice (see Cook's note below)

1 tbsp finely chopped stem ginger

2½ tsp espresso coffee powder dissolved in 1 tbsp boiling water

1 tsp Madagascan vanilla extract

freshly grated zest and juice of 1 large orange

For the topping powder (optional):

1 tbsp caster (superfine) sugar

1 tsp raw cacao nibs

1 tsp caraway seeds

½ tsp ground cinnamon

6. If you're making the topping powder, put all the ingredients in a clean coffee grinder and grind until a fine powder forms.

7. Use two-thirds of the filling to sandwich the cakes together. Spread the remaining filling on top to 8cm 3¼in of the edge. Sift the cocoa powder or optional topping powder liberally onto the plain outer edge of the cake, just catching the edge of the icing as well.

8. To finish, sprinkle cacao nibs over the topping. Chill for at least 1 hour but no more than 12 hours before serving.

Cook's note:

To make ginger juice, finely grate 1–2 heaped tablespoons of unpeeled fresh ginger. Place it in kitchen paper (paper towels) and twist and squeeze hard, catching the drops underneath.

VARIATIONS

Dairy-free option
Replace the butter in the cake mixture with an equal amount of softened hard margarine or raw coconut oil. Replace the mascarpone in the filling and icing with equal quantities of vegan cream cheese.

Lower-sugar option
Replace the sugar in the cake mixture with 225ml/8fl oz/ 1 cup agave or rice syrup. Replace the sugar in the filling and icing with the same quantity of xylitol or 125ml/4fl oz/½ cup agave or rice syrup. Replace the sugar in the topping with xylitol. If the filling is too sloppy to hold its shape, add up to 2 tbsp ground psyllium husks (page 22). Omit the chopped ginger and replace it with 1 tsp ground ginger.

CARROT PASSION CAKE

Serves 8 | Prep 30 minutes, plus at least 1 hour chilling | Bake 30–40 minutes
Dairy-free option | Gluten free | Nut free | Vegan version (page 207)

This is a moist, substantial version of the classic and most of my customers are surprised – and dare I say, some are simply thrilled – to discover it's gluten free. This recipe is one of the reasons my regulars are regulars. An added bonus is that it freezes well.

250g/9oz/1 cup plus 2 tbsp butter, softened

225g/8oz/1 cup plus 2 tbsp sugar

4 eggs (total weight 225g/8oz in shells)

1 tsp Madagascan vanilla essence

freshly grated zest and juice of 1 large orange

500g/1lb 2oz/2¾ cups carrots, peeled and finely grated

115g/4oz/¾ cup brown rice flour

115g/4oz/1⅓ cups soya (soy) flour, toasted

4 tsp gluten-free baking powder

1 tsp ground cinnamon

1 tsp freshly grated nutmeg

¼ tsp ground cloves

85g/3oz/¾ cup dried cranberries, soaked and drained

raw cacao nibs, to decorate (optional)

strands of orange zest, to decorate (optional)

For the filling and icing:

500g/1lb 2oz/2¼ cups mascarpone

115g/4oz/½ cup plus 1 tbsp sugar

4 tbsp lemon juice

1 tsp Madagascan vanilla extract

1 tsp ground mace

1. Follow steps 1 (lining tins) and 3 (batter mixing) of the Beetroot & Chocolate Cake recipe (page 190), omitting the molasses and adding orange juice in place of the melted chocolate.

2. Place the grated carrots in a large bowl. Add the rice and soya (soy) flours, baking powder, ground spices, cranberries and orange zest and mix together. Scoop the orange-flavoured mixture on top and mix together thoroughly with your hands.

3. Fill the tins, then bake, cool and unmould the cake following steps 6 and 7, page 191.

4. Meanwhile, to make the filling and icing, beat all the ingredients together. Use two-thirds of the mixture to sandwich the cakes together, spreading the rest on top. Decorate with cacao nibs and orange zest, if you like. Chill for at least 1 hour, but not longer than 12 hours before serving.

VARIATIONS

Dairy-free option
Replace the butter in the cake mixture with margarine or raw coconut oil. Replace the mascarpone in the filling and icing with vegan cream cheese.

MACROBIOTIC CARROT CAKE

Serves 8 | Prep 20 minutes | Cook 50 minutes
Dairy free | Gluten free | Lower sugar | Vegan

This firm-textured vegan cake includes cooked grain (quinoa is my choice) and, while something of an acquired taste, my vegan customers really appreciate this offering. It is low in sugar with masses of carrots. The recipe is inspired by The Devon School of Macrobiotic Cookery, now known as The Holistic Cooking School. This cake has a warming effect.

500g/1lb 2oz/2¾ cups carrots, scrubbed and *finely* grated

175g/6oz/scant ½ cup chestnut purée

4 tbsp light tahini

115g/4oz/1⅓ cups soya (soy) flour, toasted

115g/4oz/¾ cup brown rice flour

125ml/4fl oz/½ cup agave, date or rice syrup

225g/8oz/heaped 1 cup any cooked grain

4 tbsp dried goji berries (optional)

4 tbsp raw coconut oil, melted, or sunflower oil

225ml/8floz/1 cup unsweetened apple juice

½ tsp sea salt

4 tbsp fresh ginger juice (Cook's note page 201)

1 tbsp sesame seeds, toasted, to decorate

For the filling:
250g/9oz/1 cup plus 2 tbsp vegan cream cheese or silken tofu

4 tbsp pomegranate molasses or unsweetened apple juice concentrate

175g/6oz/scant ½ cup chestnut purée

2 tbsp umeboshi plum paste

½ tsp ground star anise

1 tsp Madagascan vanilla extract

ground psyllium husks, to thicken (optional)

1. Preheat the oven to Fan 160°C/Fan 325°F/Gas 4. Line the bases and sides of two 20cm/8in cake tins with parchment paper. Cut two 20cm/8in circles of parchment paper and set aside.

2. Mix all the cake ingredients, except the sesame seeds, together thoroughly, then press into the prepared tins.

3. Place both tins on a baking sheet. Cover the surface of each cake with the parchment circles, then place another baking sheet on top to prevent them drying out. Bake for 50 minutes, or until the cakes are firm and evenly cracked. Leave the cakes to cool on wire racks, then un-mould and peel off the paper.

4. Meanwhile, beat all the filling ingredients, except the psyllium husks, together. You may need up to 2 tbsp of the ground husks to thicken (page 28). Use the filling to sandwich the cakes, then sprinkle with sesame seeds.

VEGAN BEETROOT & CHOCOLATE CAKE

Serves 8 | Prep 35 minutes, plus at least 1 hour chilling | Bake 30–40 minutes
Dairy free | Gluten free | Lower-sugar option | Nut-free option | Vegan

Here is an extended vegan version of the ever-popular classic, together with my five bestselling vegan variations to boot. Still moist Hades gets to marry his dark virgin in vegan paradise. This is a very versatile and good-natured vegetable cake recipe with which you can be endlessly inventive.

115g/4oz/¾ cup brown rice flour

115g/4oz/1⅓ cups soya (soy) flour, toasted

1 tbsp gluten-free baking powder

500g/1lb 2oz/2¾ cups raw beetroot (beets), scrubbed and finely grated

125ml/4fl oz/½ cup water

115g/4oz/½ cup raw coconut oil

175g/6oz/¾ cup plus 2 tbsp sugar

1 tbsp blackstrap molasses

115g/4oz/scant ½ cup unsweetened apple sauce

115g/4oz/½ cup mashed avocado or banana

115g/4 oz dairy-free 70 per cent dark chocolate, chopped

2 tbsp light tahini

1 tsp Madagascan vanilla extract

1 tsp bicarbonate of soda (baking soda)

unsweetened cocoa powder, for dusting

raw cacao nibs and dried, fresh or sugared unsprayed rose petals, to decorate (optional)

1. Preheat the oven to Fan 160°C/Fan 325°F/Gas 4. Line the bases and sides of two 23cm/9in springform tins, 5cm/2in deep, with parchment paper, leaving a 5cm/2in rim.

2. Combine the flours and baking powder in a large bowl. Add the beetroot (beets) and toss together using your hands until well mixed, then set aside.

3. Heat the water, coconut oil, sugar and molasses in a saucepan over a medium heat, stirring until the sugar dissolves.

4. Add the apple sauce, avocado, chocolate, tahini and vanilla, stirring until the chocolate melts and the mixture is steaming hot, but not boiling. Remove the pan from the heat, add the bicarbonate of soda (baking soda) and watch the mixture froth.

5. Add the hot mixture to the beetroot mixture and quickly and gently mix together by hand, wearing rubber gloves.

For the filling and icing:

500g/1lb 2oz/2¼ cups vegan cream cheese

4 tbsp sugar

2 tsp Madagascan vanilla extract

4 tbsp chopped well-toasted hazelnuts

175g/6oz raspberries, defrosted and drained, if frozen

ground psyllium husks, to thicken (optional)

VARIATIONS

Lower-sugar option
Use no-added-sugar dairy-free 70 per cent dark chocolate. Replace the sugar in the cake mixture with the same quantity of xylitol or 175ml/6fl oz/¾ cup agave or rice syrup. Replace the sugar in the filling and icing with the same quantity of xylitol or agave or rice syrup. If the filling is too sloppy to hold its shape, add up to 2 tbsp ground psyllium husks (page 22).

Nut-free option
Replace the coconut oil with 125ml/4fl oz/½ cup sunflower oil, and replace the hazelnuts in the filling and icing with ground toasted sesame seeds.

6. Gently dollop equal handfuls into the prepared cake tins and smooth the tops. Bake for 40–50 minutes until the surface is cracked all over and the centre is springy to the touch. Leave the cakes to cool on wire racks, then un-mould and peel off the paper.

7. Meanwhile, to make the filling and icing, beat together the cream cheese, sweetener and vanilla. Mix in the nuts, then fold in the raspberries until everything is thoroughly combined. If the mixture becomes too sloppy, stir in up to 2 tbsp ground psyllium husks (page 22).

8. Use two-thirds of the filling to sandwich the cakes together. Spread the rest over the top of the cake, leaving a clear border round the edge. Dust the border liberally with cocoa powder just catching the outer edge of the icing. Decorate with cacao nibs and rose petals, if you like. Cover and chill for at least 1 hour or up to 12 hours before serving.

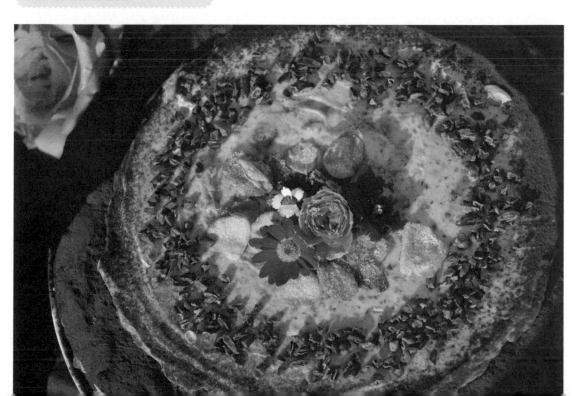

VEGAN VEGETABLE CAKE VARIATIONS

You can use my Vegan Beetroot & Chocolate Cake recipe on page 204 as a template to make vegan versions of all the non-vegan cakes in this chapter. I recommend using the lower-sugar option for each of the variations listed below.

I've given you an all-purpose vegan filling and icing recipe with the Vegan Beetroot & Chocolate Cake recipe (page 205), or you can use the vegan Silky Chocolate & Avocado Mousse recipe (opposite) or the filling for the Macrobiotic Carrot Cake (page 203). You can also adapt the non-vegan filling and icing recipes in this chapter by replacing the mascarpone with vegan cream cheese.

VEGAN SWEET POTATO, PECAN & CAPPUCCINO CAKE

Follow step 1 of the Vegan Beetroot & Chocolate Cake (page 204). Add 1 tsp ground cardamom and ½ tsp ground ginger to the flours and replace the beetroot with the same quantity of grated, peeled sweet potatoes in step 2. In step 3, replace the molasses with 1 tbsp sweetener of your choice and add 2½ tsp espresso coffee powder dissolved in 1 tbsp boiling water. Follow steps 4–9, omitting the chocolate and making the vegan filling and icing of your choice. Cover the cake and chill for at least 1 hour or up to 2 days before serving.

VEGAN TROPICAL PARSNIP & POLENTA CAKE

Follow step 1 of the Vegan Beetroot & Chocolate Cake (page 204). In step 2, add 1 tsp ground cardamom, ½ tsp ground ginger, 30g/1oz/⅓ cup ground almonds, 55g/2oz/⅓ cups fine polenta and the freshly grated zest of 1 lemon to the flours and replace the beetroot with the same quantity of grated and peeled parsnips.

In step 3 (the melting stage) replace the molasses with 1 tbsp sweetener of your choice. Follow steps 4–9, omitting the chocolate and making the vegan filling of your choice. Cover the cake and chill for at least 1 hour or up to 2 days before serving.

VEGAN COURGETTE, WHITE CHOCOLATE & MINT CAKE

Follow step 1 of the Vegan Beetroot & Chocolate Cake (page 204). Use grated dairy-free white chocolate and add it to the flours un-melted. Add 55g/2oz/⅓ cup fine polenta and 55g/2oz/1 cup finely chopped mint to the flours and replace the beetroot with the same quantity (squeezed weight) of finely grated courgettes in step 2. Omit the molasses and add an extra 1 tbsp sweetener of your choice in step 3 (the melting stage). Replace the dark chocolate with dairy-free white chocolate and gently melt, stirring occasionally. Follow steps 4–9, sprinkling 1 tbsp toasted pine nuts over one of the cake mixtures before baking. Make the vegan filling and icing of your choice. Cover the cake and chill for at least 1 hour or up to 12 hours before serving.

VEGAN MOROCCAN AUBERGINE & ROSE CELEBRATION CAKE

Follow step 1 of the Vegan Beetroot & Chocolate Cake (page 204). Use 115g/4oz/1 cup wholegrain buckwheat flour, instead of the brown rice flour, and 115g/4oz/1⅓ cups toasted soya (soy) flour in step 2. Add 85g/3oz/¾ cup chopped toasted pecans, the grated zest and juice of 1 (blood) orange, 1½ tsp ground ginger, ½ tsp each ground cardamom and chilli powder and 1 tbsp toasted unsalted pistachio kernels and replace the beetroot with the same quantity of finely chopped aubergines. Replace the molasses with 1 tbsp sweetener of your choice in step 3. Follow steps 4–9, omitting the chocolate and sprinkling 3 tbsp rose water over the cooled cake halves and making the vegan filling and icing of your choice.

VEGAN JUMPIN' JAMAICAN SWEET POTATO & ORANGE CAKE

Follow step 1 of the Vegan Beetroot & Chocolate Cake (page 204). Replace the brown rice flour with 115g/4oz/1¼ cups chestnut flour in step 2, then add 2 tbsp blue poppy seeds, 2 tsp finely grated fresh ginger, 2 tsp ground ginger, 1 tbsp caraway seeds, ½ tsp ground cinnamon and the grated zest of 2 large oranges to the flours and replace the beetroot with the same quantity of finely grated sweet potatoes. Follow steps 3–9, omitting the chocolate and making the vegan filling and icing of your choice. Cover and chill for at least 1 hour or up to 12 hours before serving.

VEGAN CARROT PASSION CAKE

Follow step 1 of the Vegan Beetroot & Chocolate Cake (page 204). Add 1 tsp ground cinnamon, 1 tsp freshly grated nutmeg, ¼ tsp ground cloves and 85g/3oz/¾ cup soaked and drained cranberries and the grated zest of 1 large orange and replace the beetroot with the same amount of finely grated carrots in step 2. Follow steps 3–9, omitting the chocolate and making the vegan filling and icing of your choice. Cover and chill for at least 1 hour or up to 2 days before serving.

SILKY CHOCOLATE & AVOCADO ICING

My daughter Zuleika is responsible for bringing this vegan delight to my attention. It's a versatile recipe that fills and ices one 20cm/8in cake, ices 12 muffins or 12 cupcakes and makes 3 ramekins of mousse. Melt 85g/3oz chopped dairy-free 70 per cent dark chocolate. Place the melted chocolate in a blender or food processor with 2 pitted, peeled and smashed avocados, 85g/3oz/1 cup unsweetened cocoa powder, 5 tbsp maple, agave or rice syrup, 3 tbsp hazelnut, rice or soya (soy) milk and 1 tsp Madagascan vanilla extract, then blitz until silky smooth. If the filling is too sloppy to hold its shape, add up to 2 tbsp ground psyllium husks (page 22). Cover and chill for at least 2 hours before using.

Blondies, Brownies & Flapjacks

If you're looking for that little something to go with your cuppa, look no further! Soft or chewy, healthy or pure indulgence – take your pick, or better still, judiciously munch your way through the year and know teatime blues to be a thing of the past.

You'll find two divine vegan chocolate brownie recipes, one of which uses adzuki beans and has a lower-sugar fudge topping. The blond pistachio angel makes an appearance, as does an awesome series of stuffed flapjacks. Make sure you buy only the certified gluten-free oats if serving them to coeliacs. Any leftovers are good chopped into home-made vanilla ice cream and served with a hot rum and butterscotch sauce. Heavenly!

All the delights in this chapter freeze well. Layer them between silicone parchment paper in a sealed container and they'll keep for up to three months.

CHOCOLATE & HAZELNUT BROWNIES

Makes 30 | Prep 20 minutes | Bake 35 minutes
Dairy-free option | Gluten free | Nut-free option

These little beauties have been a hit from the very first day we sold them. One sample taster and these go straight into the brown bag for customers to take home. They are very quick to make, and should be eaten on their own so you enjoy the full impact!

200g/7oz 70 per cent dark chocolate, chopped

175g/6oz/¾ cup unsalted butter, softened

375g/13oz/1¾ cups plus 2 tbsp sugar

4 eggs

1 tsp Madagascan vanilla extract

175g/6oz/1¾ cups ground almonds

225g/8oz/scant 1⅔ cups blanched and toasted hazelnuts, chopped

4 tsp gluten-free baking powder

unsweetened cocoa powder, for dusting

VARIATIONS

Dairy-free option
Use dairy-free 70 per cent dark chocolate. Replace the butter with the same quantity of raw coconut oil or hard margarine.

Nut-free option
Replace the hazelnuts with 225g/8oz/1¾ cups pumpkin seeds, toasted and coarsely chopped, and the ground almonds with 175g/6oz/1⅓ cups sesame seeds, finely ground.

1. Preheat the oven to Fan 160°C/Fan 325°F/Gas 4. Line the base and sides of a 40×30cm/16×12in baking tin with a single sheet of parchment paper.

2. Melt the chocolate in a heatproof bowl set over a saucepan of simmering water, stirring until smooth; leave to cool slightly.

3. Beat the butter and sugar together until fluffy and pale. Beat in the eggs, one at a time, then add the vanilla and melted chocolate. Mix together the ground almonds and hazelnuts with the baking powder, then stir into the mixture (batter).

4. Pour the mixture into the baking tin, smoothing it into the corners. Bake in the oven for 30–35 minutes, or until set.

5. Leave to cool in the tin set on a wire rack, then turn out and peel off the paper. Trim the edges and cut into 30 equal-sized brownies. Sift a little cocoa powder over the top, then store in an airtight container for up to 7 days.

WHITE CHOCOLATE & PISTACHIO BLONDIES

Makes 30 | Prep 20 minutes | Bake 35 minutes
Gluten free

I woke up one morning filled with a deep need to bring this recipe into the world! Many thanks to my partner, Brian, for fine-tuning the ingredients. Eat these in a quiet place, savouring each exquisite mouthful. They are sweet and chewy, and could easily end up crumbled into vanilla ice cream!

175g/6oz/¾ cup unsalted butter, softened

325g/11oz/1½ cups plus 2 tbsp sugar

4 eggs

1 teaspoon Madagascan vanilla extract

225g/8oz white chocolate, grated or finely chopped

200g/7oz/2 cups ground almonds

200g/7oz/1⅔ cups unsalted pistachio kernels, toasted and chopped

4 tsp gluten-free baking powder

1 tbsp icing (confectioners') sugar mixed with 1 tbsp unsweetened cocoa powder, for dusting

1. Preheat the oven to Fan 160°C/Fan 325°F/Gas 4. Line the base and sides of a 40×30cm/16×12in baking tin, 4cm/1½in deep, with a single sheet of parchment paper.

2. Beat the butter and sugar together until fluffy and pale. Gradually beat in the eggs, one at a time, then add the vanilla.

3. Mix together the white chocolate, ground almonds and pistachios, then toss with the baking powder and stir into the mixture (batter). Pour the mixture into the tin, smoothing it into the corners. Bake for 30–35 minutes, or until set.

4. Cool in the tin set on a wire rack, then turn out and peel off the paper. Trim the edges and cut into 30 equal-sized blondies.

5. Sift a layer of the chocolate icing (confectioners') sugar over each blondie, then dust with cocoa powder. Serve immediately or store in an airtight container for up to 7 days.

ADZUKI BEAN FUDGE BROWNIES

Makes 20 | Prep 20 minutes, plus melting the chocolate | Bake 35–40 minutes
Dairy free | Gluten free | Lower sugar | Vegan

My daughter India is responsible for marrying these dark, melting mouthfuls with my friend Lizi's awesome chocolate, velvety icing. The combination is so fantastic I can't keep up with the demand. They satisfy everyone, being gluten free, lower sugar and vegan, and are best enjoyed slowly nibbled and savoured.

200g/7oz/1⅓ cups pitted dates, soaked in hot water for at least 15 minutes, then drained and hand chopped

115g/4oz no-added-sugar 70 per cent dark chocolate, melted

3 tbsp nut butter

2 tbsp light tahini

1 tbsp Madagascan vanilla extract

½ tsp sea salt

2 tsp espresso coffee powder dissolved in 2 tsp boiling water

300g/10oz/1⅓ cups cooked adzuki beans, drained and rinsed if canned

85g/3oz/1 cup unsweetened cocoa powder

2 tbsp dried goji berries (optional)

4 tbsp toasted and chopped blanched hazelnuts (optional)

edible gold powder, to decorate (optional)

For Lizi's Vegan Velvet Chocolate Icing

100g/3½oz/7 tbsp raw coconut oil

150ml/5fl oz/⅔ cup agave or rice syrup

55g/2oz/⅔ cup unsweetened cocoa powder

2–3 tbsp soya (soy) milk

½ tsp Madagascan vanilla extract

1. Preheat the oven to Fan 160°C/Fan 325°F/Gas 4. Line the base and sides of a 37×26cm/14½×10½in baking tin, 4cm/1½in deep, with parchment paper.

2. Put the dates, chocolate, nut butter, tahini, vanilla, salt and coffee in a blender or food processor and pulse until a thick paste forms.

3. Add the beans and pulse again, blending well to obliterate the skins. If your blender struggles with this quantity, then blend in batches.

4. Scrape the paste onto the work surface and knead in the remaining ingredients. Then transfer to the baking tin, press evenly into the corners and smooth. Bake for 20–25 minutes until small cracks appear all over the surface.

5. Leave to cool in the tin set on a wire rack, then turn out and peel off the paper.

6. Meanwhile, make the icing. Put the coconut oil, syrup and the cocoa powder in a small pan over a medium-high heat. Stir to mix, then gently bring to the boil. Immediately remove the pan from the heat. Stir in the soya (soy) milk and vanilla until the icing thickens. Allow to cool a little before using.

7. Spread the brownie with the icing and leave for 15 minutes before cutting into 20 brownies. Store in the fridge for up to a week. For a luxurious finish, sprinkle with edible gold powder before serving.

PIXIE'S IRRESISTIBLE VEGAN CHOCOLATE BROWNIES

Makes 20 | Prep 10 minutes, plus making the icing (optional) | Bake 25–35 minutes
Dairy free | Gluten-free option | Lower-sugar option | Vegan

Why do we need another vegan brownie recipe? Why did Gaia make chocolate? Well, rhetorical questions aside, I thought the vegan world could handle another wonderful offering, fresh from Wales, via my friend Awi, an amazing vegan cook, who was given this recipe by her friend Pixie.

325g/11oz/2¼ cups plus 2 tbsp half white and half wholegrain spelt flours

250g/9oz/1¼ cups rapadura sugar

70g/2½oz/¾ cup plus 1½ tbsp unsweetened cocoa powder

1½ tsp gluten-free baking powder

1 tsp sea salt

5 tbsp chopped, toasted nuts or seeds, chopped dairy-free 70 per cent dark chocolate or dried cranberries (optional)

200ml/7fl oz/¾ cup plus 2 tbsp vegetable oil or melted raw coconut oil

200ml/7fl oz/¾ cup plus 2 tbsp water

1 tsp Madagascan vanilla extract

1 quantity Silky Chocolate & Avocado Icing (page 207) or unsweetened cocoa powder for dusting (optional)

1. Preheat the oven to Fan 180°C/Fan 350°F/Gas 6. Line the base and sides of a 37×26cm/14½×10½in baking tin, 4cm/1½in deep, with parchment paper.

2. Mix together the flours, rapadura, cocoa powder, baking powder and salt in a large bowl. Stir in the nuts or seeds, if using, and make a well in the centre.

3. Mix the oil, water and vanilla together in another bowl, then add to the dry ingredients, stirring to mix thoroughly. Pour the mixture (batter) into the baking tin, smoothing it into the corners.

4. Bake for 25 minutes until just set, or 5–10 minutes longer for a firmer texture. Cool in the tin set on a wire rack, then turn out and peel off the paper.

5. Spread the icing over the brownie cake or dust liberally with cocoa powder. Trim the edges and cut into equal-sized brownies. Store in an airtight container for up to 7 days.

VARIATIONS

Gluten-free option
Replace the spelt flours with 150g/5½oz/1⅔ cups chestnut flour and 150g/5½ oz/1¾ cups toasted soya (soy) flour.

Lower-sugar option
Replace the rapadura sugar with the same quantity of xylitol or 250ml/9fl oz/1 cup plus 2 tbsp agave or rice syrup. Use chopped no-sugar-added 70 per cent dark chocolate if that is the optional ingredient you are adding.

BLACKJACK

Makes 24 | Prep 35 minutes, plus several hours cooling | Bake 45 minutes
Dairy-free option | Gluten free | Lower-sugar option | Nut free | Vegan option

I earned a lot of parental brownie points when I used to send boxes of these away with my children on school trips. The sophisticated mix of tart blackcurrants and dark chocolate includes rice syrup, which creates a chewier and less crumbly result than you might expect. Buy fresh blackcurrants in season, pick over, lay on a tray, open freeze and bag up. They will keep for ages.

500g/1lb 2oz/2¼ cups butter

225ml/8fl oz/1 cup agave or rice syrup

225g/8oz/1 cup plus 2 tbsp rapadura sugar

500g/1lb 2oz/5½ cups gluten-free porridge oats (rolled oats)

300g/10oz/3½ cups gluten-free jumbo oats (old-fashioned rolled oats)

700g/1lb 9oz blackcurrants, defrosted if frozen and picked over to remove any stalks and leaves, or 700g/1lb 9oz/2cups blackcurrant conserve

350g/12oz 70 per cent dark chocolate, chopped

VARIATIONS

Dairy-free and Vegan options
Replace the butter with the same amount of hard margarine or raw coconut oil. Use dairy-free 70 per cent dark chocolate.

Lower-sugar option
Replace the rapadura sugar with 500ml/18fl oz/2¼ cups agave or rice syrup. The texture will be softer and the taste will be less sweet. Use no-added-sugar 70 per cent dark chocolate.

1. Preheat the oven to 160°C/325°F/Gas 4. Line the base and sides of a 40×30cm/16×12in baking tin, about 4cm/1½in deep, with parchment paper.

2. Stir the butter, syrup and sugar in a saucepan over a medium heat until the sugar dissolves. Bring to the boil and bubble just until the mixture is well blended and turns a pale golden colour.

3. Beat briefly, then stir in all the oats. Stir well over a low heat for 5 minutes, or until the mixture at the bottom of the pan begins to turn a pale nutty colour.

4. Press just under half the oat mixture into the tin, pressing it well into the corners. Cover with an even layer of blackcurrants or jam, then add the remaining oat mixture. Press down firmly.

5. Bake for 35–45 minutes until golden brown. Cool in the tin, then turn out and peel off the paper.

6. Melt the chocolate in a heatproof bowl over a pan of simmering water. Spread in 4 broad swathes over the top of the flapjack. Cool until set, which will take several hours. Cut into 24 flapjacks (bars). Store for up to 2 weeks in an airtight container.

LOVEJACK

Makes 24 | Prep 35 minutes, plus several hours cooling | Bake 45 minutes
Dairy-free option | Gluten free | Nut free | Vegan option

I once overdosed on this indecently named flapjack. This is a great way of using up any sad, old bananas languishing in the fruit bowl. For a less decadent version, you *can* always leave out the chocolate. Ideal for lunchboxes, these luscious, nutritious bars are popular with all ages.

700g/1lb 9oz ripe bananas

freshly grated zest and juice of 2 lemons, kept separate

4 tbsp dried goji berries, fresh or dried cranberries or fresh blueberries, or a mixture

½ tsp ground cinnamon

½ tsp ground mace

500g/1lb 2oz/2¼ cups butter, softened

225ml/8fl oz/1 cup agave or rice syrup

225g/8oz/1 cup plus 2 tbsp rapadura sugar

500g/1lb 2oz/5½ cups gluten-free porridge oats (rolled oats)

300g/10oz/3½ cups gluten-free jumbo oats (old-fashioned rolled oats)

175g/6oz/1⅓ cups mixed seeds, such as poppy, pumpkin, sesame and sunflower

350g/12oz white chocolate, chopped

> ### VARIATIONS
> **Dairy-free and Vegan options**
> Replace the butter with the same quantity of hard margarine or raw coconut oil. Use dairy-free white chocolate, grating it over the hot flapjack as soon as it comes out of the oven.

1. Preheat the oven to 160°C/325°F/Gas 4. Line the base and sides of a 40×30cm/16×12in baking tin, 4cm/1½in deep, with a single sheet of parchment paper, making a 5cm/2in rim.

2. Mash the bananas with the lemon juice, then add the dried berries, cinnamon and mace; set aside.

3. Stir the butter, syrup and sugar in a saucepan over a medium heat until the sugar dissolves. Bring to the boil, and boil briefly just until the mixture is well blended and turns a pale gold colour.

4. Beat briefly, then add all the oats, seeds and lemon zest and stir over a low heat for a couple of minutes until thoroughly amalgamated.

5. Press just under half the oat mixture into the lined tin, pressing it into the corners. Cover with an even layer of the banana mixture, then crumble the rest of the oat mixture over the top, pressing down firmly.

6. Continue with steps 5–6 of the Blackjack recipe (page 215), melting the white chocolate.

PIÑA COLADA FLAPJACK

Makes 24 | Prep 35 minutes, plus several hours cooling | Bake 45 minutes
Dairy-free option | Gluten free | Vegan option

Another classic taste transposition that jazzes up the 'ol' timer', making it a quick kudos generator for bring-and-share parties. You can omit the alcohol and the chocolate for a less fancy version. My teenagers make endless variations of flapjacks, and this is one such favourite that has made it to the stall.

700g/1lb 9oz fresh pineapple, peeled, cored and chopped into medium-sized chunks, or drained, if canned

freshly grated zest and juice of 2 limes, kept separate

500g/1lb 2oz/2¼ cups butter

225ml/8fl oz/1 cup agave or rice syrup

225g/8oz/1 cup plus 2 tbsp rapadura sugar

4 tbsp grated block creamed coconut

500g/1lb 2oz/5½ cups gluten-free porridge oats (rolled oats)

300g/10oz/3½ cups gluten-free jumbo oats (old-fashioned rolled oats)

350g/12oz white chocolate, melted

125ml/4fl oz/½ cup dark rum`

1. Preheat the oven to 160°C/325°F/Gas 4. Line the base and sides of a 40×30cm/16×12in baking tin with a single sheet of parchment paper.

2. Toss the pineapple with the lime juice in a non-metallic bowl and set aside.

3. Stir the butter, rice syrup and sugar in a saucepan over a medium heat until the sugar melts. Bring to the boil, and boil just until the mixture is well blended and turns a pale gold colour; beat briefly. Add the creamed coconut and stir until it melts.

4. Stir in the oats and lime zest over a low heat until thoroughly amalgamated.

5. Press just under half the oat mixture into the tin, pressing it into the corners. Cover this layer with an even layer of the pineapple chunks, then add the rest of the flapjack mixture, pressing to flatten.

6. Continue with steps 5–6 of the Blackjack recipe (page 215), sprinkling the flapjack with rum as soon as it comes out of the oven and brushing with white chocolate. Store for up to 5 days in an airtight container.

VARIATIONS

Dairy-free and Vegan options
Replace the butter with the same quantity of hard margarine or raw coconut oil. Use dairy-free white chocolate and grate it over the hot flapjack as soon as it comes out of the oven. Do not melt dairy-free white chocolate.

SPICES & SEASONINGS

Dairy free | Gluten free | Nut free | Vegan

You can buy most of the spices, seasonings and curry paste I've included here, but I think it's worth making your own as they add a real depth of flavour to your dishes. Make them up when you have a spare minute and, stored according to instructions, they'll keep for several months and be ready for use when you need them.

Ras-el-Hanout Paste

4 tsp freshly ground cumin

2 tsp ground allspice

2 tsp ground cardamom

2 tsp ground cinnamon

2 tsp chilli powder

2 tsp garlic granules

2 tsp ground culinary lavender, or 1 drop lavender oil

2 tsp ground mace

2 tsp ground nutmeg

2 tsp turmeric

1½ tsp ground cloves

1 tsp smoked paprika

1 tsp sea salt

2 tsp freshly ground coriander

2–3 drops rose oil

150ml/5fl oz/⅔ cup sunflower or olive oil, plus extra to cover

55g/2oz piece of fresh ginger

2 tsp freshly grated or bottled galangal (optional)

freshly grated zest and juice of 4 lemons

1. Combine all the ground spices in a blender or food processor.

2. Add the oils, ginger, galangal (if using) and lemon juice and zest and blitz to blend.

3. Transfer to a container with a tight-fitting lid, cover with a layer of oil and store in the fridge. Keeps for up to a month, but be sure to keep topped up with oil between uses.

Thai Curry Paste

4 tsp cumin seeds

1 tsp coriander seeds

1 tsp black peppercorns

450g/1lb fresh coriander (cilantro), including roots, stalks and leaves, roughly chopped

7.5cm/3in piece galangal or fresh ginger, peeled and roughly chopped

20 fresh green chillies, de-seeded

12 garlic cloves, peeled

4 bunches spring onions (scallions), chopped

2 lemongrass stalks, outer leaves removed, finely chopped

4 green (bell) peppers, de-seeded and roughly chopped

4 tsp freshly grated lime zest

2 tsp ground mace

2 tsp ground nutmeg

sea salt, to season

150ml/5fl oz/²⁄₃ cup sunflower oil, for storing

1. Heat a frying pan over a medium heat. Add the cumin and coriander seeds and dry-roast, stirring, for 3–5 minutes, until they are aromatic. Remove from the heat and put the seeds into a clean coffee grinder. Add the peppercorns and then grind into a fine powder.

2. Next, place the fresh coriander (cilantro), galangal, chillies, garlic, spring onions (scallions) and lemongrass in a food processor and blend until you have a fine paste. Add the green (bell) peppers, lime zest, mace, nutmeg and ground spices, and blend again. Season to taste.

3. Store in an airtight container in the fridge, covered with 2.5cm/1in extra oil, for up to 1 week, or freeze in small containers or in an ice-cube tray for up to 3 months.

Kashmiri Spice Mix

1 tbsp coriander seeds

1 tbsp cumin seeds

1 tbsp black peppercorns

1 tbsp ground cinnamon

1 tbsp mace

1 tbsp nutmeg

1 tsp ground cloves

1 tsp ground cardamom

1. Heat a frying pan over a medium heat. Add the coriander seeds, cumin seeds and black peppercorns, and dry-roast for 3–5 minutes, stirring, or until they are aromatic.

2. Remove the spices immediately from the heat and grind them to a fine powder in a clean coffee grinder or spice mill.

3. Mix the freshly ground spices with the cinnamon, mace, nutmeg, cloves and cardamom. Store in an airtight jar in a dark cupboard for up to 4 months.

Piri-piri Spice Mix

2 tsp ground piri-piri or chilli powder

2 tsp Himalayan pink salt or rock salt

2 tsp sweet paprika

2 tsp ground sumac

1 tsp dried chilli flakes

½ tsp ground bay leaves

½ tsp garlic powder (smoked)

½ tsp onion powder

½ tsp dried oregano

½ tsp ground cardamom

½ tsp coriander

½ tsp ginger

½ tsp sweet paprika

1. Combine the ground piri-piri and Himalayan pink salt with the sweet paprika and ground sumac.

2. Add the dried chilli flakes, ground bay leaves (look for them in southeast Asian food shops), garlic powder, onion powder and dried oregano and stir well.

3. Complete by adding the cardamom, coriander, ginger and sweet paprika. Store in an airtight jar in the fridge for up to 2 months.

Tomato & Avocado Salsa

1 garlic clove, smashed and finely chopped

1 small red onion, finely chopped

1 fresh red chilli, de-seeded and finely chopped (optional)

1 tbsp chopped coriander (cilantro) leaves

½ tsp smoked paprika

freshly squeezed juice of 1 lime

225g/8oz ripe tomatoes

2 ripe avocados

sea salt and black pepper, to season

1. Combine the garlic, onion and chilli, if using, in a non-metallic bowl with the coriander (cilantro), smoked paprika, lime juice, salt to taste and a few grinds of pepper.

2. Use a small, curved knife to remove the tough cone-shaped core at the top of each tomato. Finely dice the flesh and add to the other salsa ingredients.

3. Split an avocado in half lengthways, then smack a large knife into the stone and twist – the stone should come out with ease. Repeat with the other avocado, then peel and dice them. Add to the salsa and gently mix together, then adjust seasoning and serve.

THE FOOD CODE

Many years ago I remember asking my father, who was the chemical fertilizer sales rep for ICI India, a seemingly innocuous question. I wanted to know who was responsible for taking care of environmental concerns, and he told me, 'Oh, there's a department that deals with that kind of thing.' And that was the end of the conversation.

Having watched *The Future of Food*, a widely praised 2004 documentary revealing the irrevocable corruption of global food supplies through governmental and corporate collusion, I recalled his words with growing concern. As I gradually realized the deep personal implications of a world, albeit one generation removed, that I had been unwittingly involved in creating, I felt no judgement, but was nevertheless shocked by my own ignorance.

Since then I have researched the history of the green revolution, and the related implications of using food as a political tool of global control: in particular, the new legislation contained in the EU document *Codex Alimentarius* or 'food code'. I began sharing this information and talking to customers about their views on the issue of genetically modified food and the future of organic farming. Unsurprisingly, I had a very mixed response, ranging from full agreement to complete indifference, and also outrage that I, a mere food seller, should expect customers to consider such matters at all! Uplifted, emboldened and occasionally depressed, I felt I was beginning to find an answer to my dilemma: What can I do to make a real difference?

Sustainable Sourcing

The questions of self-care and sustainability seem to me to be related. How we live our lives is reflected in the world around us, and to be a bystander is no longer, if it ever was, a healthy occupation. Taking care of ourselves means taking on more responsibility for our personal and planetary health, and there has never been a more vital occupation as the ill effects of passive consumerism make themselves known. I believe we underestimate the power contained in human intention, and I know from personal experience that all manner of hindrances, namely doubt, fear and hatred, live in the gap between saying and doing.

I also believe that biodynamic farming practices, which are contained and informed by holistic infrastructures, potentially possess the ability to heal and restore the earth from these and many other ravages. However, to be successful, such enterprises require communities of individuals to relate to one another in new ways. My message is simple: Choose, or be chosen for. We live in exciting times where possibility can lead everywhere – or nowhere.

RESOURCES

Recommended Viewing

Codex Alimentarius: The UN Plan to Eradicate Organic Farming and to Destroy the Natural Health Industry (2009)
Inspirational and informative talk by Ian R. Crane.

Food, Inc. (2008)
An unflattering look inside America's corporate-controlled food industry. The Soil Association is the film's official charity partner.

The Future of Food (Lily Films, 2004)
Documents the effects of the green revolution.

Julie & Julia (2009)
Joyous foodie biopic that faithfully commemorates the late Julia Child, American author of the sublime *Mastering the Art of French Cooking*.

Like Water for Chocolate (1993)
Sensuous film of Laura Esquivel's novel. Powerful emotions are stirred, ground and chopped into every meal in this romantic, bittersweet movie.

We Become Silent: The Last Days of Health Freedom (2005)
Documentary detailing attempts by major pharmaceutical and food companies to limit access to herbs and vitamins to maintain a monopoly on health care.

What the Bleep Do We Know!? (2004)
Cutting-edge film documentary feature that explores the spiritual connection between quantum physics and the power of conscious intention.

The World According to Monsanto (2008)
Documentary based on Marie Monique Robin's three-year-long investigation into the controversial corporate practices of the US multinational Monsanto.

Recommended Reading

Chill, a Reassessment of Global Warming Theory, by Peter Taylor (2009)
Peter Taylor, ex-Greenpeace ecologist and governmental scientist, presents a fascinating alternative view of global warming.

Codex Alimentarius, compiled and edited by Scott Tipps (2007)
A compendium of articles concerning health-freedom issues and the Codex Alimentarius Commission.

The Constant Gardener, John le Carré (2001)
This gripping fictional account of the unmasking of a pharmaceutical conspiracy sends a strong social message.

Seeds of Deception, Jeffrey Smith (2003)
Fraudulent GM lab results revealed by a scientific journalist.

Seeds of Destruction, William Engdahl (2007)
Masterly chronological analysis exposing the political manipulations that forced GM foods onto the global food markets.

Cookbooks

Gluten-Free Diet: A Comprehensive Resource Guide, Shelley Case (Case Nutrition Consulting, 2002)

The Gluten-Free Gourmet: Living Well Without Wheat, Bette Hagman (Holt Paperbacks, 2000)

Living Gluten-Free for Dummies, Danna Korn (For Dummies, 2010)

Recipes for Self-Healing, Daverick Leggett (Meridian Press, 1999)
Traditional Chinese medicine informs this gorgeous book with delicious recipes and their food energetics all on the same page.

Vegetarian Cooking Without, Barbara Cousins (Thorsons, 2000)
Simple recipes free from added gluten, sugar, yeast and dairy products.

Useful UK Websites

www.allergyuk.org
Comprehensive information on many types of food allergy and intolerance.

www.coeliac.org.uk
Authoritative source of advice and support for people with coeliac disease.

www.foodsmatter.com
Articles and research on allergy, intolerance and sensitivity, and related health problems.

www.coeliac.org.uk/gluten-free-diet-and-lifestyle/crossed-grain-magazine
Crossed Grain Magazine: the UK's leading quarterly magazine for gluten-free living.

www.glutenfreebaking.co.uk
Relevant information, live cookery classes, courses and digital downloads.

Useful US Websites

www.celiac.nih.gov (National Institutes of Health Celiac Disease Awareness Campaign)

www.csaceliacs.org (Celiac Support Association)

www.delightglutenfree.com (*Delight* Gluten-Free magazine)

www.dr-rath-foundation.org
The Dr. Rath Health Foundation campaigns for a new global health-care system.

www.ethicalconsumer.org
Consumer organization with consumer reports and tips on ethical buying.

www.glutenfreeliving.com (*Gluten-Free Living* magazine)

www.glutenfreemom.com
Site aimed at parents of children who need to follow a gluten-free diet.

www.gluten.net
Gluten Intolerance Group that offers support to those with gluten sensitivities.

www.healingwithwholefoods.com
Offers articles and recipes focusing on the whole food approach.

www.livingwithout.com (*Living Without* magazine)

UK Suppliers

www.ethicallyessential.coop
Ethically Essential: a Bristol-based online co-operative featuring a wide range of ethical, organic and Fairtrade foods, including store-cupboard essentials, herbs and spices.

www.healthysupplies.co.uk
Healthy Supplies: online supplier of no-nonsense healthy food. UK delivery by post or courier. Stockists of kinako/toasted soya (soy) flour.

www.hollandandbarrett.com
Holland & Barrett: high-street stockist of a wide range of health foods, including gluten-free flours and psyllium husks. Also stocks Neal's Yard whole foods.

www.melburyandappleton.co.uk
Melbury & Appleton: family-owned business supplying a large selection of international food ingredients. You will find toasted soya (soy) flour and crystallized violets.

www.nealsyarddairy.co.uk
Neal's Yard Dairy: Suppliers of farm cheeses from the British Isles, available online and through retail outlets nationwide.

www.riverfordfarmshop.co.uk
Riverford Farm Shop: Devon-based stockist of organic vegetables, local organic milk and cheeses, organic whole foods, ecologically-friendly cleaning products.

www.ticklemorecheese.co.uk
Ticklemore Cheese, Totnes: wonderful, Devon handmade cheeses including goats' curds and ricotta. The site has a list of nationwide stockists.

US Suppliers

www.bobsredmill.com/gluten-free
Wide range of gluten-free flours and other products, including cookbooks.

www.celiac.com/glutenfreemall
Popular brands of gluten-free foods; also supplements and cookbooks.

www.gfmall.com
Useful directory of gluten-free products, stores and vendors in the USA and Canada.

ACKNOWLEDGEMENTS

There is not the space to name all those who have eased this cookbook into its several publications; however, my gratitude goes to everyone I know who has supported me along the meandering wayside!

Carole Salmon, whose beautiful photographs grace many of these pages and without whose practical and moral support this book is unlikely to have seen the light of day.

John Platt, for his beautiful drawings and steadfast enthusiasm for the project.

Brian Jones, India and Zuleika Connolly Jones, and Sarah Connolly, who willingly test-drove recipes and offered invaluable feedback on all aspects of this work.

John Meredith, whose generous eleventh-hour expertise coaxed yet more gorgeous photographs from dark February days.

Michelle Pilley at Hay House, whose unerring sense of time and place has enabled this book to reach a global audience.

Carolyn Thorne at Hay House, whose patient vision has brought order and direction to this diverse venture.

Beverly LeBlanc, whose prodigious editing skills were exercised beyond the call of duty, bringing finesse to a raw manuscript.

Julie Oughton at Hay House, whose calm efficiency and vision brought coherent pagination to the light of day.

To everyone else at Hay House who has helped birth this cookbook.

Rick Smaridge, who so willingly stepped in to fill the photographic gaps.

To Wendy Cook, whose own inspirational books *Foodwise* and *The Biodynamic Food and Cookbook* gave me the courage to conceive of publishing my own recipes.

To Wilhelmina Swindell, whose practical support initially got the book off the ground.

To Toby Tobias, for his generous sharing of the Mini Millet Burger recipe.

To all my lovely customers and well-wishers, both past and present, whose enthusiastic encouragement has made this book possible.

INDEX

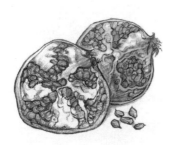